P9-CRS-609

# HONEST WORK:
## *A Business Ethics Reader*
### THIRD EDITION

Joanne B. Ciulla
Clancy Martin
Robert C. Solomon

Source material from:
**Ciulla, Martin, and Solomon**, *Honest Work: A Business Ethics Reader, 3rd ed.*
978-0-19-994420-0


Oxford   New York
OXFORD UNIVERSITY PRESS

# OXFORD

UNIVERSITY PRESS

Oxford University Press is a department of the University of Oxford. It furthers the University's
objective of excellence in research, scholarship, and education by publishing worldwide.

Oxford   New York
Auckland   Cape Town   Dar es Salaam   Hong Kong   Karachi
Kuala Lumpur   Madrid   Melbourne   Mexico City   Nairobi
New Delhi   Shanghai   Taipei   Toronto

With offices in
Argentina   Austria   Brazil   Chile   Czech Republic   France   Greece
Guatemala   Hungary   Italy   Japan Poland   Portugal   Singapore
South Korea   Switzerland   Thailand   Turkey   Ukraine   Vietnam

ISBN 978-0-19-022914-6

# Contents

# CASES

# 1

# On the Job

## *Everyday Ethics at Work*

## Introduction

Most workplaces are like zoos. They are filled with a variety of people, some like you and some quite exotic. When you go to work, you navigate your way through a complex web of relationships with people who often seem to be of different species. Some of them are dominant, some are docile, some are cooperative, others are contentious, some are kind, and some will bite you. When you think of it, work is basically about the interaction of people toward some common goals, and ethics is about how they treat each other. The work zoo is an emotional place where employees experience anger, pain, fear, joy, satisfaction, and even love, sometimes all at once and in the same building. Not only do these people have different titles and different job descriptions, they also carry with them different lives shaped by gender, race, ethnicity, religion, health, and personal values, experiences, and cultural and personal preferences. Almost everyone you work with lives in another world with other responsibilities at home and at play. Before they go to work, some drop their children off at day care or school, others leave behind an elderly parent or a seriously ill spouse or partner, and still others say good-bye to their faithful dog or an empty apartment. After work, there are those who go off to help their favorite charity, those who go to the health club, and still others who head for the nearest bar. But they are all fellow members of this human zoo that we call work and, as such, deserve to be treated fairly and with respect.

When you think about it, what most upsets you about your job are the times when you either don't feel like you are treated with respect or don't think you are treated fairly. Throughout the history of modern work, one hears the same refrain from workers, "We just want to be treated like adults!" In the workplace, respect means treating someone as an autonomous person on the job, while at the same time knowing where to draw the line between the employee's job and the employee's personal life. You may have noticed that this line between work and private life is not easy to draw, especially if you socialize with coworkers, check your office email from home or are on call after hours via a pager or cell phone. But as your work life and your "personal" life converge, the question becomes even more pressing: What is the relation between the two? Is it OK for you to do whatever you want to in your personal life as long as you do your job well? What is the proper realm of privacy? And what are the employer's and employee's rights and responsibilities to each other?

Many great thinkers, such as Immanuel Kant, believe that respect for our common humanity is the most important principle of ethics. This chapter begins with a discussion of how Kant's ideas about respect for persons apply to the workplace. One aspect of respecting people is appreciating that they have feelings. In "Exploring the Managed Heart," Arlie Hochschild describes the emotional labor that flight attendants and others in the service industry do every day. Her article raises the question, When does the requirement to be nice to customers compromise the dignity and autonomy of a person? Where does one draw the line between politeness and humiliation? This leads us to the issue of an employee's right to express him or herself at work. Bruce Barry's article, "The Cringing and the Craven: Freedom of Expression in the Workplace," explores the question, Should employees have the same freedom of expression on the job as they have in their personal lives? Do employers have the right to punish employees for expressing their views on things such as politics?

The workplace can be a dangerous place, which raises questions about the obligations of employers to look after the physical, mental, and financial well-being of employees. Employers have power over employees and sometimes they abuse it. Loraleigh Keashly's article looks at one of the darker aspects of human nature—bullying. Bullying has the potential to inflict both physical and emotional damage on employees. Another way that work can be dangerous is when employers ask employees to work in dangerous places. An article from the *Economist* explores some of the ethical problems with putting employees in harm's way. Perhaps the most dangerous thing about the workplace in the twenty-first century is that most businesses are subject to increasingly volatile national and international economic conditions. As a result of this, most employees can lose their jobs at the drop of a hat because of a financial or environmental crisis at home or abroad. In an era where there is little, if any, job security left, what obligations do employers have to employees? Harry J. Van Buren III explores this question in his article, "Boundaryless Careers and Employability Obligations."

The last article in this chapter addresses the question of how your physical appearance affects your employment prospects. People come in all shapes, colors, and sizes, and their faces tell us about their race, ethnicity, and gender. The article "Facial Discrimination" offers us a broad way to think about how employers intentionally and unintentionally discriminate against job applicants because of the way that they look.

The first case in this chapter is from the classic novel *The Man in the Gray Flannel Suit*. It will give you an opportunity to think about who you are and how you want to present yourself to potential employers. We then go from a case on hiring to John Boatright's case on firing, which allows us reflect on how to respect the dignity of a person when you fire him or her. The rest of the cases in this chapter are all true stories that Joanne Ciulla has collected from participants in corporate seminars and students. They have been disguised for use in this text. These cases illustrate the old adage that "truth is stranger than fiction." The first case is about a manager who discovers that a man that his company was planning on promoting beats his wife. The next one is about matching clients with employees who share the same interests and gender. This is a very controversial issue in businesses that provide client services and sales. Should you pair a salesperson who golfs with a client who likes to golf? Is that different from pairing a male salesman with a client who does not seem to respect women? Since most people do not leave their feelings at home when they go to work, we explore a case where an employee chooses a supplier in part because she finds the company rep attractive. The last case is about an intern who discovers pornography on his boss's computer and then does something really stupid.

Since this chapter is about the everyday ethical problems of working with a variety of personalities and problems in the workplace, it offers cases that look at the large and small ethical problems that people face when they work together. All of the cases challenge us to think about our moral obligations to each other. Respect for persons and fairness are both moral obligations, but they are more than that. They are at the core of what makes us good people and represent a good part of what motivates us to cooperate with one another. Thus, a solid sense of what is personally fair (and unfair) lies at the heart of personal, social, and professional success. People have known this for a long time. Around the eighth century B.C., the poet Hesiod wrote, "Neither famine nor disaster ever haunt men who do true justice; but lightheartedly they tend the fields which are all their care."

---

To: You
From: The Philosopher
Subject: "Sloth: The Noonday Demon"

Have you ever noticed how the seventh deadly sin, sloth, seems almost out of place with the first six? I always thought it was worse to be greedy or lustful than to be just plain lazy, but it turns out that sloth isn't simply about not wanting to work, it's about being bored, listless, and simply not caring about work. In the fourth century, the Egyptian monk Evagrius called sloth the "Noonday Demon" that attacked monks after lunch and made the day seem as if it lasted 50 hours. He said:

> [The Noonday Demon] causes the monk continually to look out the windows and forces him to step out of his cell and to gaze at the sun to see how far it is from the ninth hour and to look around, here and there, whether any of his brethren is near.*

It makes you wonder how many people are attacked by this demon every day at work either because of a mind-numbing job, a big lunch, or sheer exhaustion.

*Siegfried Wenzel. *The Sin of Sloth: Acedia* (Chapel Hill, NC: University of North Carolina Press, 1967). p. 5.

---

Norman E. Bowie | # Respecting the Humanity in a Person

Norman E. Bowie is a professor of management at the University of Minnesota.

*Part of the power of Kant's ethics lies in the extent of its ability to answer questions that Kant himself did not consider.*

*—Barbara Herman*

## INTRODUCTION

If the average American has a second moral principle to supplement the Golden Rule, it is probably a principle that says we should respect people. Respecting people is thoroughly interwoven into the fabric of American moral life. There is no one in the business community that has challenged the respect for persons principle as a principle in business ethics the way Albert Carr challenged the application of the Golden Rule in business. Yet, ironically, many of the moral criticisms of business practice are directed against policies that do not respect persons, e.g., that business human relations policies often invade privacy or relegate people to dead-end jobs where they cannot grow. In addition, there is considerable controversy, even among ethicists, as to what a respect for persons principle requires. . . .

I want to begin with an example which, although oversimplified, represents a standard discussion of the application of Kant's respect for persons principle to business. After presenting the example, I shall provide Kant's justification of the respect for persons principle and, using contemporary scholarship, explain what Kant means by the principle. With that in hand I will be able to apply the principle to more complex business examples.

I recall from my undergraduate ethics class more than 30 years ago that we struggled with the issue of whether buying a product, like vegetables in the supermarket, violated the respect for persons requirement of the second formulation of the categorical imperative. In buying our groceries did we merely use the clerk who rang up our purchases on the register? The first issue to be decided was whether we treated the sales person as a thing. Somewhat naively we decided that we did not merely use people in business transactions because we could accomplish our goal—buying carrots or potatoes—but that we could still show respect to those on the other end of the transaction. A casual observer in a supermarket can usually distinguish those patrons who treat the cashiers with respect from those who do not.

Our "solution" in this undergraduate class did not address business exchanges that involve tradeoffs between human and nonhuman sources. Any introductory economics text establishes that the efficient producer is instructed always to rearrange capital, land, machines, and workers so that their proportional marginal productivity is equal. The requirement of equal proportional marginal productivity works as follows: If the price of machines rises with respect to labor, substitute labor for machines. If the price of labor rises with respect to machines, substitute machines for labor. Both substitutions are equivalent.[1]

At first glance it looks as if a Kantian would say that the two substitutions are not morally equivalent. The first is morally permissible; the second is not morally permissible. It looks as if the employees are used as a means merely for the enhancement of the profits of the stockholders. It is morally permissible to use machines that way but it is not morally permissible to use people that way. Unlike the grocery-store example, the managers who act on behalf of the stockholders are not in a personal face-to-face

From Norman E. Bowie, *Business Ethics: A Kantian Perspective* (Oxford: Blackwell Publishers, 1999), 63–78 (edited).

relationship with the employees and thus they cannot avoid the charge of merely using the employees by saying that in the transaction they treated the other party to the transaction with respect. It doesn't matter if the manager was nice to the employees when she laid them off—a fact of some importance in contemporary discussions of downsizing because many managers think that when they fire people in a nice way, as opposed to firing them cruelly, they are off the moral hook. It is morally better to be nice than to be cruel, but the real issue is whether the firing can be morally justified. How would a Kantian using the respect for persons principle justify these contentions? To answer that question some explanation of Kant's respect for persons principle is in order.

## THE RESPECT FOR PERSONS PRINCIPLE

Kant's second formulation of the categorical imperative says "Act so that you treat humanity whether, in your own person or in that of another, always as an end and never as a means only."[2] Kant did not simply assert that human beings are entitled to respect; he had an elaborate argument for it. Human beings ought to be respected because human beings have dignity. For Kant, an object that has dignity is beyond price. That's what is wrong with the principle that says a manager should adjust the inputs of production to the point where the marginal productivity of each is equal. And further, the denial of dignity is what makes much downsizing unjust. In these cases, that which is without price, human beings, are treated as exchangeable with that which has a price. Human employees have a dignity that machines and capital do not have. Thus, managers cannot manage their corporate resources in the most efficient manner without violating the respect for persons principle—or so it seems. But why do persons possess a dignity which is beyond all price?

They have dignity because human beings are capable of autonomy and thus are capable of self-governance. As autonomous beings capable of self-governance they are also responsible beings, since autonomy and self-governance are

the conditions for responsibility. A person who is not autonomous and who is not capable of self-governance is not responsible. That's why little children or the mentally ill are not considered responsible beings. Thus, there is a conceptual link between being a human being, being an autonomous being, being capable of self-governance, and being a responsible being.

Autonomous responsible beings are capable of making and following their own laws; they are not simply subject to the causal laws of nature. Anyone who recognizes that he or she is autonomous would recognize that he or she is responsible (that he or she is a moral being). As Kant argues, the fact that one is a moral being enables us to say that such a being possesses dignity.

> Morality is the condition under which alone a rational being can be an end in himself because only through it is it possible to be a lawgiving member in the realm of ends. Thus morality, and humanity insofar as it is capable of morality, alone have dignity.[3]

It is the fact that human beings are moral agents that makes them subjects worthy of respect.

———

As I read Kant this is his argument for the necessity of including other persons within the scope of the respect for persons principle (treating the humanity in a person as an end and never as a means merely). It is based on consistency. What we say about one case, namely ourselves, we must say about similar cases, namely about other human beings.

———

Kant begins the third section of the *Foundations* as follows:

> What else, then, can freedom of the will be but autonomy (the property of the will to be a law to itself)? The proposition that the will is a law to itself in all its actions, however, only expresses the principle that we should act according to no other maxim than that which can also have itself as a

universal law for its object. And this is just the formula of the categorical imperative and the principle of morality. Therefore a free will and a will under moral laws are identical.[4]

Freedom and the ability to make laws are necessary and sufficient for moral agency. Moral agency is what gives people dignity. The importance of rationality comes when one explicates the meaning of freedom. Freedom is more than independence from causal laws. This is negative-freedom. Freedom is also the ability to make laws that are universal and to act on those laws in the world. As Kant says:

> The sole principle of morality consists in independence from all material of the law (i.e., a desired object) and in the accompanying determination of choice by the mere form of giving universal law which a maxim must be capable of having. That independence, however, is freedom in the negative sense, while this intrinsic legislation of pure and thus practical reason is freedom in the positive sense.[5]

---

Thus, we have shown why Kant believes persons have dignity and in this world are the only beings who have dignity. Kant has thus grounded our obligation to treat humanity in a person as an end and never as a means merely.

## NOTES

1. Richard Parker has correctly pointed out that if the substitution of the machines made the jobs of the remaining workers more meaningful, then Kant would not oppose the substitution of machines for people just because the cost of machines went down relative to the costs of people.

2. Immanuel Kant, *Foundations of the Metaphysics of Morals* (New York: Macmillian, 1990), p. 46.

3. Ibid. p. 52.

4. Ibid. p. 64.

5. Immanuel Kant, *Critique of Practical Reason*, (Upper Saddle River, NJ: Prentice Hall, 1993), pp. 33–34.

## QUESTIONS

1. What does the "respect for persons" principle mean in terms of the policies and practices of an organization?

2. If you simply are a means to your employer's ends, and you understand that this is the case when you are hired, would you care if you were treated as a means?

3. Do you agree with the idea that because humans are moral agents they are worthy of respect? What about people who are morally despicable?

---

To: You
From: The Philosopher
Subject: W. D. Ross on Prima Facie Duties

I like my work but I hate my job because of my boss. He treats most of the people in the office like they are garbage. We work like dogs and he never even bothers to say thank you. The other day he started yelling at the cleaning lady for making too much noise when she was emptying the trash in his office. The poor woman was almost in tears. My friend Sarah asked him if she could take a training seminar, so that she could get a promotion and he laughed and said, "you can hardly do your current job, let alone a job in management." He then promised Sarah that he would let her take the course in a year if her performance improved. It did improve, but then he told her he changed his mind.

My boss needs a good lesson on how to treat people. Sometimes I fantasize about tattooing the British philosopher W. D. Ross's list of prima facie duties on his chest—backwards so that he could read it in the mirror every day. "Prima facie" means "on the face of it" or "on first view." A prima facie duty or obligation is one that you should exercise all the time unless there is a very good moral reason not to do so. Ross's list of duties offer a simple guide to how you should treat people. It goes like this*:

1. Justice          Be just, prevent injustice and future injustice, and rectify existing injustices.
2. Non-injury       Avoid harming people.
3. Fidelity         Keep promises.
4. Veracity         Tell the truth.
5. Reparation       Apologize or make amends when you do something wrong.
6. Beneficence      Do good deeds for others and contribute to the development of their virtue, knowledge, or happiness.
7. Self-improvement Better yourself.
8. Gratitude        Express appreciation for good deeds.

* W. D. Ross, *The Right and the Good*, Oxford University Press, 1930.

Arlie Hochshild

# Exploring the Managed Heart

Arlie Hochshild is a professor of sociology at the University of California at Berkeley.

*The one area of her occupational life in which she might be "free to act," the area of her own personality, must now also be managed, must become the alert yet obsequious instrument by which goods are distributed.*

—C. Wright Mills

In a section in *Das Kapital* entitled "The Working Day," Karl Marx examines depositions submitted in 1863 to the Children's Employment Commission in England. One deposition was given by the mother of a child laborer in a wallpaper factory: "When he was seven years old I used to carry him [to work] on my back to and fro through the snow, and he used to work 16 hours a day. . . . I have often knelt down to feed him, as he stood by the machine, for he could not leave it or stop." Fed meals as he worked, as a steam engine is fed coal and water, this child was "an instrument of labor."[1] Marx questioned how many hours a day it was fair to use a human being as an instrument, and how much pay for being an instrument was fair, considering the profits that factory owners made. But he was also concerned with something he thought more fundamental: the human cost of becoming an "instrument of labor" at all.

From Arlie Hochshild, *The Managed Heart* (Berkeley: University of California Press, 1983), pp. 3–9.

On another continent 117 years later, a twenty-year-old flight attendant trainee sat with 122 others listening to a pilot speak in the auditorium of the Delta Airlines Stewardess Training Center. Even by modern American standards, and certainly by standards for women's work, she had landed an excellent job. The 1980 pay scale began at $850 a month for the first six months and would increase within seven years to about $20,000 a year. Health and accident insurance was provided, and the hours were good.[2]

The young trainee sitting next to me wrote on her notepad, "Important to smile. Don't forget smile." The admonition came from the speaker in the front of the room, a crewcut pilot in his early fifties, speaking in a Southern drawl: "Now girls, I want you to go out there and really *smile*. Your smile is your biggest *asset*. I want you to go out there and use it. Smile. *Really* smile. Really *lay it on.*"

The pilot spoke of the smile as the *flight attendant's* asset. But as novices like the one next to me move through training, the value of a personal smile is groomed to reflect the company's disposition—its confidence that its planes will not crash, its reassurance that departures and arrivals will be on time, its welcome and its invitation to return. Trainers take it as their job to attach to the trainee's smile an attitude, a viewpoint, a rhythm of feeling that is, as they often say, "professional." This deeper extension of the professional smile is not always easy to retract at the end of the workday, as one worker in her first year at World Airways noted: "Sometimes I come off a long trip in a state of utter exhaustion, but I find I can't relax. I giggle a lot, I chatter, I call friends. It's as if I can't release myself from an artificially created elation that kept me 'up' on the trip. I hope to be able to come down from it better as I get better at the job."

As the PSA jingle says, "Our smiles are not just painted on." Our flight attendants' smiles, the company emphasizes, will be more human than the phony smiles you're resigned to seeing on people who are paid to smile. There is a smile-like strip of paint on the nose of each PSA plane. Indeed, the plane and the flight attendant advertise each other. The radio advertisement goes on to promise not just smiles and service but a travel experience of real happiness and calm. Seen in one way, this is no more than delivering a service. Seen in another, it estranges workers from their own smiles and convinces customers that

---

To: You
From: The Philosopher
Subject: "Robert C. Solomon, *The Passions*"

I have a British friend who is always amazed by how service employees act in America. The first time she went to a bank here she said, "the teller acted as if she just happened to be there and was delighted that I had dropped by to see her." Emotions are a part of your job and your life. You shouldn't abuse them or fail to cultivate the right ones. As philosopher Robert C. Solomon noted:

> Emotions are the meanings of life. It is because we are moved, because we feel, that life has a meaning. The passionate life is the meaningful life. Of course, it all depend on *which* passions. There are the grand passions, the driving forces of life, a life well-lived. And then there are the petty passions, defensive and self-undermining, "which drag us down with their stupidity," as Nietzsche says. Some meanings, in other words, are de-meaning.

on-the-job behavior is calculated. Now that advertisements, training, notions of professionalism, and dollar bills have intervened between the smiler and the smiled upon, it takes an extra effort to imagine that spontaneous warmth can exist in uniform—because companies now advertise spontaneous warmth, too.

At first glance, it might seem that the circumstances of the nineteenth-century factory child and the twentieth-century flight attendant could not be more different. To the boy's mother, to Marx, to the members of the Children's Employment Commission, perhaps to the manager of the wallpaper factory, and almost certainly to the contemporary reader, the boy was a victim, even a symbol, of the brutalizing conditions of his time. We might imagine that he had an emotional half-life, conscious of little more than fatigue, hunger, and boredom. On the other hand, the flight attendant enjoys the upper-class freedom to travel, and she participates in the glamour she creates for others. She is the envy of clerks in duller, less well-paid jobs.

But a close examination of the differences between the two can lead us to some unexpected common ground. On the surface there is a difference in how we know what labor actually produces. How could the worker in the wallpaper factory tell when his job was done? Count the rolls of wallpaper; a good has been produced. How can the flight attendant tell when her job is done? A service has been produced; the customer seems content. In the case of the flight attendant, the *emotional style of offering the service is part of the service itself*, in a way that loving or hating wallpaper is not a part of producing wallpaper. Seeming to "love the job" becomes part of the job; and actually trying to love it, and to enjoy the customers, helps the worker in this effort.

In processing people, the product is a state of mind. Like firms in other industries, airline companies are ranked according to the quality of service their personnel offer. Egon Ronay's yearly *Lucas Guide* offers such a ranking; besides being sold in airports and drugstores and reported in newspapers, it is cited in management memoranda and passed down to those who train and supervise

flight attendants. Because it influences consumers, airline companies use it in setting their criteria for successful job performance by a flight attendant. In 1980 the *Lucas Guide* ranked Delta Airlines first in service out of fourteen airlines that fly regularly between the United States and both Canada and the British Isles. Its report on Delta included passages like this:

> [Drinks were served] not only with a smile but with concerned enquiry such as, "Anything else I can get you, madam?" The atmosphere was that of a civilized party—with the passengers, in response, behaving like civilized guests. . . . Once or twice our inspectors tested stewardesses by being deliberately exacting, but they were never roused, and at the end of the flight they lined up to say farewell with undiminished brightness. . . .
>
> [Passengers are] quick to detect strained or forced smiles, and they come aboard wanting to *enjoy* the flight. One of us looked forward to his next trip on Delta "because it's fun." Surely that is how passengers ought to feel.[3]

The work done by the boy in the wallpaper factory called for a coordination of mind and arm, mind and finger, and mind and shoulder. We refer to it simply as physical labor. The flight attendant does physical labor when she pushes heavy meal carts through the aisles, and she does mental work when she prepares for and actually organizes emergency landings and evacuations. But in the course of doing this physical and mental labor, she is also doing something more, something I define as *emotional labor*.[4] This labor requires one to induce or suppress feeling in order to sustain the outward countenance that produces the proper state of mind in others—in this case, the sense of being cared for in a convivial and safe place. This kind of labor calls for a coordination of mind and feeling, and it sometimes draws on a source of self that we honor as deep and integral to our individuality.

Beneath the difference between physical and emotional labor there lies a similarity in the possible cost of doing the work: the worker can become estranged or alienated from an aspect of self—either the body or the margins of the soul—that is *used* to do the work. The factory boy's arm functioned like a piece of machinery used to produce wallpaper. His employer, regarding that arm as an instrument, claimed control over its speed and motions. In this situation, what was the relation between the boy's arm and his mind? Was his arm in any meaningful sense his *own?*[5]

This is an old issue, but as the comparison with airline attendants suggests, it is still very much alive. If we can become alienated from goods in a goods-producing society, we can become alienated from service in a service-producing society. This is what C. Wright Mills, one of our keenest social observers, meant when he wrote in 1956, "We need to characterize American society of the mid-twentieth century in more psychological terms, for now the problems that concern us most border on the psychiatric."[6]

When she came off the job, what relation had the flight attendant to the "artificial elation" she had induced on the job? In what sense was it her *own* elation on the job? The company lays claim not simply to her physical motions—how she handles food trays—but to her emotional actions and the way they show in the ease of a smile. The workers I talked to often spoke of their smiles as being *on* them but not *of* them. They were seen as an extension of the makeup, the uniform, the recorded music, the soothing pastel colors of the airplane decor, and the daytime drinks, which taken together orchestrate the mood of the passengers. The final commodity is not a certain number of smiles to be counted like rolls of wallpaper. For the flight attendant, the smiles are a *part of her work*, a part that requires her to coordinate self and feeling so that the work seems to be effortless. To show that the enjoyment takes effort is to do the job poorly. Similarly, part of the job is to disguise fatigue and irritation, for otherwise the labor would show in an unseemly way, and the product—passenger contentment—would be damaged.[7] Because it is easier to disguise fatigue and irritation if they can be banished altogether, at least for brief periods, this feat calls for emotional labor.

The reason for comparing these dissimilar jobs is that the modern assembly-line worker has for some time been an outmoded symbol of modern industrial labor; fewer than 6 percent of workers now work on assembly lines. Another kind of labor has now come into symbolic prominence—the voice-to-voice or face-to-face delivery of service—and the flight attendant is an appropriate model for it. There have always been public-service jobs, of course; what is new is that they are now socially engineered and thoroughly organized from the top. Though the flight attendant's job is no worse and in many ways better than other service jobs, it makes the worker more vulnerable to the social engineering of her emotional labor and reduces her control over that labor. Her problems, therefore, may be a sign of what is to come in other such jobs.

Emotional labor is potentially good. No customer wants to deal with a surly waitress, a crabby bank clerk, or a flight attendant who avoids eye contact in order to avoid getting a request. Lapses in courtesy by those paid to be courteous are very real and fairly common. What they show us is how fragile public civility really is. We are brought back to the question of what the social carpet actually consists of and what it requires of those who are supposed to keep it beautiful. The laggards and sluff-offs of emotional labor return us to the basic questions. What is emotional labor? What do we do when we manage emotion? What, in fact, is emotion? What are the costs and benefits of managing emotion, in private life and at work?

## NOTES

1. Karl Marx, (1977) *Capital,* Vol. 1. "Intro". By Ernest Mandel Tr. Ben Fowkes. New York: Vintage, pp. 356–357, 358.

2. For stylistic convenience, I shall use the pronoun "she" when referring to a flight attendant, except when a specific male flight attendant is being discussed. Otherwise I shall try to avoid verbally excluding either gender.

3. *Lucas Guide 1980*, p. 66.

4. I use the term *emotional labor* to mean the management of feeling to create a publicly observable facial and bodily display; emotional labor is sold for a wage and therefore has *exchange value*. I use the synonymous terms *emotion work* or *emotion management* to refer to these same acts done in a private context where they have *use value*.

5. *Lucas Guide 1980*, pp. 66, 76. Fourteen aspects of air travel at the stages of departure, arrival, and the flight itself are ranked. Each aspect is given one of sixteen differently weighted marks. For example, "The

friendliness or efficiency of the staff is more important than the quality of the pilot's flight announcement or the selection of newspapers and magazines offered."

6. C. Wright Mills (1956), *White Collar.* New York: Oxford University Press.

7. Like a commodity, service that calls for emotional labor is subject to the laws of supply and demand. Recently the demand for this labor has increased and the supply of it drastically decreased. The airline industry speed-up since the 1970s has been followed by a worker slowdown. The slowdown reveals how much emotional labor the job required all along. It suggests what costs even happy workers under normal conditions pay for this labor without a name. The speed-up has sharpened the ambivalence many workers feel about how much of oneself to give over to the role and how much of oneself to protect from it.

## QUESTIONS

1. What are the various types of emotional labor found in the workplace today?

2. What kinds of emotional labor are acceptable and what kinds are unacceptable in the workplace? What ethical principles would you use to draw the line?

3. Does emotional labor violate your personal autonomy and freedom of expression?

<br/>

Bruce Barry

# The Cringing and the Craven: Freedom of Expression in the Workplace

Bruce Barry is the Brownlee O. Currey, Jr., Professor of Management at the Owen Graduate School of Management and Professor of Sociology at Vanderbilt.

In September 2004, Lynne Gobbell was fired from her job as a factory machine operator in Decatur, Alabama, because her automobile in the company's parking lot displayed a bumper sticker supporting John Kerry for president. In 2001, Clayton Vernon was fired by the Enron Corporation after posting on an Internet message board his opinion that Enron CEO Kenneth Lay is "a truly evil and satanic figure." In 1998, Edward Blum resigned his position as a stockbroker in Houston after (as he alleged) the firm pressured him to curtail his off-work political activities in support of a municipal ballot initiative on affirmative action. In August 2004, a web developer named Joyce Park was fired from her job at an online social network website company for mentions of her employer in writings posted to her blog. Gonzalo Cotto, an aircraft factory worker in Connecticut, sued his employer after he was fired for refusing to display an American flag at his workstation during a Gulf War celebration. After several appeals, Connecticut's highest court rejected Cotto's claim that his dismissal violated a state law protecting constitutional rights in the workplace.

These incidents share a common theme: punishment or retaliation by an employer for employee actions that involve expressive behavior—verbal or symbolic actions that would, in other domains of social life and in many countries, be regarded as protected speech. Freedom of speech and expression are bedrock tenets of liberty found in the legal frameworks of most nations having systems of civil democracy or republican government. Yet as these examples indicate, the scope of free expression in and around the workplace can be quite limited (especially in the United States compared to many other "Western" democracies). Work is a place where many adults devote significant portions of their waking lives, but it is also a place where civil liberties, including but not limited to freedom of speech, are significantly constrained.

## DEFINING WORKPLACE FREEDOM OF EXPRESSION

Workplace speech as a liberty having roots in law, policy, custom, or ethics has received limited scholarly attention, but when it has, the focus has typically been constrained to speech at work or about work. For example, Campbell, a philosopher, defined *workplace freedom of expression* as "the capacity of employees to have and express opinions in their workplace about their workplace and the organisation that employs them." Estlund, a legal scholar, defined *freedom of speech in the workplace* as "the freedom to speak out at or about the workplace free from the threat of discharge or serious discipline." Lippke defined *work-related speech* as "speech that occurs within the workplace, but also speech which is sufficiently about work so that though it occurs outside the workplace, it is subject to employer sanction."

The incident mentioned at the outset involving a worker discharged for a political message affixed to an automobile in a factory parking lot moves beyond these cited definitions in two ways: by involving content that is plainly unrelated to work or workplace and by taking the form of expression that is not spoken (not literally "speech"). Accordingly, I define expression broadly here. Free speech theorist Scanlon defined an act of expression as "any action that is intended . . . to communicate to one or more persons some proposition or attitude" including acts of speech, publication, displays, failures to display, and artistic performances. Baker critized Scanlon's definition as too narrow, noting that it excludes self-expressive and creative forms of communication.

Siding with Baker, I encompass within "expression" actions that convey a proposition or attitude, or that involve a personal display of self-expression or creativity. The construct of interest in this article, then, is *workplace freedom of expression*, which I define as *the ability to engage in legally protected acts of expression at or away from the workplace, on subjects related or unrelated to the workplace, free from the threat of formal or informal workplace retribution, discipline, or discharge.*

This definition is expansive, incorporating the wide canvas of expression that might be legally protected in a constitutional democracy, but is delimited by its focus on expression that is discouraged, proscribed, or regulated by an employer. To illustrate the breadth of acts potentially within its purview, I show in Figure 1-1 a simplified taxonomy of expression in three dimensions. Acts of expression of potential interest for this analysis vary by *venue* (occurring at the workplace or away from it), by *topic* (addressing matters related to work or organization, or not), and by *publicness* (occurring through channels and contexts that make the conveyence one-to-one/few vs. one-to-many). Of the eight types implied within the figure, the two comprising the upper-left quadrant have garnered the most attention from researchers studying interaction processes in organizations, and understandably so. One can assume that the octant in the lower right—expression that occurs away from the workplace, on off-work topics, in private settings—is the expressive form of least interest presumably to employers, and by extension to this analysis (although by no means wholly irrelevant).

A renewed interest in and analysis of free expression in the workplace is warranted for several reasons. First, the legal climate regarding free speech in the workplace has evolved in significant ways since Ewing and Werhane were writing about employment rights.

Second, the workplace itself is changing in ways that render rights to expression both more threatened and more important. Yamada developed this argument, describing several factors that raise concerns about employers' inclination to

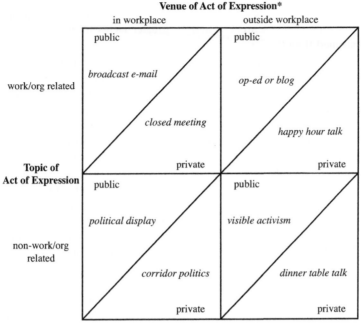

FIGURE 1-1 Taxonomy of acts of expression.

limit workplace expression: individual economic insecurity that breeds self-censorship at work, a rise in electronic surveillance of workers, a decline in unionization, an expansion in corporate political partisanship (which ostensibly chills employee expression that might deviate from the preferred point of view), and the simple fact that people work longer hours than in the past.

The notion that people spend more time at work bridges into a third rationale for more attention to workplace expression: the role of the workplace, given that many individuals spend the bulk of their waking hours there, as a building block for community engagement and a critical site for exchanges of views and public debate around political and social issues. Moreover, if individuals are spending more time on the job, then opportunities to engage in expression outside the workplace inevitably diminish. The relevance of speech rights to broader notions of

citizenship and community in a free society is a subject to which I will return later.

Fourth, advances in information technology, and individuals' ability to use technology for expressive purposes, change the landscape of free expression in and around the workplace (and everywhere else). A currently prominent illustration is found in cases where individuals are sanctioned or dismissed for comments about the workplace that appear in online web sites such as blogs; these in a sense are technology-enabled "publication" outlets that were previously unavailable. Workplace freedom of expression has occupied new terrain in an era of web sites, email, instant messaging, blogs, vlogs, wikis, and podcasts, compared to what existed before.

Lastly, renewed attention to free speech at work is warranted by the abundance (noted earlier) of research on related topics within the fields of organizational behavior and labor relations. As a consequence of this progress, researchers and managers are more attuned than they were twenty years ago to the role of workplace expression and participation in organizational processes and outcomes.

A generation ago there was optimism that employee rights were expanding not only as a matter of evolving practice, but as a veritable movement building toward radical change in corporate life. In 1974 an editor at the *Harvard Business Review* wrote:

> Within the management castle, as well as out in the woods and fields, there is growing support for employee rights. . . . [T]he notion of a "bill of rights" for corporate employees has been advocated in the *Harvard Business Review* and will doubtless find its way soon into other management journals.[1]

Ewing predicted a "sea change" in the social and intellectual environment of organizations. Thirty years later, it would be delusional to suggest that Ewing's predictions have come to fruition. The law in the United States (from an employment law perspective) has not significantly expanded its accommodation of employee expression, even as exceptions to employment-at-will have grown wider. Outside of academic writing, connections between speech, other civil liberties at work, and the state and health of larger civil society remain elusive. As Balkin wrote in an essay chronicling the evolution of free speech doctrine in the twentieth century, "speech in the workplace is not considered speech in the same sense as political or expressive speech generally, but is thought to be utilitarian, pedestrian, and incidental to the performance of work."

The proposition that people at work deserve greater rights to expression than the law, management practice, or conventional wisdom allow is not a utopian call for a fundamental transformation of economic relations in employment, or even for a broadly democratized workplace. It is merely an assertion that a market economy can still flourish when adults sell their time and their labor but not all of their liberties. Where suppression of one's power to think, speak, and dissent is conventionally accepted in workplaces, the ideology of management is given license to run free, not just at work, but everywhere. This places at risk the liberty interests of individuals, but also jeopardizes the health of civil democracy in community and society. Justice Hugo Black put it this way over a half-century ago: "Our own free society should never forget that laws which stigmatize and penalize thought and speech of the unorthodox have a way of reaching, ensnaring and silencing many more people than at first intended. We must have freedom of speech for all or we will in the long run have it for none but the cringing and the craven."

## NOTE

1. David W. Ewing, "Free Speech from Nine to Five." *The Nation* 218:755–56, 1974.

## QUESTIONS

1. What kinds of speech can be justifiably prohibited in the workplace?

2. Does freedom of speech protect an employees right to say what he or she knows is true at any time?

3. To what extent do managers have the right to tell employees what they can say and not say in regards to their work?

Loraleigh
Keashly

# Workplace Bullying

Loraleigh Keashly is Associate Professor of Communication and Director of the MA program in Dispute Resolution at Wayne State University.

## WORKPLACE BULLYING: THE NATURE OF THE BEAST

Workplace bullying is a special case of workplace aggression. Workplace aggression refers to efforts by individuals to harm others with whom they work. Before addressing workplace bullying's unique features, it is important to discuss aggressive behaviors more generally. I never cease to be amazed at the range and type of behaviors that fall within this domain. To more completely map out this behavioral space, Neuman and Baron utilized Buss's approach of three dimensions to define the space. The dimensions are:

1. Physical (deeds)—verbal (words, tone)
2. Active (doing a behavior)—passive (withholding or "failures to do")
3. Direct (at the target)—indirect (at something or someone the target values)

This approach describes the "methods of attack." This is not a comprehensive listing of all possible behaviors, but it will give an idea of ways in which bullying can be conducted.

1. **Threat to Professional Status.** Questioning competence, belittling opinion, professional humiliation in front of colleagues, negative comments about intelligence, questioning a person's ability to supervisors; spreading rumors or gossip. These are primarily active behaviors.
2. **Threat to Personal Standing.** Name-calling, insults, verbal abuse, tantrums, intimidating behaviors, devaluing with reference to age,

gender, race/ethnicity or appearance, hostile gestures. These are predominantly active behaviors

3. **Isolation.** Exclusion from work-related gatherings, silent treatment, withholding information, ignoring contributions, not taking concerns seriously, preventing access to opportunities or promotion, poisoning others against the target. These behaviors tend to be passive in nature.
4. **Overwork/Unreal Expectations.** Undue pressure, impossible deadlines, unnecessary disruptions, setting up to fail, unreal or ambiguous expectations; more so than for others in the same environment.
5. **Destabilization.** Others take credit for work; assigning meaningless tasks, removing responsibility, denied raise or promotion without reason; excessive monitoring.

I have several observations regarding these behaviors. First, what is particularly unique about workplace bullying is that it is often about what people **do not do** rather than what they do, i.e., "lack of action" such as withholding information, excluding from meetings, the silent treatment. This poses particular challenges for the target, bystanders, managers, and third parties to whom these concerns are brought. Thus, it is important for ombudsmen to note that most aggressive behavior at work is psychological in nature and often passive or "failures to do" behaviors.

Second, the nature of the relationship between the target and actor will influence the specific expressions of hostility. This has to do with the means and opportunity available to the actor. For example, a supervisor due to his/her control over rewards and job assignments has the opportunity and the means to bully through overwork and destabilization types of behaviors. Opportunities available to peers may have more to do with information sharing and other working relationships. Thus, behaviors falling under threats to personal and professional standing as well as isolation are more likely under their control. Subordinates, due to their less powerful organizational position, may engage in more indirect kinds of behaviors such as rumors or gossip or withholding of information. These examples of actor means and opportunity illustrate that bullying is not limited to one type of relationship. Indeed, bullying can be top-down (boss–subordinate), horizontal (peer-peer) or bottom-up (subordinate–boss). Thus, workplace bullying is considered to be **relational** in nature— harming others through purposeful manipulation and damage of relationships. This is important for ombudsmen to know as it requires that the relational context of the experience be assessed. Thus, investigations will need to involve at the very least assessment of target and actor and consideration of the nature of their relationship organizationally, e.g., the kind of contact that is typically required for this type of relationship.

Third, identifying the behaviors, while necessary, is insufficient for understanding workplace bullying. Indeed, in isolation, each of these behaviors may be seen as minor and people may wonder what all the fuss is about (So he glared at you? So what?). What makes these behaviors more than they appear is their **frequency** and the **duration of exposure**. Workplace bullying and its related constructs are **repeated** and **enduring** forms of workplace aggression. **Persistency** is the core feature that distinguishes workplace bullying from more occasional aggressive treatment. The defining characteristics are as follows:

1. **Negative Actions that Are Repeated and Patterned.** This element captures both frequency of occurrence (daily, weekly, monthly) and variety (more than one type of behavior). Regardless of the construct, it is the frequency of exposure to hostile behaviors that has been directly linked to a variety of negative individual (health, job attitudes and behaviors) and organizational (productivity, turnover) outcomes, i.e., the greater the exposure, greater the impact. Being exposed to a number of

different hostile behaviors contributes to this sense of frequency. We found that the number of different events uniquely contributed to negative individual outcomes beyond the mean frequency of exposure. But the number of behaviors and the frequency of occurrence do not adequately capture the nature of exposure. Frequency of exposure must also be considered in terms of the overall frequency of contacts with the actor. For example, perhaps the boss only yells at an employee once a month but if the employee only sees him/her once a month that is 100% of the time. The implications of that for a target are very different than for a target whose actor behaves this way once a month but they see him/her daily, i.e., they are exposed to other behaviors, hopefully positive, that will influence their overall experience. Further, the frequency of exposure can be created (or enhanced) by the target reliving the experience, i.e., rumination. Finally the repeated nature of exposure may be linked to the involvement of more than one actor, i.e., mobbing. The repeated and patterned nature of these behaviors highlights the importance of investigating a pattern of behavior rather than each incident as a separate item. Further the frequency of contact that would be required organizationally "normally" for the relationship is also important to consider in any assessment.

2. **Prolonged Exposure over Time (Duration).** It is duration that is particularly distinctive about workplace bullying. Researchers have used timeframes for assessing these actions ranging from six months (which is typical in the European literature) to a year. These timeframes pale in comparison to the reports of those who self-identify as targets of workplace bullying. They report exposure ranging up to 10 years. Zapf and Gross report that average duration of those who were bullied by one person was 28 months, for those who were bullied by two to four people or more than 4 people (i.e., mobbing), it was 36 months and 55 months, respectively. Thus, the question

of "how long is too long" is important to consider in this discussion of workplace bullying. While researchers often specify at least one event weekly for a minimum period of 6 or 12 months, this timeframe does not necessarily appeal to those for example, in Human Resources or indeed, ombudsmen who will want to be able to address a developing hostile situation as quickly as possible, before irreversible damage sets in. Thus, codifying a specific minimum duration in policy may hamper reporting of problems and ultimately effective management. It is sufficient to note that bullying tends to occur over an extended period of time.

Fourth, while persistence or chronicity is the important marker of workplace bullying, it is also important to recognize that the nature and intensity of behaviors directed at the target do not stay the same throughout. Long-standing bullying situations will often show a progression or escalation of aggression from covert and indirect behaviors to increasingly overt, direct and in some situations physical. Research suggests that such escalation will have the effect of rendering target attempts to constructively and actively respond ineffective. This puts the target at increased risk for injury psychologically, emotionally, and physically (see further discussion below). The failure of constructive methods also may promote target resistance and retaliation behaviors that may further an escalatory spiral. Such spirals can result in drawing others into the situation, often as actors and may even result in secondary spirals or cascades of aggression elsewhere in the unit or organization, i.e., the development of a hostile work environment.

Given the above description, a question is often raised as to how workplace bullying, particularly at advanced stages is different from an escalated conflict between employees. What appears to distinguish bullying from "normal" workplace conflict is the existence of a power imbalance. This imbalance can be preexisting in the structure of the workplace (boss-subordinate) or it can develop as a conflict escalates and one party becomes disadvantaged

relative to the other. The importance of the imbalance is the potential impact on the target's resources and ability to defend him/herself as well as the actor's ability to continue their actions. This has implications for the nature and intensity of negative effects and highlights the importance of prevention and early intervention, as well as the necessity of strategies for remediation of effects.

Taken together, the prolonged exposure to repeated hostile actions with an inability to defend creates a situation in which the target becomes increasingly disabled. Further such a relationship, if allowed to continue, has the potential to not only spread its impact beyond the immediate dyad to others in the organization (e.g., witnesses) but it also has the possibility of creating hostile work environments where many workers are now "behaving badly". The bullying process with its progression and its span of impact illustrates the **communal** nature of workplace bullying. That is, a variety of different parties are involved in or impacted by workplace bullying. This communal nature requires that ombudsmen will need to engage a number of people in the investigation and ultimately the management of the bullying.

### *Cyberspace: The Next (and Current) Frontier*

Before leaving this section on bullying's nature, It is Important to acknowledge modern technological devices as the new medium for bullying, e.g., bullying through the internet, email, text messaging, video/picture clips and social networking sites. Lois Price Spratlen ombudsman for the University of Washington at the time was among the first to identify how email was being used to bully and harass others. Known as cyberbullying or cyber-aggression, several unique features of the medium conspire to make it a particularly virulent and destructive forum for and form of bullying. Some of these features are:

(a) the ability of the actor(s) to be anonymous making it more difficult for both targets and those investigating to identify the source. By reducing detection, actors may become emboldened to engage in more extreme and destructive attacks on the person's reputation;

(b) span of impact from a few organizational members to millions of new media users globally; and

(c) once these messages or images are released, they are difficult to expunge from cyberspace, creating a situation in which exposure can be continually renewed and thus relived, increasing damage to the target and others.

It is critical that researchers and professionals focus their efforts on understanding the nature and impact of cyberbullying and to seek ways to manage its use and impact.

## QUESTIONS

1. Do you think that bullying is a serious problem in the workplace?

2. What is the difference between being criticized by your boss for substandard work and bullying?

3. How can you tell if your boss is engaging in passive bullying rather than simply ignoring you?

---

*The Economist*     |     # Doing Business in Dangerous Places

Setting up a business abroad has always been risky, and not just financially. To create the colony of 90,000 white settlers that, in the late 17th century, earned enormous profits from growing tobacco in Virginia required the immigration of around 116,000 people. The chaps who sailed for India a century later had to endure even worse. "The variety of means by which a man could be carried off was quite bewildering," observes a recent book on the East India Company. "Malaria, typhoid or enteric fever, cholera, dysentery and smallpox were the most common diseases, and the bites of scorpions and mad dogs were frequently lethal."

Those who today run businesses in the nastier parts of the world also face a bewildering range of threats to the safety and health of their employees. Indeed, there are many more disagreeable places to choose from than there were a generation ago. In the days of the Cold War, there was usually a government to deal with, or at worst a rebel authority. These days, a growing number of countries, or large tracts of them, are run (if at all) by shifting coalitions of warlords or local bullies. Such power vacuums create potentially lethal uncertainty. They also aggravate more mundane (but no less burdensome) risks, from life-threatening driving conditions to the spread of diseases such as AIDS and malaria.

Moreover, some of the protection once offered by a white face, a red cross, a neutral flag or the passport of a Great Power has now vanished. As a result, many places that have long been dangerous have become even more so. Last month, Médecins Sans Frontières (MSF), an aid group that specialises in sending medical staff to countries in conflict, shut all its programmes in Afghanistan after five of its staff were killed in a deliberate attack on a clearly marked MSF vehicle. Taliban spokesmen said that aid organisations such as MSF were helping the Americans, something the charity vehemently denies. Anyone doing business in a conflict zone runs similar risks: driving a truck or building a telecoms network may not seem a political act to the company that undertakes the task, but followers of Osama bin Laden think otherwise.

*The Economist*, "Doing Business in Dangerous Places," August 14, 2004, p. 11.

## HOW TO BE SAFER

For most employers, health and safety issues are generally about avoiding minor injuries and malfunctions. To send employees to regions where injury or death are real possibilities involves, on the face of it, quite a different approach. Sending staff to work in Iraq or Colombia might appear to be the reverse of good health-and-safety practice. In fact, whereas some of the principles of protecting employees in dangerous places are different, others are surprisingly similar.

For example, the greatest risks even in some of the scariest parts of the world are not of kidnap or murder, but of illness, traffic accidents or violent crime. In the heyday of the East India Company, the single biggest cause of death of the company's employees was not mad dogs or scorpions, but the familiar drug of alcohol (aggravated by bad diet and lack of exercise). In Congo today, malaria is a far bigger risk for expatriates than murder. The good news: such threats are easier to deal with than the terrors of ambush or armed attack. One of the simplest ways to lessen risk is to get all expats, their families and local staff to wear seatbelts: prosaic but effective.

Employers sending people to dangerous places need, first of all, to be honest about what they are doing. That means thinking early about the risks involved. Too many companies entering markets in backward countries, even those not at war, greatly underestimate the cost of security. Employers also need to decide early on how big a threat to their staff would force them to withdraw. That will vary from firm to firm. KBR, part of Halliburton, has lost 42 employees in Iraq and Kuwait and yet stayed put. Many other companies would have retreated at a serious threat to just one staff member.

Being honest with employees entails—as far as possible—avoiding pressure on them to go somewhere dangerous. That is sometimes easier said than done: the oil-company engineer willing to work only in comfy places is unlikely to thrive. It also means giving staff good advance training, especially in first aid. And it means using people with experience where possible. For instance, South Africans, accustomed to working in some of the riskier parts of their continent, may understand how to deal with a threat much better than someone coming to Africa for the first time. Inexperienced staff need more specialist support, perhaps from one of the companies in the burgeoning threat-management business.

## SIMMERING

Inexperienced staff may also be eager to go for the wrong reasons—to be able to boast that they have risked death for their work and survived. One constant hazard is the "boiling frog" syndrome. Where danger is mounting, as it seems to be now in Saudi Arabia, people on the ground may not realise it, or may prefer to pretend otherwise, until too late. Even if they do acknowledge the risk, they may stay on out of exaggerated loyalty to clients or misplaced zeal to outlast competitors. Wise companies make sure that the judgment of independent security experts goes to head office, not the local boss, and that risks are kept under constant review.

What about using local staff? They may have a better sense of danger and be less conspicuous than expatriates. Many employers in dangerous parts of the world try to keep the use of foreigners to a minimum. That is fine if they also take their responsibilities to local staff seriously, but not if the locals are put at greater risk than expatriates because they are considered more expendable.

Why go, if the risks are great? There are good reasons for operating in dangerous lands. There are people who need help, and countries to rebuild. But for companies, the lure is usually the one that led early Virginians to endure the privations of America or the British to colonise India: if the risks are great, then so too are the rewards. What matters is that the rewards are not earned at the cost of putting employees in more danger than, once properly informed, they choose to accept.

## QUESTIONS

1. To what extent should companies be held responsible for employees who get kidnapped or murdered while working in a foreign country?

2. In an era of terrorism, are there some places or conditions under which no company should send employees?

3. Is a company responsible for risks that employees take on their own volition in dangerous places?

Harry J. Van
Buren III

# Boundaryless Careers and Employability Obligations

Harry J. Van Buren III is associate Professor
of Management at the Anderson Schools of
Management, University of New Mexico.

Few issues in the academic study of management
are as contentious as observed (and potential)
changes in career patterns. The idea that employers
and employees increasingly do not expect to have
lifelong relationships has been the subject of much
academic study and public debate. Optimists believe
that boundaryless careers, defined as careers that
unfold in multiple employment settings, provide
opportunities for personal fulfillment and economic
prosperity while freeing people from the demands
of moribund organizational structures. A person
following the boundaryless career (whether by
choice or not) expects as a matter of course to
work for a number of organizations in a temporary
capacity; each employment relationship is in effect a
transactional contract of limited duration. Pessimists
suspect that changing career patterns are really
driven by employers' desires to be rid of as many
costly permanent employees (and their benefits) as
possible. It is not surprising, therefore, that passions
run high on both sides of the debate.

## WHAT ARE BOUNDARYLESS CAREERS?

Before discussing "boundaryless careers," it is helpful to define "career." A person's career is the unfolding sequence of his or her work experiences overtime.
For the purposes of this paper, everyone—not just
professionals—is understood to have a career. A
career can consist of one job held in an organization
for a long time, many jobs held in the same organization, the same job in many different organizations,
or many jobs in many organizations; the sum total of

one's work experiences in one or several organizations is her career. The term "boundaryless career"
did not come into existence until the early 1990s, and
was the theme of the 1993 Academy of Management
annual meeting.

Career theory has traditionally focused on the
unfolding of a person's work experiences with one
organization over time. The "boundaryless career"—
a career that unfolds over time in multiple employment settings—describes a variety of changes in
career patterns that have been recently observed.
Employment practices like downsizing and the
use of temporary/contingent workforces illustrate
how organizational preferences for flexibility have
affected career patterns. The traditional view of
careers noted above—and the stable employment
relationships assumed thereunder—has been largely
replaced by a new view that emphasizes employer
flexibility.

## WHO IS HARMED BY THE BOUNDRYLESS CAREER?

Although many studies of boundaryless careers have
focused on contexts like Silicon Valley, in which
employees with rare skills have significant market
power, a more difficult ethical question is posed
by the advent of boundaryless career practices for
employees with fungible skills. The ethical challenge posed by boundaryless careers is not the plight
of well-compensated employees whose stock options
and other forms of compensation equilibrate effort
and reward, but rather the individuals whose talents
mark them for lowlypaid, dead-end jobs. Workers
with rare and valuable skills are most likely to have
the sorts of contractual arrangements that ensure (1)
their assent to the terms of the exchange relationship between themselves and the organization and

(2) explicit guarantees of remuneration and benefits. For those workers whose labor is a not a scarce commodity, their treatment by employers is quite different: Such employees are not likely to be given the sorts of benefits and due process protections enjoyed by workers who are thought to have rare and valuable skills. The notion that employees have less power than employers in negotiating the terms of exchange agreements can be traced back to Smith, who noted that "many workmen could not subsist a week, few could subsist a month, and scarcely any a year without employment. In the long run the work-man may be as necessary to his master as his master is to him, but the necessity is not so immediate."

The effect of boundaryless careers is to exacerbate the negative effects of the two-tiered workforce in most industrialized societies, composed of

1. a small top tier of highly sought-after employees with rare skills whose market power enables them to demand and receive fair treatment from employers and
2. a large second tier of employees whose skills are fungible and easily replaced. As a quasi-commodity, the pay and benefits of people in this tier will likely fall rather than rise in real terms unless they are able to acquire skills that move them closer to the first tier.

The first tier is largely able to demand and to receive equitable treatment. As Meyer has put it, "them who has, gets." The second tier faces a more tenuous existence; unless their skills are constantly upgraded, they will face greater competition for, and declining benefits from, jobs requiring fungible skills.[4] Second-tier workers are more likely to be negatively affected by boundaryless careers than first-tier workers.

## RISK SHARING, FAIRNESS, EMPLOYABILITY, AND THE BOUNDARYLESS CAREER

The central issue with regard to boundaryless careers is this: who assumes what risk in the employment relationship? It is true, of course, that employees traditionally have borne risk when working for an organization. Although it is commonly held that shareholders—as residual claimants—bear the most risk in a publicly held enterprise, employees also bear risks. Employees face health and safety risks, the risk that the organization will go bankrupt, and (in the case of firms that have employee stock ownership plans) the risk that the company's stock will lose value. These risks are faced by almost every employee. But employees—whether in a boundaryless career pattern or not—also face the risk that the firm-specific investments that they make in a particular employer will not be fairly compensated.

In any employment relationship, two kinds of skills are used by employees. The first sort of skill is general to the particular task that a particular employee performs. A computer professional, for example, uses a set of skills that are transferable across organizations. But employees—even in very short-term occupations—also use firm-specific skills that are not salable on the external labor market. Such skills may include things as mundane as knowledge of organizational logistics. or as fundamental as information about the firm's values and mission. Skills therefore are transferable across organizations but require firm-specific knowledge in order to be useful in a particular firm. When an employee works for a particular firm, she is (or should be) making investments in both general skills (salable on external labor markets) and firm-specific skills (generally not salable on external labor markets).

In a traditional, long-term employment relationship, there is some element of mutuality and risk sharing between employers and employees: the organization invests in the general and firm-specific skills of employees and in turn employees exhibit some level of loyalty to the firm. Of course, employee investments in a particular firm are subject to abuse by employers; employers can, and do, change the terms of exchange relationships with employees—and employees are generally not able to force the organization to live up to the old "agreement," and employees tend to prefer the predictability of stable employment relationships to the unpredictability of more ephemeral arrangements. Further, there is some balancing of risk in firms that seek to maintain stable employment relationships: The firm makes investments in employees and compensates them for their lost opportunity costs by providing further (general and firm-specific) skill investment and employment stability, and employees in turn voluntarily agree to stay with that employer long enough to allow the employer to earn returns from such investments in employees. It should be noted that agreements between employers and employees in this sort of arrangement are implicit rather than explicit in nature, following the logic of psychological rather than written contracts.

In the boundaryless career, however, employees still need to bring general and firm-specific skills into their employment relationships. (Even short-term employment relationships do not obviate the need for firm-specific knowledge.) But the terms of exchange between employers and employees are different in a firm that uses a boundaryless career model than in a firm that maintains strong internal labor markets and career ladders. Now employees not only bear the burden of maintaining their general skills and acquiring firm-specific knowledge, but they cannot rely on any promise of a long-term employment relationship with a particular employer. The risk to the employee increases dramatically in a boundaryless-career relationship as compared with a more traditional relationship: the employee not only bears all of the burdens common to any job, but also becomes responsible for acquiring general and firm-specific skills without any promise of a long-term relationship or of equitable risk sharing.

Further, the sorts of protections available to workers in more stable employment relationships are absent for short-term employees. Union protections, for example, are largely absent. Many temporary workers actually work for (and draw a paycheck from) a temporary agency—not the particular employer to which the employee is assigned by the agency. Few if any temporary employees are willing to jeopardize future temporary assignments by seeking union representation. Similarly, contract workers are loath to jeopardize the possibility of future work, either with their current "employer" or another employer. The countervailing force that union representation creates is therefore absent for many employees in boundaryless-career relationships. Similarly, labor and employment law in general—whether in terms of benefits, worker safety, or employer obligations—is an artifact of an industrial relations system designed in the 1930s and 1940s at a time when union representation (or the threat thereof) was a powerful check on managerial autonomy.

## THE INADEQUACY OF EMPLOYMENT CONTRACTS FOR PRESERVING EMPLOYEE RIGHTS

Even if it is the case that boundaryless careers shift risk from employers to employees, it might be the case that this problem can be addressed through the use of employment contracts. But this is not a likely solution to the problem.

First and foremost, it should be noted that to the degree that contracts exist at all in boundaryless career-like relationships, they are generally contracts of adhesion created by employers that employees must either agree to or be denied employment. Ehrenreich, for example, found that even (or perhaps especially) for low-wage jobs, employees are required to submit to drug tests as a condition for continued employment. Ehrenreich argues that employees are powerless to resist demands for drug testing as one condition of employment among many that are forced upon them. Similarly, employees in short-term and/or temporary employment relationships—the kinds of employment arrangements most consistent with the boundaryless career model—are often in no position to negotiate the terms of exchange. Such workers possess little power to make demands on their employees, whether for increased remuneration, benefits, or training. Their ability to negotiate for skill enhancement that would maintain their employability is limited.

Second, all contracts are incomplete, and especially so with regard to employment relationships.

It is conceivable that some employees—particularly those with rare and valuable skills or the decreasing portion of the U.S. workforce that is represented by union contracts—might be able to include language germane to employability obligations in their employment contracts. (The vast majority of employees, however, would fit into neither category.) Even for such employees, however, the likelihood that they could develop an employment contract that ensures employability is limited by the incompleteness of any contract. It would be difficult indeed to write contractual language that would bind an employer to maintain an employee's employability, now and in the future. Although the problem of incompleteness in employment contracting is common to most relationships, the ephemeral nature of boundaryless career obligations makes it even harder for such employees to protect themselves through contractual means.

Finally, to adapt McCall's approach, there is little evidence that boundaryless careers provide wage premiums to employees over and above wages paid to employees in more stable employment relationships to compensate the former for the increased risks they assume. As noted previously, workers tend to prefer stable to unstable employment relationships. Further, the risk to employees (including risks associated with making investments in human capital that may not be rewarded by future employers and the risk of not having long-term job tenure) of boundaryless career employment relationships—which are by definition short-term in nature with no promise of access to internal labor markets or career ladders—is significantly higher. Yet—although more empirical research needs to be done in this area—employees whose employment patterns fit the boundaryless career model neither command wage premiums nor even keep pace with permanent employees with regard to wages and non-wage benefits. Were contracts a sufficient way in which employees in boundaryless career relationships could protect their interests and gain compensation for the increased risks they assume, such wage and benefit premiums would be expected.

In short, there is a fairness problem inherent to the boundaryless career: Employees assume a disproportionate share of the risks without commensurate marginal benefits (as compared with long-term employment relationships). The inequality of bargaining inherent to most employment relationships—after all, organizations find it easier to go without the labor of a particular employee than that employee can forego a paycheck in search of better exchange terms—is exacerbated by the kinds of short-term employment relationships (in which employment-related risk is shifted from the employer to the employee) engendered by the boundaryless career model. How, then, can the moral value of fairness be partially obtained in employment relationships based on the boundaryless career model?

## THE RIGHT TO EMPLOYABILITY

The main ethical problem posed by boundary less careers is unfairness in terms of shifting risk from employers and employees without corresponding benefits for employees. A partial solution to this problem is therefore the vesting of employability rights to employees that must be satisfied by employers. Recall that employability was defined as "not a guarantee of continuity of employment with one company but a commitment to enhancing the skills and competencies of the employees so they can protect and continuously improve their options for gainful employment in the external labor market" and (1) greater information about employment prospects and (2) greater opportunities for enhancing skills that are salable in the external labor market (in contrast to firm-specific human capital investments).

Note that this is a partial solution to the problem of unfairness previously identified. This paper does not take a position with regard to whether boundary less career patterns are de facto unethical. Neither does employability satisfy or exhaust all of the ethical obligations of employers to employees—whether in short-term employment relationships consistent with the boundaryless career model or not. Rather, the ethical claim being made in this paper is more modest: if employers use the boundaryless career model as a way of organizing employment relationships and gaining flexibility, then satisfying the rights of employees to continued employability is *one* ethical obligation of employers. Such a right is derivative rather than basic and moral, rather than legal. What is deserving of protection in defining an employee's right to employability in the boundaryless career model is (1) employees' ability to maintain their ability to earn a living while (2) shifting some of the risks that they assume back to employers.

In the absence of employability rights, therefore, employers will be able to shift the risks associated with employment relationships almost entirely to employees while gaining the flexibility that employers seek by using the kinds of employment practices (temporary, contingent, contract) consistent with the boundaryless career model. Employment contracts are either absent or inadequate to protect employee interests in this regard. Countervailing forces—whether unions or government agencies—are similarly poorly situated to protect employability rights. Therefore, employability obligations should accrue to employers who benefit most from boundaryless career relationships, and they are best placed to protect and ensure employee employability.

In practical terms, positing a right of employees to employability means that corporations must invest in the skill development of each employee in an employment relationship consistent with the boundaryless career model sufficient to allow him to remain employable on the external labor market. Further,

information about internal employment prospects must be offered to allow employees to assess whether or not to maintain the employment relationship with the organization or to disengage. In turn, of course, employees owe the organization an obligation to use their skills and abilities as contracted for in the employment agreement (whether written or oral).

The analysis of the ethical issues posed by boundaryless careers should yield presumptive grounds for defining a right to employability that would be enjoyed by employees whose careers and employment relationships are consistent with it. The imbalance in relations between employers and employees, combined with the risk shifting from employers to employees engaged in boundaryless career patterns, can thus be partially remedied through employability rights—and, in so doing, helping to promote the moral value of justice in employer-employee relations.

## QUESTIONS

1. What is the ethical argument for having employers to invest in employees' future employability?
2. How might adopting an employability approach to managing employees positively and negatively impact a business?
3. In the boundaryless career model, what are the employees' responsibilities?

# Ethical Management of Uncertain Employment
## Rosabeth Moss Kanter

Ideas for building an ethical workplace in a time when no one's job is secure:

- Recruit for the potential to increase in competence, not simply for narrow skills to fill today's slots.
- Offer ample learning opportunities, from formal training to lunchtime seminars—the equivalent of three weeks a year.
- Provide challenging jobs and rotating assignments that allow growth in skills even without promotion to higher jobs.

- Measure performance beyond accounting numbers and share the data to allow learning by doing and continuous improvement—turning everyone into self-guided professionals.
- Retrain employees as soon as jobs become obsolete.
- Emphasize team building, to help our diverse work force appreciate and utilize fully each other's skills.
- Recognize and reward individual and team achievements, thereby building external reputations and offering tangible indicators of value.
- Provide three-month educational sabbaticals, external internships, or personal time-out every five years.
- Find growth opportunities in our network of suppliers, customers, and venture partners.
- Ensure that pensions and benefits are portable, so that people have safety nets for the future even if they seek employment elsewhere.
- Help people be productive while carrying family responsibilities, through flex-time, provision for sick children, and renewal breaks between major assignments.
- Measure the building of human capital and the capabilities of our people as thoroughly and frequently as we measure the building and use of financial capital.
- Encourage entrepreneurship—new ventures within our company or outside that help our people start businesses and create alternative sources of employment.
- Tap our people's ideas to develop innovations that lower costs, serve customers, and create new markets—the best foundation for business growth and continuing employment, and the source of funds to reinvest in continuous learning.*

* Rosabeth Moss Kanter, *Men and Women of the Corporation*, 2nd ed. (New York: Basic Books, 1993, 330–331).

Harvard Law
Review

# Facial Discrimination

*"He had but one eye, and the popular prejudice runs in favour of two."*
—Charles Dickens, Nicholas Nickleby

## THE PHENOMENON OF APPEARANCE DISCRIMINATION

To be human is to discriminate. Humans constantly evaluate people, places, and things and choose some over others. The premise of antidiscrimination law is that in some areas, such as employment and housing, certain criteria are not permissible bases of selection. Antidiscrimination law has yet to state a general model of discrimination that describes precisely which criteria are "illegitimate." Despite the difficulty of developing such criteria, some inner and outer bounds are clear. In the domain of employment, for example, members of racial and religious minority groups are legally protected from discrimination. Those who score poorly on employment aptitude tests found to bear a legitimate relation to the job generally are not.

One approach to antidiscrimination law would protect any member of a minority group who faces discrimination because of membership in that group. This approach is consistent with Louis Wirth's influential definition of a minority: "a group of people who, because of their physical or cultural characteristics, are singled out from the others in the society in which they live for differential and unequal treatment and who therefore regard themselves as objects of collective discrimination." Physically unattractive people do not fall precisely within Wirth's formulation. First, the physically unattractive do not constitute a cohesive group; a thin person with an unattractive face, for example, may feel little kinship with an obese person. In addition, physical attractiveness is a continuum, and neat determinations of who is "unattractive" are impossible. Nevertheless, the physically unattractive share many of the burdens of Wirth's minority groups. Although our society professes a commitment to judge people by their inner worth, physically unattractive people often face differential and unequal treatment in situations in which their appearance is unrelated to their qualifications or abilities. In the employment context, appearance often functions as an illegitimate basis on which to deny people jobs for which they are otherwise qualified.

### Appearance Discrimination Generally

People in our society often have a visceral dislike for individuals whom they find unattractive. The bias is so strong that it is not deemed inappropriate to express this dislike; the physically unattractive are a frequent subject of derisive humor. People frequently believe, either consciously or unconsciously, that people with unattractive exteriors were either born with equally unattractive interiors or gradually developed them. By contrast, people tend to think, often with very little basis, that people they find physically attractive are generally worthy and appealing or that, as the title of one study has it, "What Is Beautiful Is Good."

Social science studies have shown that people attribute a wide range of positive characteristics to those whom they find physically attractive. These studies also indicate that when less attractive people are compared to more attractive people, the less attractive men and women are accorded worse treatment simply because of their appearance. This less-favored treatment apparently begins as early as the first few months of life. Throughout childhood, unattractive children face parents who have lower expectations for their success than for more attractive children, teachers who have lower expectations for their academic success, and contemporaries who prefer more attractive children as friends. This less generous treatment of unattractive people continues through adulthood. For example, studies of "helping behavior"—the willingness of subjects to do small favors for a stranger—show that such behavior varies directly with the stranger's attractiveness. Likewise, simulation studies of court proceedings have found that unattractive people receive higher sentences in criminal cases and lower damage awards in civil lawsuits.

Physical appearance can also warp the functioning of ordinarily "objective" evaluations of individuals' work. This distortion has been shown in studies in which subjects were asked to evaluate a written essay that was accompanied by a photograph of the purported author. When copies of the same essay were evaluated with a photograph of an attractive or an unattractive person attached, the essays with the more attractive purported author were judged to have better ideas, better style, and more creativity. Moreover, studies have shown that in general, attractive people are disproportionately likely to receive credit for good outcomes, whereas the good outcomes of unattractive people are more likely to be attributed to external factors, such as luck. Such biases might easily lead an employer to underrate the talents of an unattractive job applicant.

Empirical research on the real-world effects of appearance discrimination supports the results of these simulation exercises. Considerable empirical research has been done in the area of obesity. One study showed that obese high school students were significantly less likely than non-obese students to be admitted to selective colleges, when academic achievement, motivation, and economic class were held constant; another found that obese adults were discriminated against in the renting of apartments.

Appearance discrimination thus seems to occur in a wide variety of situations. Clearly, the law cannot intervene directly to prevent all such discrimination; no law, for example, can itself make a teacher have more faith in an unattractive child's academic success. The law can, however, address discrimination in discrete areas. One such area is employment selection, in which appearance discrimination is widespread.

### Appearance Discrimination in Employee Selection

Physical appearance is a significant factor in employee selection, regardless of the nature of the job or the relevance of appearance to the task at hand. One of the primary methods of assessing applicants for all levels of jobs is the personal interview, in which the applicant's appearance is a central criterion. One survey found that appearance was the single most important factor in determining candidate acceptability for a wide variety of jobs, regardless of the level of training of the interviewers. Another study asked 2804 employment interviewers throughout the United States to give "favorability" scores to a variety of characteristics of applicants for various positions. Interviewers considered as important positive characteristics such factors as "Has a good complexion" and rated as important negative characteristics factors such as "Is markedly overweight," and, for men, "Physique appears feminine." Interview manuals written for employers make clear the importance of physical appearance in the selection process. One general employment handbook places "Appearance" first on its list of "hire appeal" factors.

Research in specific areas of physical difference reinforces the claim that appearance discrimination pervades the job market. The National Association to Aid Fat Americans found that fifty-one percent of its members who responded to a survey reported instances of employment discrimination. A report of the State of Maryland's Commission on Human Relations concluded that it may well be easier to place a thin black person on a job than a fat white person. Extremely short people also experience severe employment discrimination.

There have as yet been no direct challenges to appearance discrimination, although appearance issues have been raised in other lawsuits. Hiring practices based on explicit evaluations of applicants' physical appearance were challenged in the courts for the first time in the 1960s and early 1970s in lawsuits charging airlines with sex and race discrimination in the hiring of flight attendants. One Equal Employment Opportunity Commission hearing of a race discrimination claim revealed that an interview form contained the written comment that a black applicant had "unattractive, large lips. The Commission found that this negative evaluation of a race-related aspect of the applicant's appearance provided reasonable cause to believe that unlawful racial discrimination had taken place. More recently, a computer programmer successfully sued under New York State law a company that failed to hire her because she was obese. The challenge alleged, however, that obesity was a medical handicap, and did not raise the broader issue of appearance discrimination.

### Restructuring Employment Selection To Reduce Appearance Discrimination

Even if employers agreed in principle that considerations of physical appearance should ideally be eliminated from the hiring process, this ideal would be difficult to achieve in practice. As long as hiring is based on face-to-face interviews, physical appearance will inevitably have an impact on impressions. This problem can be avoided, however, by restructuring the hiring process to eliminate or reduce information about applicants' appearance when applicants are evaluated and hiring decisions are made.

The regulations promulgated by the HHS bar "preemployment inquiries" concerning a job applicant's handicapped status, unless the inquiries specifically concern the applicant's ability to do the job. To meet this requirement, employers could publicly announce a policy of not soliciting information about an applicant's appearance, other than grooming and neatness, and of not considering appearance as a factor in employee selection. The standard face-to-face interview, in which the applicant's appearance is highly salient, in many ways resembles just such a statutorily forbidden preemployment inquiry into appearance handicaps. To conform with the ban on preemployment inquiries, employers should reevaluate their commitment to the standard employment interview.

To be sure, interviews undoubtedly have some informational value beyond permitting illegitimate appearance evaluations. An employer may justifiably be concerned, for example, with an applicant's interpersonal skills. But this information can be obtained in ways that avoid the prejudicial process of face-to-face interviews. One possible method is the expanded use of telephone interviews. Another possibility, which could work well for many kinds of jobs, is the adoption of the practice used by virtually every American symphony orchestra to avoid discrimination and favoritism in hiring: auditions conducted behind screens. Such an interview process would provide employers with useful information about an applicant, revealing factors such as a "pleasant personality," without prejudicing the selection process by injecting appearance into the calculus.

Employers could also reduce or eliminate appearance discrimination through less dramatic modifications in the selection process. They could, for example, set a rigid dividing line between the person who meets and interviews job applicants and the person who makes the decision about whom to hire. The interviewer could pass along a form to the decision-maker that includes only job-related information and impressions. Although the applicant's appearance might still influence the interviewer's perceptions of other subjective qualities, it would nevertheless be a considerable reform.

Objections that employment decisions will be difficult or "random" under such a new regime are misplaced. Workable selection procedures and criteria can be maintained without permitting appearance discrimination. Employers could continue to use the battery of legitimate, work-related criteria: they could ask about education, prior work experience, and success in school and at previous jobs. And they could administer bona fide, work-related, nondiscriminatory tests. Indeed, to the extent that these reforms eliminate irrelevant criteria, they should lead to a greater weighting of job-relevant criteria and hence a fairer overall process.

## Moving From "Efficiency" to Equality

Efforts to eliminate appearance discrimination would significantly restructure employment practices. Inevitably, such proposed reforms raise questions about the sort of criteria on which our society should permit employment decisions to be based. One objection to eliminating physical appearance as a criterion for hiring is an argument about economic efficiency. If an employer can show that an applicant's appearance makes him or her more profitable, why should this not be a valid criterion for employment? The response to this objection is that "efficiency" is not always an acceptable basis on which to make distinctions in the employment process.

In fact, many sorts of discrimination may be "economically efficient." For example, a restaurant owner in a racist neighborhood might enlarge his or her clientele—and thus increase profits—by refusing to hire black waiters and waitresses. Yet in all forms of antidiscrimination law we proclaim that our society has some principles of equality that it holds more dear than efficiency.

## CONCLUSION

The implications of appearance discrimination go beyond the sizeable number of people who experience its effects firsthand. Physical attractiveness discrimination provides a window on the criteria that our society uses to distinguish among people. It represents one of the ways in which we use hazy and illegitimate criteria to separate good from bad, acceptable from unacceptable, and normal from deviant. Stereotypes of all kinds are linked. Together they form a larger "web of stereotypes" that leads people at times to treat racial minorities, women, the elderly, and the disabled as "other" and to exclude them. One strand of otherness that is woven deeply into this web is that of appearance.

Appearance discrimination is sometimes closely connected to related kinds of discrimination. One significant aspect of prejudice against blacks, old people, or people in wheelchairs is a negative reaction to the way they look. Conversely, people may well dislike certain appearance characteristics—such as broad noses or wrinkled skin—because they associate them with groups they disfavor. Decreasing appearance discrimination would help to unravel this entire web of stereotypes. As we expand our conception of what people in certain jobs can look like, we open these jobs up further to once excluded groups.

Ultimately, as with the eradication of all forms of discrimination, people's attitudes must change before appearance discrimination will cease. The first step in this process is recognizing the existence of the problem. As Sander Gilman has written:

> The need for stereotypes runs so deep that I do not think it will ever be thwarted; nor do I think that it will ever be converted to purely harmless expression. But I believe that education and study can expose the ideologies with which we structure our world, and perhaps help put us in the habit of self-reflection.

## QUESTIONS

1. Is discrimination based on gender, race, ethnicity, and sexual orientation also facial discrimination?

2. In what cases is it ethical to hire people based on the way that they look?

3. Is an employer ever justified in not hiring someone who is qualified for a job because they are obese, ugly, disfigured, or with some other unattractive physical abnormality?

---

To: You
From: The Philosopher
Subject: "John Stuart Mill on the Greatest Good and Expediency"

A friend of mine just started working at a bank. On his first day of work, he had to take a drug test. He asked his manager why and she said, "The reason why new employees have to take drug tests is to help protect our clients and the bank from potential problems. After all, if we got in trouble, we'd have to let employees go. So, while it may be unpleasant for you, it's best everyone."

When I heard this argument, I thought, they certainly don't seem to believe in Kant's idea of treating people as ends in themselves. She sort of sounded like John' Stuart Mill.

> The multiplication of happiness is, according to utilitarian ethics, the object of Virtue: the occasions on which any person (except one in a thousand) has it in his power to do this on an extended scale, in other words to be a public benefactor, are but exceptional; and on these occasions alone, is he called on to consider public utility; in every other case, private utility, the interest or happiness of some few persons, is all the he has to attend to.*

But Mill also made a distinction between utility and expedience:

> [T]he expedient, in the sense in which it is opposed to the Right, generally means that which is expedient for the particular interest of the agent himself. . . . When it means anything better than this, it means that which is expedient for some immediate object, some temporary purpose, but which violates a rule whose observance is expedient in a much higher degree. The Expedient, in this sense instead of being the same thing as what is useful, is a branch of the hurtful."**

\* John Stuart Mill, "What Is Utilitarianism?" in *Utilitarianism and other Essays*, ed. Alan Ryan (New York: Penguin Books, 1987), p. 282.
\*\* Ibid., p. 283.

# CASES

## CASE 1.1
## The Job Interview
Sloan Wilson

"Why do you want to work for the United Broadcasting Corporation?" Walker asked abruptly.

"It's a good company . . .," Tom began hesitantly, and was suddenly impatient at the need for hypocrisy. The sole reason he wanted to work for United Broadcasting was that he thought he might be able to make a lot of money there fast, but he felt he couldn't say that. It was sometimes considered fashionable for the employees of foundations to say that they were in it for the money, but people were supposed to work at advertising agencies and broadcasting companies for spiritual reasons.

"I believe," Tom said, "that television is developing into the greatest medium for mass education and entertainment. It has always fascinated me, and I would like to work with it. . . ."

"What kind of salary do you have in mind?" Walker asked. Tom hadn't expected the question that soon. Walker was still smiling.

"The salary isn't the primary consideration with me," Tom said, trying desperately to come up with stock answers to stock questions. "I'm mainly interested in finding something useful and worth while to do. I have personal responsibilities, however, and I would hope that something could be worked out to enable me to meet them. . . ."

"Of course," Walker said, beaming more cheerily than ever. "I understand you applied for a position in the public-relations department. Why did you choose that?"

Because I heard there was an opening, Tom wanted to say, but quickly thought better of it and substituted a halting avowal of lifelong interest in public relations. "I think my experience in working with *people* at the Schanenhauser Foundation would be helpful," he concluded lamely.

"I see," Walker said kindly. There was a short silence before he added, "Can you write?"

"I do most of the writing at the Schanenhauser Foundation," Tom said. "The annual report to the trustees is my job, and so are most of the reports on individual projects. I used to be editor of my college paper."

"That sounds fine," Walker said casually. "I have a little favor I want to ask of you. I want you to write me your autobiography."

"What?" Tom asked in astonishment.

"Nothing very long," Walker said. "Just as much as you can manage to type out in an hour. One of my girls will give you a room with a typewriter."

"Is there anything in particular you want me to tell you about?"

"Yourself," Walker said, looking hugely pleased. "Explain yourself to me. Tell me what kind of person you are. Explain why we should hire you."

"I'll try," Tom said weakly.

"You'll have precisely an hour," Walker said. "You see, this is a device I use in employing people—I find it most helpful. For this particular job, I have twenty or thirty applicants. It's hard to tell from a brief interview whom to choose, so I ask them all to write about themselves for an hour. You'd be surprised how revealing the results are. . . ."

He paused, still smiling. Tom said nothing.

From Sloan Wilson, *The Man in the Gray Flannel Suit* (Simon & Schuster, 1955), pp. 13–14.

"Just a few hints," Walker continued. "Write anything you want, but at the end of your last page, I'd like you to finish this sentence: 'The most significant fact about me is . . .'"

"The most significant fact about me is . . .," Tom repeated idiotically.

"The results, of course, will be entirely confidential." Walker lifted a bulky arm and inspected his wrist watch. "It's now five minutes to twelve," he concluded. "I'll expect your paper on my desk at precisely one o'clock."

Tom stood up, put on his coat, said, "Thank you," and went out of the room. . . .

Tom sat down in the chair, which had been designed for a stenographer and was far too small for him. Son of a bitch, he thought—I guess the laws about cruel and unusual punishment don't apply to personnel men. He tried to think of something to write, but all he could remember was Betsy and the drab little house and the need to buy a new washing machine, and the time he had thrown a vase that cost forty dollars against the wall. "The most significant fact about me is that I once threw a vase costing forty dollars against a wall." That would be as sensible as anything else he could think of, but he doubted whether it would get him the job. He thought of Janey saying, "It isn't *fair!*" and the worn linoleum on the kitchen floor. "The most significant fact about me is. . . ." It was a stupid sentence to ask a man to finish.

I have children, he thought—that's probably the most significant fact about me, the only one that will have much importance for long. Anything about a man can be summed up in numbers. Thomas R. Rath, thirty-three years old, making seven thousand dollars a year, owner of a 1939 Ford, a six-room house, and ten thousand dollars' worth of G.I. Life Insurance which, in case of his death, would pay his widow about forty dollars a month. Six feet one and a half inches tall; weight, 198 pounds. He served four and a half years in the Army, most of it in Europe and the rest in the South Pacific.

Another statistical fact came to him then, a fact which he knew would be ridiculously melodramatic to put into an application for a job at the United Broadcasting Corporation, or to think about at all. He hadn't thought about this for a long while. It wasn't a

thing he had deliberately tried to forget—he simply hadn't thought about it for quite a few years. It was the unreal-sounding, probably irrelevant, but quite accurate fact that he had killed seventeen men. . . .

Such things were merely part of the war, the war before the Korean one. It was no longer fashionable to talk about the war, and certainly it had never been fashionable to talk about the number of men one had killed. Tom couldn't forget the number, "seventeen," but it didn't seem real any more; it was just a small, isolated statistic that nobody wanted. His mind went blank. . . .

"The most significant fact about me is that I detest the United Broadcasting Corporation, with all its soap operas, commercials, and yammering studio audiences, and the only reason I'm willing to spend my life in such a ridiculous enterprise is that I want to buy a more expensive house and a better brand of gin."

That certainly wouldn't get him the job.

"The most significant fact about me is that I've become a cheap cynic."

That would not be apt to get him the job.

"The most significant fact about me is that as a young man in college, I played the mandolin incessantly. I, champion mandolin player, am applying to you for a position in the public-relations department!"

That would not be likely to get him far. Impatiently he sat down at the typewriter and glanced at his wrist watch. It was a big loud-ticking wrist watch with a black face, luminous figures, and a red sweep hand that rapidly ticked off the seconds. He had bought it years ago at an Army post exchange and had worn it all through the war. The watch was the closest thing to a good-luck charm he had ever had, although he never thought of it as such. Now it was more reassuring to look at than the big impersonal clock on the wall, though both said it was almost twelve-thirty. So far he had written nothing. What the hell, he thought. I was a damn fool to think I wanted to work here anyway. Then he thought of Betsy asking, as she would be sure to, "Did you get the job? How did it go?" And he decided to try.

"Anybody's life can be summed up in a paragraph," he wrote. "I was born on November 20, 1920, in my grandmother's house in South Bay, Connecticut. I was graduated from Covington Academy in 1937, and from Harvard College in

1941. I spent four and a half years in the Army, reaching the rank of captain. Since 1946, I have been employed as an assistant to the director of the Schanenhauser Foundation. I live in Westport, Connecticut, with my wife and three children. From the point of view of the United Broadcasting Corporation, the most significant fact about me is that I am applying for a position in its public-relations department, and after an initial period of learning, I probably would do a good job. I will be glad to answer any questions which seem relevant, but after considerable thought, I have decided that I do not wish to attempt an autobiography as part of an application for a job."

He typed this paragraph neatly in the precise center of a clean piece of paper, added his name and address, and carried it into Walker's office. It was only quarter to one, and Walker was obviously surprised to see him. "You've still got fifteen minutes!" he said.

"I've written all I think is necessary," Tom replied, and handed him the almost empty page.

Walker read it slowly, his big pale face expressionless. When he had finished it, he dropped it into a drawer. "We'll let you know our decision in a week or so," he said.

## QUESTIONS

1. What values does Tom struggle with in the job interview?

2. What does this story say to you about the relationship between the individual and the organization?

3. To what extent would you be willing to say things that you do not believe to please an interviewer? Where would you draw the line?

## CASE 1.2

## A "State of the Art" Termination

John R. Boatright

Monday had been the most humiliating day of Bill Collin's life. Rumors of downsizing had been swirling for months, and every computer analyst in Bill's department knew that the ax would fall on some of them. Bets had even been taken on who would stay and who would go. When the news was finally delivered, Bill was not surprised. He also understood the necessity of reducing the computer support staff in view of the merger that had made many jobs redundant, and he felt confident that he would find a new job fairly quickly. What upset him was the manner in which he had been terminated.

Bill arrived in the office at eight o'clock sharp to find a memo on his desk about a nine-thirty meeting at a hotel one block away. Since this site was often used for training sessions, he gave the notice little thought. Bill decided to arrive a few minutes early in order to chat with colleagues, but he found himself being ushered quickly into a small conference room where three other people from his department were already seated. His greeting to them was cut short by a fourth person whom Bill had never seen before. The stranger explained that he was a consultant from an outplacement firm that had been engaged to deliver the bad news and to outline the

From John R. Boatright, *Ethics and the Conduct of Business*, 2nd edition (Upper Saddle River, NJ: Prentice Hall, 1997), pp. 255–256. Notes were deleted from the text.

benefits the company was providing for them. Once he started talking, Bill felt relieved: The package of benefits was greater than he had dared hope. All employees would receive full salary for six months plus pay for accrued vacation time; medical insurance and pension contribution would be continued during this period; and the outplacement firm would provide career counseling and a placement service that included secretarial assistance, photocopying and fax service, and office space. The consultant assured the four longtime employees that the company appreciated their years of service and wanted to proceed in a caring manner. It was for this reason that they hired the best consulting firm in the business, one that had a reputation for a "state-of-the-art" termination process.

Bill's relief was jolted by what came next. The consultant informed the four that they were not to return to their office or to set foot inside the corporate office building again; nor were they to attempt to contact anyone still working for the company. (At this point, Bill suddenly realized that he had no idea how many employees might be in other four-person groups being dismissed at the same time.) The contents of their desks would be boxed and delivered to their homes; directories of their computer files would be provided, and requests for any personal material would be honored after a careful review of their contents to make sure that no proprietary information was included. The consultant assured them that all passwords had already been changed, including the password for remote access. Finally, they were instructed not to remain at the hotel but to proceed to a service exit where prepaid taxis were stationed to take them home.

Bill regretted not being able to say goodbye to friends in the office. He would have liked some advance warning in order to finish up several projects that he had initiated and to clear out his own belongings. The manner in which he had been terminated was compassionate up to a point, Bill admitted, but it showed that the company did not trust him. A few days later, Bill understood the company's position better when he read an article in a business magazine that detailed the sabotage that had been committed by terminated employees who had continued access to their employer's computer system. Some disgruntled workers had destroyed files and done other mischief when they were allowed to return to their offices after being informed of their termination. One clever computer expert had previously planted a virtually undetectable virus that remained dormant until he gained access long enough through a co-worker's terminal to activate it. The advice that companies were receiving from consulting firms that specialize in termination was: Be compassionate, but also protect yourself. Good advice, Bill thought, but the humiliation was still fresh in his mind.

## QUESTIONS

1. Is firing someone with dignity an oxymoron?
2. Is there a way to fire people that will encourage them to act with dignity?
3. How does the way that a company fires people affect the rest of the employees?

# CASE 1.3
## Does Home Life Matter at Work?
Joanne B. Ciulla

Over the past month, you and your colleagues have been reviewing applications for regional manager. The regional manager's job involves overseeing and coordinating the operations of a large portion of the western United States. On Friday afternoon, your committee finally makes its selection and plans to announce its choice on Monday morning. Out of a number of talented managers, it selected John Deer. John's peers often used the words "brilliant" and "genius" to describe him. He held a consistent record of excellence in every task that he accomplished for the company.

A quiet, polite man, John rarely attended social functions, and when he did, he never brought his wife. When you arrive at your office on Monday morning, you are surprised to get a call from John's wife Edith, whom you've never met. Her voice sounds shaky, and you can hardly hear her. She says:

> I'm sorry to be a bother, but I needed to talk to you. My husband John has been tense lately because he. really wants the regional manager's job. Anyway, last night John gave me a very bad beating. Our two children saw the whole thing and were terrified. I took the children and ran out of the house. We are now staying at the Chicago shelter for battered women. Over the years, John has hit me on numerous occasions, but never like this. He's basically a good man, but he's very high strung. Anyway, the reason why I am calling is to beg you to give the job to John. Maybe then he'll feel happier and things will be better for our family.

The phone call is so bizarre that you decide to check out Mrs. Deer's story. You call the Chicago shelter to find out if she is indeed there. The shelter director says that it is against its policy to give out the identity of clients or any information on them. Then in the background you hear some confusion as Mrs. Deer grabs the phone from the director. Mrs. Deer tells the director to get on the other line and demands that she answer your questions. The director protests, but does as she is asked. She reports that Mrs. Deer and her two children, ages 2 and 6, were admitted to the shelter last night at midnight after being treated at City Hospital. Mrs. Deer had a broken rib and bruises on the face, arms, and neck that were apparently caused by a blunt object.

It is now 10:30 a.m. The formal announcement is scheduled for noon. At this point, John may already know that he got the job. You are angry and disgusted, but you know that you will have to put your personal feelings aside and consider a number of issues before you make any decisions about John. Since Mrs. Deer has no plans to press charges against her husband, you put aside legal considerations and think about your ethical obligations in this situation.

## QUESTIONS

1. Given that there is no legal action taken against an individual, is the way that a person treats his or her spouse or other family member relevant in hiring and promotion decisions?

2. If you were the manager in this case, how would you fill your moral obligations to all the stakeholders who are involved in it?

3. When do you think the manager's moral obligations to John Deer and his wife and children begin and end?

# CASE 1.4
## The Best Person for the Job?
Joanne B. Ciulla

Sam, one of your senior professionals, has resigned unexpectedly to join one of your competitors. He was responsible for transactions with Magnolia Corporation, where he had a close relationship with the CEO, J. W. Crawford. You know that there is a good chance that Magnolia may go with Sam if you don't put a knowledgeable and experienced person on the account. This is your largest account, and you don't want to lose it. In the past, both the company and Sam have made a lot of money from various deals with Magnolia.

You know from Sam's client notes and from your previous visits to Magnolia that J. W. belongs to the "old school" and is most comfortable dealing with "one of the boys." Last year, when Sam was visiting Magnolia, he went on a hunting trip with J. W. The final night of the trip, J. W. surprised them with a "special treat." He invited a stripper to entertain them after a long dinner and plenty of drinks. On another occasion, Sam invited Elaine Jones, one of the firm's top account executives, to attend a meeting with J. W. Sam wanted her advice on an investment. During the meeting, J. W. paid little attention

to what Elaine had to say and kept referring to her as "honey." On the way out of the meeting, J. W. gave her a pat on her behind.

Elaine is really the only person who knows J. W.'s business and has the expertise and seniority to take Sam's place. Ordinarily, there would be no question of her taking over this client because of her experience and track record. Elaine is not known to turn down potentially lucrative deals; however, knowing what you do about J. W., you wonder if she's the person for the job.

### QUESTIONS

1. Who should be responsible for making this decision?

2. What are the larger long-term ramifications of this decision for the firm and its stakeholders?

3. In businesses where client relationships are important, is it fair to consider an employee's personal interests as qualifications for working with a particular client? For example, would it be ethical to give a client who plays golf to a salesperson who plays golf, even if there are other salespeople who may be better qualified to work with that client?

# CASE 1.5
## Attraction or Business as Usual?
Joanne B. Ciulla

Your company is in the process of opening a new office. You are in charge of purchasing software that will be used for billing and payroll. There are really only three software systems that will meet your businesses needs.

Last week, each of the three vendors came in to give a demonstration of their product and get an assessment of your computing needs. You spoke with salespeople from two of the companies. However, the third company that you talked to, Agape, sent along a salesperson and a systems expert. The systems expert was named Hank Smith. The salesman explained that Agape likes its customers to meet the technician whom they would be working with if they purchased the system.

Hank Smith was very knowledgeable and answered all your questions clearly. He was also honest about the strengths and weaknesses of the system. The three of you talked for about two hours, and then the salesperson said that he had another appointment, but that Hank would stay to answer any further questions. Hank suggested that you continue over lunch. You said that would be fine, but only if you could pay.

At lunch Hank talks more about the software system, but you realize that you aren't really listening. Hank isn't just handsome, he's gorgeous and *very* charming. You find yourself looking at his hands to see if he is married. There is no wedding ring, so you turn the conversation to other matters. He tells you that he has an apartment in the city and, through a series of questions, you finally discover that he is not married and that he lives alone. You sense that Hank feels a similar attraction to you. Nonetheless, you realize that you can't do or say anything because of your business relationship.

Over the next few days, you keep thinking about Hank and hoping that Agape will come in with the lowest bid. Finally the bids arrive. Agape and Hi-Tech come in at about the same price. The third company's bid is significantly higher. You discuss the three options with your manager. The software packages offered by Agape and Hi-Tech are similar; either system would be adequate. The more expensive system does not offer much more, so you eliminate it.

Your manager says that since it's a toss-up between Agape and Hi-Tech, the decision is up to you. For a moment you think about your intense attraction to Hank. But then you think, "I am a professional woman, and this is a decision that could be made by the toss of a coin. So why not choose Agape?" You buy the Agape software, but to your great disappointment, they send another systems expert to work with your company. It makes you wonder if you really made the best decision and if the company sent Hank to work his charm on you.

## QUESTIONS

1. Would it be wrong if Agape sent Hank because it knew a single woman was making the decision on the software?

2. Is this a conflict of interest on the purchaser's part, or is it just a case of her interests coinciding with the company's interests?

3. Is there anything wrong with doing a little flirting to make a sale?

# CASE 1.6
# Pornography and the Boss's Computer
Joanne B. Ciulla

Carlton Smith, an undergraduate business major, was very excited about his summer internship at the public relations company James and Madison in New York. The firm serves a number of high-profile clients ranging from Fortune 500 companies to religious organizations and NGOs. People inside and outside of the industry consider James and Madison the gold standard for integrity in the industry. This was where Carlton aspired to work at after he graduated. James and Madison had an extensive code of ethics that they required everyone in the firm, including interns, to sign. The code focuses on issues related to professional conduct, confidentiality, and the use of office computers for personal purposes. It requires all employees to report any infractions of the code to senior management.

The internship proved to be everything that Carlton had hoped it would be. A senior VP named Todd Williams took Carlton on as his assistant. The work that Carlton did for Todd exposed him to many aspects of the public relations business. Most of Carlton's work involved gathering information for Todd and providing support when Todd gave presentations to potential clients.

One day, about halfway into the internship, Todd called Carlton from L.A., where he was working with a client. Todd was in the middle of a meeting and he needed Carlton to quickly look up an article related to his client's business. Todd said that he could not remember how he searched for the article, but that he remembered pulling it up on his computer right before he left town. Carlton figured that instead of searching for it on his computer, it would be faster to retrieve it from the search history on Todd's Mac.

Carlton then went into Todd's office and pulled up Todd's search history to see if it is there. Just as Todd said, it was the first one on the list.

Carlton could not help but notice that the next few items in the search history had very odd names that sounded like pornography sites. Maybe these sites were research that Todd was doing for another client, but it did not seem likely. Curiosity got the best of him. Without thinking, he clicked on one site that had some very sick pictures of sadistic sex. Carlton then realized that he should not have done this. Since he sent the email from Todd's computer, Todd might know that he saw his search history and went to one of the sites. Carlton realized that he might be in a serious fix.

## QUESTIONS

1. What did Carlton do wrong here?
2. What are his ethical obligations and to whom?
3. What would you do if you were Carlton?

---

# Sexual Harassment Guidelines

Sexual harassment is covered Under Title VII of the Civil Rights Act of 1964. The act states that it is unlawful for an employer to discriminate against an employee based on a person's sex. It prohibits discrimination in decisions involving compensation, terms, conditions, or privileges of employment. There are two types of sexual harassment:

1. *Quid pro quo*: Harassment that pressures an employee for sexual favours as a condition of employment or for benefits, such as promotions, job assignments, etc.
2. *Hostile Environment*: Behavior that does not affect and employee's economic benefits. It consists of unwelcome advances or sexual, verbal, and/or physical conduct of a sexual nature. This conduct has the purpose or effect of interfering with an individual's work performance or creating an intimidating, hostile, or offensive working environment.*

Key elements of sexual harassment:

1. Harassment was unwelcome.
2. Harassment was based on gender
3. Harassment was sufficiently severe or pervaisve
4. Hostile enviornment affects a person's ability to perform at work and/or causes psychological harm.

* Anja Angelica chan, *Women and Sexual Harassment* (New York: Harrington Park Press, 1994), pp. 5–6.

# CHAPTER QUESTIONS

1. What are the underlying conditions of the employer–employee relationship that make it a challenge for organizations to respect the humanity of persons in the workplace?

2. What claim does an employer have on a person's feelings, rights, and privacy? What rights are you willing to give up to be employed? What rights can an employer justifiably limit in the workplace?

3. The old social contract of most workplaces was, "if you do your job well, you can keep it." In today's uncertain employment environment, what kind of reciprocal agreements can employers have with employees?

# 9

# Things Fall Apart

## *Product Liability and Consumers*

## Introduction

During a brief strike at your company, all the managers—regardless of their status or position—are farmed out to the various company functions that are normally handled by the striking employees. You are put in charge of the walk-in Complaint Department. The second day, a fellow walks in with one of your company's products, mangled almost beyond recognition. It is immediately obvious to you that the consumer has misunderstood the assembly instructions, and his rambling explanation confirms it. You tell him, politely, that you think that this is what happened, but he, in turn, gets irritated and a bit abusive. He threatens to sue. You are not used to this sort of behavior, and you are getting pretty irritated yourself. You think of a number of terse and sarcastic responses, but you keep your cool and some semblance of a smile. Your manager has told you to handle all cases as best you can and has given you a free hand to give refunds or replace products at your discretion. But there is no advice or policy about what to do when a customer abuses the product through stupidity or incompetence. In your view, should the company honor the complaints of this customer? Or should you (politely) tell him what he should do?

"Sooner or later, life makes philosophers of us all" wrote minor French philosopher Maurice Riseling. In the same vein, "Shit Happens" is the crude philosophical message of one of the ruder bumper stickers you see around town these days. "Accidents happen," the more polite way of putting the same point, is an inescapable part of business life. Even high-quality products break. Good intentions get frustrated. It would be good and useful experience for every manager and employee, in whatever industry, to spend a few days working in the Complaint Department. (In the most trusted corporations, every person in the company is, in effect, a mini-Complaint Department, responsible for making good on the company's claims and liabilities.) The aim of a business, we are told, is to make a profit by selling high-quality products at a reasonable price. But this makes it sound as if most business transactions are one-shot deals, without an aftermath, sort of like buying something on eBay or at a garage sale. But most business is not like this. It involves multiple transactions, often over a prolonged period. (It is often pointed out that getting a new customer costs a business ten times what it costs to retain an old one.) It thus involves the building of relationships, and this means not just continuing to provide high-quality products and services, but "making good" when they go wrong. How a business responds to flaws and failure, whether or not the company is strictly responsible, can fix the fate of a business relationship. A dissatisfied consumer will end his or her relationship and, even after many years, cease to do business with the company. The defensive response that we hear too often, "so what d'ya want me to do about it?" signals the end of many business relationships.

Businesses are responsible for what happens because of their operations and products. The extent and nature of that responsibility depends on the product, the situation, the extent of the damage caused, the character of the company, the consumer, and the community. If something bad happens because an already-hated company or industry does something wrong, the reaction will be much more ferocious than when a well-loved local business makes a mistake. Sometimes, the mistake in question is a broken or flawed product. Sometimes, as was described earlier, the mistake is the consumer's, not the company's at all, but, nevertheless, the company has to deal with it. Sometimes the harm done is inherent to the product itself. No one any longer pretends that smoking doesn't cause cancer and all sorts of other horrid diseases, but there is still considerable controversy surrounding the selling and marketing of tobacco products. An important question is to what extent the consumer is a fully responsible agent, which is why marketing to teenagers is so much in focus. Sometimes the harm is not from the product, but from the production process, for example, when a manufacturing process causes severe pollution or building a new factory strains the infrastructure of a small community. Sometimes the potential harm of a product or a line of products is just not known, for instance, the new bioengineered foods or the radiation from cell phones. But after the fact, companies may still be liable, as evidenced by the still-lingering asbestos-poisoning cases from decades ago.

Complicating the basic observation that most people consider companies to be responsible for their products and services are a number of issues that are both basic to human psychology and emergent in the new world of tort law and strict liability. On the human psychology side, there is the fact that when something goes wrong, people want to *blame* someone. Thus, the relationship between company and consumer when something goes wrong often starts on a confrontational, if not hostile, note, and the first concern of any wise company or agent of the company is to defuse the accusations of blame and re-present the situation as a shared problem. On the side of tort law, there has been a ballooning— especially in America—of product liability and malpractice cases and verdicts. Some of these verdicts have been well publicized and quite understandably strike fear in the hearts of anyone who tries to supply products or services to the public. Some strike most people as ridiculous—the original multi-million-dollar award to the woman who spilled McDonald's hot coffee on herself (the award was considerably reduced on appeal), but others, for instance, when medical products have caused serious illnesses and deaths, do not strike most people as ridiculous. Deterring such irresponsibility, of course, is why the plaintiffs' attorneys defend the current system of sometimes-huge verdicts. It is not enough to punish an allegedly wrong-doing company (when it is usually possible to absorb the verdict as just another cost of doing business). The aim is to put the company out of business.

Further complicating the emerging portrait of the tort system is the concept of "strict liability." Most people accept the idea that when someone does something wrong or causes harm that could or should have been avoided, he or she should be held responsible. But strict liability bypasses that commonsense practice and holds companies responsible—at least financially responsible—even in the absence of any argument that they could have or should have avoided the harm in question. Thus, it has become common practice for plaintiffs to sue not only those who are immediately responsible for a harm, but those who are simply in the chain of causation. For instance, after an automobile accident, one might expect the wrongful or careless driver to be sued. But current law allows for the pursuit of the company that manufactured the car as well, even if there was no design flaw that contributed to the accident. Feeding this practice is the notion of "deep pockets," the idea that those who are immediately responsible may not have funds to pay any substantial award, but someone down the line may well have the resources to do so. It is, in part, because of this practice, but also the enormous size of some of the recent awards, that tort law has been declared a kind of "crisis" by many in the business community.

In this chapter, we explore a family of issues surrounding the concepts of risk and responsibility, both on an individual and on a corporate level, and their effects on society as a whole. The issues are economic, to be sure, but they also have a great deal to do with fairness and our attitudes toward life. Accordingly, they are of interest to both the law and philosophy and the basic question of how much risk are we willing to take in our lives. Economically, on the one hand, there is the need to provide recourse for consumers and communities who are hurt by business practices and products and to deter and punish companies that act irresponsibly. On the other hand, the cost of litigation and the irresponsible use of litigation do indeed hurt innocent businesses and compromises the free enterprise system. In the readings that follow, we take a look at some of the situations that are most in the news and both some of the charges against the tort system and the arguments for it. We start with a selection from Peter Huber's polemical book on the liability crisis and the need for tort reform, which has now become a major campaign by many prominent politicians. The numbers are still in dispute, but the seriousness of the problem is very much on the national agenda.

In response to Huber, we offer different perspectives on the problem, including various considerations about both the difficulties of risk assessment and fairness. John Nesmith discusses the difficulty of calculating risks in his "Calculating Risks: It's Easier Said Than Done." From inside the insurance industry, Stanley J. Modic explains "How We Got into This Mess." Henry Fairlie chastizes us all for failing to acknowledge the role of risks in our lives in his "Fear of Living," and former Chief Justice Warren E. Burger reflects on the situation of "Too Many Lawyers, Too Many Suits" in *The New York Times* (1991). We focus on one of the most publicized liability cases in the past several decades, the case of the once-popular Ford Pinto, which exploded on impact because of a fixable design flaw. Mark Dowie presents the original case in his "Pinto Madness," from *Mother Jones* in 1977, but philosopher and business ethicist Patricia Werhane urges us to be cautious in considering such cases. She compares the Pinto case with the classic Japanese movie, *Rashomon*, in which we get four different accounts of a murder and no clear resolution in favor of any one of them. Judith Jarvis Thomson shows many of the complications that arise when we examine more closely the relationship between harm, liability, and how harm is caused. In the cases, you will be asked to examine more examples of liability and the law. Finally, Bob Sullivan shows that the "annoying fine print" that is supposed to protect companies from consumer lawsuits may not even be legal.

# 41

Peter Huber | # Liability

Peter W. Huber is a lawyer, a Senior Fellow of the Manhattan Institute for Policy Research, and the author of *Liability*.

It is one of the most ubiquitous taxes we pay, now levied on virtually everything we buy, sell, and use. The tax accounts for 30 percent of the price of a step-ladder and over 95 percent of the price of childhood vaccines. It is responsible for one-quarter of the price of a ride on a Long Island tour bus and one-third of the price of a small airplane. It will soon cost large municipalities as much as they spend on fire or sanitation services.

Some call it a safety tax, but its exact relationship to safety is mysterious. It is paid on many items that are risky to use, like ski lifts and hedge trimmers, but it weighs even more heavily on other items whose whole purpose is to make life safer. It adds only a few cents to a pack of cigarettes, but it adds more to the price of a football helmet than the cost of making it. The tax falls especially hard on prescription drugs, doctors, surgeons, and all things medical. Because of the tax, you cannot deliver a baby with medical assistance in Monroe County, Alabama. You cannot buy several contraceptives certified to be safe and effective by the Food and Drug Administration (FDA), even though available substitutes are more dangerous or less effective. If you have the stomach upset known as hyperemesis, you cannot buy the pill that is certified as safe and effective against it. The tax has orphaned various drugs that are invaluable for treating rare but serious diseases. It is assessed against every family that has a baby, in the amount of about $300 per birth, with an obstetrician in New York City paying $85,000 a year.

Because of the tax, you cannot use a sled in Denver city parks or a diving board in New York City schools. You cannot buy an American Motors "CJ" Jeep or a set of construction plans for novel airplanes from Burt Rutan, the pioneering designer of the *Voyager*. You can no longer buy many American-made brands of sporting goods, especially equipment for amateur contact sports such as hockey and lacrosse. For a while, you could not use public transportation in the city of St. Joseph, Missouri, nor could you go to jail in Lafayette County in the same state. Miami canceled plans for an experimental railbus because of the tax. The tax has curtailed Little League and fireworks displays, evening concerts, sailboard races, and the use of public beaches and ice-skating rinks. It temporarily shut down the famed Cyclone at the Astroland amusement park on Coney Island.

The tax directly costs American individuals, businesses, municipalities, and other government bodies at least $80 billion a year, a figure that equals the total profits of the country's top 200 corporations. But many of the tax's costs are indirect and unmeasurable, reflected only in the tremendous effort, inconvenience, and sacrifice Americans now go through to avoid its collection. The extent of these indirect costs can only be guessed at. One study concluded that doctors spend $3.50 in efforts to avoid additional charges for each $1 of direct tax they pay. If similar multipliers operate in other areas, the tax's hidden impact on the way we live and do business may amount to a $300 billion dollar annual levy on the American economy.

The tax goes by the name of *tort liability*. It is collected and disbursed through litigation. The courts alone decide just who will pay, how much, and on what timetable. Unlike better-known taxes, this one was never put to a legislature or a public referendum, debated at any length in the usual public arenas, or approved by the president or by any state governor. And although the tax ostensibly is collected for the public benefit, lawyers and other middlemen pocket more than half the take.

From Peter Huber, *Liability* (New York: Basic Books, 1990), pp. 3–39. Reprinted with permission.

The tort tax is a recent invention. Tort law has existed here and abroad for centuries, of course. But until quite recently it was a backwater of the legal system, of little importance in the wider scheme of things. For all practical purposes, the omnipresent tort tax we pay today was conceived in the 1950s and set in place in the 1960s and 1970s by a new generation of lawyers and judges. In the space of twenty years they transformed the legal landscape, proclaiming sweeping new rights to sue. Some grew famous and more grew rich selling their services to enforce the rights that they themselves invented. But the revolution they made could never have taken place had it not had a component of idealism as well. Tort law, it is widely and passionately believed, is a public-spirited undertaking designed for the protection of the ordinary consumer and worker, the hapless accident victim, the "little guy." Tort law as we know it is a peculiarly American institution. No other country in the world administers anything remotely like it.

## FROM CONSENT TO COERCION

Tort law is the law of accidents and personal injury. The example that usually comes to mind is a two-car collision at an intersection. The drivers are utter strangers. They have no advance understanding between them as to how they should drive, except perhaps an implicit agreement to follow the rules of the road. Nor do they have any advance arrangement specifying who will pay for the damage. Human nature being what it is, the two sides often have different views on both these interesting questions. Somebody else has to step in to work out rights and responsibilities. This has traditionally been a job for the courts. They resolve these cases under the law of *torts* or civil wrongs.

But the car accident between strangers is comparatively rare in the larger universe of accidents and injuries. Just as most intentional assaults involve assailants and victims who already know each other well, most unintended injuries occur in the context of commercial acquaintance—at work, on the hospital operating table, following the purchase of an airplane ticket or a home appliance. And while homicide is seldom a subject of advance understanding between victim and assailant, unintentional accidents often are. More often than not, both parties to a transaction recognize there is some chance of misadventure, and prudently take steps to address it beforehand.

Until quite recently, the law permitted and indeed promoted advance agreement of that character. It searched for understandings between the parties and respected them where found. Most accidents were handled under the broad heading of *contract*—the realm of human cooperation—and comparatively few relegated to the dismal annex of tort, the realm of unchosen relationship and collision. The old law treated contract and tort cases under entirely different rules, which reflected this fairly intuitive line between choice and coercion.

Then, in the 1950s and after, a visionary group of legal theorists came along. Their leaders were thoughtful, well-intentioned legal academics at some of the most prestigious law schools, and judges on the most respected state benches. They were the likes of the late William Prosser, who taught law at Hastings College, John Wade, Professor of Law at Vanderbilt University, and California Supreme Court Justice Roger Traynor. They are hardly household names, but considering the impact they had on American life they should be. Their ideas, eloquence, and persistence changed the common law as profoundly as it had ever been changed before. For short, and in the absence of a better term, we will refer to them as the founders of modern tort law, or just the *Founders*. If the name is light-hearted, their accomplishments were anything but.

The Founders were to be followed a decade or two later by a much more sophisticated group of legal economists, most notably Guido Calabresi, now Dean of the Yale Law School, and Richard Posner of the University of Chicago Law School and now a federal judge on the Seventh Circuit Court of Appeals. There were many others, for economists seem to be almost as numerous as lawyers, and the application of economic theory to tort law has enjoyed mounting popularity in recent years as tort law has itself become an industry. An economist, it has been said, is someone who observes what is happening in practice and goes off to study whether it is possible in theory. The new tort economists were entirely true to that great tradition. Indeed, they carried it a step forward, concluding that the legal revolution that had already occurred was not only possible but justified and necessary. Mustering all the dense prose, arcane jargon, and elaborate methodology that only the very best academic economists muster, they set about proving on paper that the whole new tort structure was an efficient and inevitable reaction to failures in the marketplace. Arriving on the scene of the great tort battle late in the day, they courageously congratulated the victors, shot the wounded, and pronounced the day's outcome satisfactory and good.

Like all revolutionaries, the Founders and their followers, in the economics profession and elsewhere, had their own reasons for believing and behaving as they did. Most consumers, they assumed, pay little attention to accident risks before the fact. Ignoring or underestimating risk as they do, consumers fail to demand, and producers fail to supply, as much safety as would be best. As a result, manufacturers, doctors, employers, municipalities, and other producers get away with undue carelessness, and costly accidents are all too frequent. To make matters worse, consumers buy less accident insurance than they really need, so injuries lead to unneeded misery and privation and some victims become public charges.

With these assumptions as their starting point, the new tort theorists concluded that the overriding question that the old law asked—how did the parties agree to allocate the costs of the accident?—was irrelevant or worse. The real question to ask was: How can society best allocate the cost of accidents to minimize those costs (and the cost of guarding against them), and to provide potential victims with the accident insurance that not all of them currently buy or can afford? The answer, by and large, was to make producers of goods and services pay the costs of accidents. A broad rule to this effect, it was argued, can accomplish both objectives. It forces providers to be careful. It also forces consumers to take accident costs into account, not consciously but by paying a safety-adjusted price for everything they

buy or do. And it compels the improvident to buy accident insurance, again not directly but through the safety tax. It has a moral dimension too: People should be required to take care before the accident and to help each other afterward, for no other reason than that it is just, right, and proper to insist that they do so.

The expansive new accident tax is firmly in place today. In a remarkably short time, the Founders completely recast a centuries-old body of law in an entirely new mold of their own design. They started sketching out their intentions only in the late 1950s; within two short decades they had achieved virtually every legal change that they originally planned. There were setbacks along the way, of course; the common law always develops in fits and starts, with some states bolder and others more timid, and the transformation of tort law was no exception. But compared with the cautious incrementalism with which the common law had changed in centuries past, an utter transformation over a twenty-year span can fairly be described as a revolution, and a violent one at that.

The revolution began and ended with a wholesale repudiation of the law of contract. Until well into the 1960s, it was up to each buyer to decide how safe a car he or she wanted to buy. Then as now, the major choices were fairly obvious: large, heavy cars are both safer and more expensive; economy cars save money but at some cost in safety. In case after case today, however, the courts struggle to enforce a general mandate that all cars be *crashworthy*. That term is perfectly fluid; it is defined after the accident by jury pronouncements; it is defined without reference to preferences and choices deliberately expressed by buyer and seller before the transaction. A woman's choice of contraceptives was once a matter largely under the control of the woman herself and her doctor, with the FDA in the background to certify the general safety and efficacy of particular drugs or devices. Today tort law has shifted that authority too from the doctor's office to the courtroom. Balancing the risks and benefits of childhood vaccination was once a concern of parents, pediatricians, the FDA, and state health authorities. But here again, the views of the courts have become the driving force in determining what may be bought and sold. Not long ago, workplace safety was something to be decided between employer and employees, often through collective bargaining, perhaps with oversight from federal and state regulators, while compensation for accidents was determined by state workers' compensation laws. Today the courts supervise a free-for-all of litigation that pits employees against both employers and the outside suppliers of materials and equipment, the latter two against each other, and both against their insurers.

What brought us this liability tax, in short, was a wholesale shift from consent to coercion in the law of accidents. Yesterday we relied primarily on agreement before the fact to settle responsibility for most accidents. Today we emphasize litigation after the fact. Yesterday we deferred to private choice. Today it is only public choice that counts, more specifically the public choices of judges and juries. For all practical purposes, contracts are dead, at least insofar as they attempt to allocate responsibility for accidents ahead of time. Safety obligations are now decided through liability prescription, worked out case by case after the accident. The center of the accident insurance world has likewise shifted, from *first-party* insurance chosen by the expected beneficiary, to *third-party* coverage driven by legal compulsion.

---

## STRICT LIABILITY

The old negligence rules had always been open to the reproach of stinginess. With the death of contract, they now promised to be hopelessly cumbersome as well. The prospect of running an ever-growing number of cases through a full postaccident inquest on how all the players had performed was discouraging; the sheer task threatened to overwhelm the courts, and the outcome would too often be compensation deferred or denied altogether. This was most vexing. The Founders had labored hard to cross the high mountains of contractual language, only to find that the valley of tort below was not exactly flowing with milk and honey.

As we saw earlier, their initial response was to rely on the contractual material already at hand, using it to spin out liability through the implied warranty. If the Mammoth Corporation had somehow *promised* to pay for any and all accidents involving its product, everything else was simple. No one had to worry about whether there had been negligence; somewhere or other down there between the lines the contract itself promised payment. The content was novel, but the forms were reassuringly familiar.

For a while, then, the reinterpretation of contract terms sufficed as a basis for inventing liability standards much stricter than negligence. And a while was all the Founders really needed. Most people are eager to believe good news, even when it is too good to be true. The public and press didn't at all mind the idea that manufacturers had suddenly begun promising (tacitly, mind you) to pay for accidents resulting from all defects in their products, regardless of negligence. Within a few years, this legal notion of "strict" producer liability had become familiar and obvious. At that point, several state courts were ready to discard the roundabout legal fictions and take a more direct route to the same result. In 1962, the California Supreme Court led the way.

For Christmas in 1955, William Greenman's wife had bought her husband a Shopsmith, a new power tool that served as a combination saw, drill, and wood lathe. Greenman was making a wooden chalice on his Shopsmith one day when a piece of wood flew out of the machine and struck him on the forehead. He sued the manufacturer, maintaining that "inadequate[ly] set screws were used to hold parts of the machine together so that normal vibrations caused the tailstock of the lathe to move away from the piece of wood being turned, permitting it to fly out of the lathe." No contract claim was possible: Greenman was not the actual buyer of the lathe, and he had failed, in any event, to comply with California contract rules that require timely notice of a pending claim. By 1962, however, when the case reached it, the California Supreme

Court was already growing tired of contracts and all their troublesome formalities and rules. It contemptuously brushed aside the notice requirement as a "booby trap for the unwary." Strict liability, the court bluntly declared, would no longer be rationalized in terms of implied warranties, fictional contracts, or anything of that sort. Product manufacturers would instead be held "strictly liable" to consumers for accidents caused by a "defect in manufacture" of their product.

This was a great leap. The need to find implied warranties and such had been a bothersome and often embarrassing barrier to contractual theories of liability. The need to find negligence had been an equally troublesome barrier to tort theories of liability. Now, at one bound, the courts could leap directly to the desired goal, at least so long as a product defect was at issue.

But there was important work still to be done. Though somewhat obscure on the point, *Greenman* seemed to cover *manufacturing defects*, which are in fact quite rare. *Design defects*, however, were quite another matter, and had not yet been officially incorporated into the new doctrine. So Barbara Evans learned in 1966. Driving her station wagon across an intersection one day, Barbara's husband was broadsided by another car and killed. The 1961 Chevrolet had an X-shaped frame; at the time, other manufacturers still used a box frame. Barbara sued General Motors, claiming misdesign. Her suit was quickly dismissed. "Perhaps it would be desirable to require manufacturers to construct automobiles in which it would be safe to collide," the court of appeals declared, "but that would be a legislative function, not an aspect of the judicial interpretation of existing law." Errors in manufacture were one thing. But in 1966 the courts were not yet ready to examine product design and declare it defective.

*Greenman*, however, had its own inexorable logic. If General Motors can be held liable for leaving a frame strut loose accidentally, why shouldn't it be liable for leaving it out deliberately? By mid-decade the design defect barrier was beginning to crumble.

David Larsen broke through this last major conceptual wall in 1968, just two years after Barbara

Evans lost her case. His 1963 Chevrolet Corvair collided head on with another car, thrusting the steering column into his head. He sued General Motors, complaining that "the design and placement of the solid steering shaft, which extends without interruption from a point 2.7 inches in front of the leading surface of the front tires to a position directly in front of the driver, exposes the driver to an unreasonable risk of injury from the rearward displacement of that shaft in the event of a left-of-center head-on collision." This time, a federal appeals court was ready to move ahead. Thereafter, the court announced, juries would be free to pin liability on defects in design as well as manufacture.

Like so many other changes in the tort rules, the step from manufacturing defects to design defects was presented as the soul of modesty. But with that simple change the courts plunged into a new and daunting enterprise. To begin with, the takes in design defect cases are much higher. A manufacturing-defect verdict condemns only a single item coming off the assembly line. But a defect of design condemns the entire production, and a loss in one case almost inevitably implies losses in many others. Moreover, design is a much more subtle business than manufacture, and identifying deficiencies is vastly more difficult.

Before long, juries across the country were busy redesigning lawn mowers, electrical switches, glass and plastic bottles, pesticides, and consumer and industrial products of every other description. A product can be defectively designed because a safety device has been omitted (e.g., a paydozer without rearview mirrors) or because certain parts are not as strong as they might have been (e.g., a car roof is not strong enough to withstand a rollover, or the impact of a runaway horse that lands on the roof after a front-end collision). A jury can find that a single-control shower faucet is defective because if one turns it on all the way to one side, it will allow only hot water to spray, or that children's cotton sleepwear is defective because it has no flame-retardant chemicals added. Sears lost a $1.2 million judgment to a man who suffered a heart attack caused (he alleged) by a lawn mower rope that was too hard to pull. The Bolko Athletic Company paid $92,500 for defectively designing the second base on a baseball diamond; a concrete anchor, the jury concluded, was unsafe for amateur-league players. Recent cases have attempted to extend strict liability (at least for the condition rather than the design of a product) to persons who sell used goods, even ordinary citizens selling cars through the classified ads, though so far most courts have declined to take this seemingly logical step.

Drugs and pharmaceutical devices were among the last products to be swept up in design defect litigation. Until well into the 1970s, most courts accepted that potent drugs often have unavoidable side effects, and they declined to repeat the difficult balancing of risks and benefits already conducted by the FDA. But this line was crossed in the end as well. Courts began to find design defects in contraceptive pills (one brand contained more hormone than another, making it both more effective and riskier), vaccines (the live but weakened polio virus is both more effective and more dangerous than the killed virus), morning sickness drugs, and intrauterine devices.

## QUESTIONS

1. What is "liability"? How does a business acquire it?
2. What are the limits on liability? How are they justified?

---

John Nesmith | # Calculating Risks: It's Easier Said Than Done

WASHINGTON—What's more dangerous? A terrorism attack involving anthrax or being struck by lightening? A plane trip or a long country drive? In these terror-haunted times, we must constantly balance risks.

We often fear the wrong things and spend money to protect ourselves from lesser evils, says David Ropeik, director of risk communications at Harvard Center for Risk Analysis.

Government and industry together spend more than $30 million a year to deal with hazardous products even though the number of people whose health is at risk from this special kind of garbage is quite low. The annual expenditure on anti-smoking campaigns, on the other hand, is only about $500 million a year, even though smoking is one of the leading preventable causes of death in America.

"This irrational response kills people," Ropeik says. "In a world of finite resources, we can only protect ourselves from so many things."

But fear often is stronger than reason.

Ropeik likes to cite the example of a hiker walking through the woods who sees a dark, crooked shape on the ground. Before he has time to ask himself whether it is a stick or a snake, and then reason that if it is a snake it could be dangerous, he jumps away, impelled by a fear programmed deep in his brain, perhaps even in his genes.

Nerve circuits convey information to the brain's fear center, or amygdala, much faster than other circuits serve the cortex, where thought and rational learning occur, Ropeik says. These messages not only trigger the physical response, but also reinforce the fear itself.

Reprinted by permission of John Nesmith of the Cox News Washington Bureau.

That means to Ropeik that fear and the emotional processes linked to it are more powerful than the rational processes with which we might make more valid assessments of our risks.

In addition to such biological factors, Ropeik says, social psychologists have identified "universal perception factors" that underlie group fears and help shape behavior. Among them are:

- Control vs. no control: We normally fear something more if we are not personally in control of it. Thus, you feel safer driving your own car through several hundred miles of bad traffic than traveling the same distance in an airliner, even though you are safer in the plane.
- Immediate vs. chronic: We are more afraid of something that can kill us suddenly and violently than we are of chronic, long-term dangers.
- Natural vs. manmade: We're less afraid of radiation from the sun than of the radiation from power lines and cell phone towers, even though the risk from the sun is far greater.
- Risk vs. benefit: We find reasons to overlook the risks brought to us by something we like. The acetone in fingernail polish is less fearsome to those who use it than the same chemical encountered in another form.
- Imposed vs. voluntary: Nonsmokers are often fearful of tobacco smoke. Smokers usually aren't.

There's even some risk in assessing risk, at least politically. The Harvard center has been criticized for accepting contributions from government-regulated industries eager to promote any suggestion that their products pose relatively little danger. Thus, the center is controversial with environmental and consumer groups.

Ropeik, who authored "Risk: A Practical Guide for Deciding What's Really Safe and What's Really

## What's Risky? Chances of Death?

The annual risks of dying of various causes in the United States:

Heart disease, 1 in 397
Cancer, 1 in 511
Stroke, 1 in 1,699
Accidents (all kinds), 1 in 3,014
Accidents (motor vehicle), 1 in 6,745
Alzheimer's disease, 1 in 5,752
Alcohol (including liver disease), 1 in 6,210
Suicide, 1 in 12,091
Homicide, 1 in 15,440
Food poisoning, 1 in 56,031
Fire, 1 in 82,977
Bicycle accidents, 1 in 376,165
Lightning, 1 in 4,478,159
Bioterrorism attack involving anthrax, 1 in 56,424,800

Harvard Center for Risk Analysis, from U.S. Centers for Disease Control and Prevention data.

Dangerous in the World Around Us," insists that some of our most expensive risks are actually "bogeymen" on which society spends inordinate sums.

"I think some people have used this to advance political or corporate agendas," he said. "Obviously, there are environmental risks that are bigger and demand more attention than we're giving them."

He cited indoor air pollution. Most Americans draw nine out of 10 breaths in indoor environments that are polluted with molds, germs and chemicals, he said.

So, with crooked sticks, solar radiation, acetone, mosquitoes and dirty indoor air surrounding us, what is our biggest risk?

Ropeik hesitated.

"Obesity," he replied. "There is better than a 50–50 chance that any given American is obese, and this causes 300,000 deaths a year. Tobacco causes about 400,000 deaths a year, but only 47 million Americans smoke. They are really neck-and-neck."

## QUESTIONS

1. What are the "universal perception factors" that are used in explaining group fear?
2. What are your biggest fears as a consumer? As a citizen? How do they control your behavior?

Stanley J. Modic

# How We Got into This Mess

Stanley J. Modic is a journalist and a member of the Press Club of Cleveland's Hall of Fame. John Anderson is a retired vice president of Allstate Insurance Co.

Product-liability problems continue to vex U.S. industry. Just about everyone concedes that something must be done, but consensus as to a solution remains elusive.

Some accuse the insurance industry of contriving a crisis to justify raising premiums. Others blame the legal profession's obsession with using tort law to extract high settlements.

Just where *does* the fault lie? And where do we go from here? Are legislative curbs needed?

The search for a remedy is mired in confusion. And the confusion stems primarily from the way in which liability insurance and tort law have combined into an organic system which has evolved over the years.

The principal catalysts feed on each other. As the system of tort law has grown and its scope has expanded, the insurance industry has responded by increasing the amounts of coverage it offers and, naturally, its premiums. Each system has prospered, in a sense, from the activities of the other. And, over the years, that has caused the product-liability problem to spiral out of control.

Roy R. Anderson, who retired as a vice president of Allstate Insurance Cos., has pondered this dilemma. As an actuary, a strategic planner, and a futurist, he has extensively analyzed the problems of our society and of the insurance industry. In retirement, he continues his interest in futurism. And, though he readily admits that accurately predicting the future is impossible, he believes that the way to get a fix on the future is to study how our systems are working today and how they got that way.

From Stanley J. Modic, "How We Got into This Mess," *Industry Week*, January 12, 1987.

## WHO PAYS?

"It is critical," Mr. Anderson stresses, "to understand that both liability insurance and tort law are organic, man-made systems that operate in accordance with the perceptions, beliefs, and values of human beings—all of which continually are shifting."

As he explains it, the tort system was originally intended to achieve two goals in situations where one person, through negligence, injured another person.

"The first was to heal the victim; the second was to punish the person at fault by making him compensate the victim."

The advent of liability insurance drastically changed things. "No longer was the person at fault punished by having to bear the full cost of compensating the victim," Mr. Anderson explains. "Instead, this 'punishment' was spread across society by means of insurance premiums."

To illustrate how social systems evolve, Mr. Anderson points out that in some respects we are returning to the days when the guilty party had to bear the full burden of compensating the victim. This happens when a person (or corporation) forgoes liability insurance—because it's not available or because the premiums are too high. It also happens when the amount of the plaintiff's award greatly exceeds the amount of liability insurance carried—an increasingly common situation which alarms many manufacturers.

## IT'S NOT WORKING

For those individuals and corporations priced out of the insurance market, the system is no longer working. The expansion of the tort system has warped beyond all reason both the financial settlements and the legal definition of what constitutes being "at fault."

"The most invidious and illogical of these distortions has been the increase in awards for punitive damages," Mr. Anderson contends. He feels that if a guilty person is to be punished for behavior that caused injury to another person, that punishment should come in the form of a fine payable to the state, rather than punitive damages awarded in a civil suit to the individual.

"This is especially true," Mr. Anderson asserts, "in the case of a guilty corporation where the fine must be very large before it gets the attention of the wrongdoer. Clearly, such cases should come under the criminal section of the law—with both the corporation and the guilty corporate executives subject to the penalty process."

Other shifts, too, have distorted the legal system. The initial concept that the guilty person had to be 100% at fault and that the victim had to be totally blameless in the cause of the injury has been eroded, Mr. Anderson points out. In addition, the definition of what constitutes an "injury" and the conditions under which a party can be deemed liable have changed; and class-action and cumulative-injury precedents have been established.

## WHY IT'S HAPPENING

The reasons for these shifts, Mr. Anderson says, include: The liberality of juries in awarding damages; the attitude of the public toward insurance companies' ability to pay; and public outrage against the questionable behavior of some corporations and professionals.

"In a nutshell, the system of liability insurance has been transformed from a system that originally compensated only blameless victims to a system that is steadily expanding to take care of all injured persons [regardless of fault]," Mr. Anderson claims.

It comes into play in our lives in many ways. The skyrocketing cost of liability insurance impacts the repair of our automobiles and the quality of our health care. It increases the cost of new products being developed—and keeps some of them off the market. More recently, it has even affected civic affairs, Little League baseball, and our leisure hours.

"If you stop to consider how much it is messing up so much of what we do, you have to wonder how we let it get so bad," says Mr. Anderson.

The former insurance executive believes that the tort law-liability insurance system started going sour with the explosion in automobile ownership following World War II. Prior to that time, liability insurance was almost a luxury for the lower and middle classes. Ordinarily, they carried only collision and comprehensive insurance, usually provided by the dealer as part of the financing package, Mr. Anderson explains. But the enactment of financial-responsibility laws shifted liability insurance from a luxury to a necessity.

"Steadily, it became apparent to the plaintiffs' [attorneys] that each time there was an automobile accident, there was a good chance that there was also an injured person—and another person involved who was at fault," Mr. Anderson says. "The existence of the 'contingent fee' provision in the tort system made it possible for the plaintiff's lawyer to finance the lawsuit for his client—and to be rewarded handsomely for his initiative if he won the case."

In terms of coverage—typically $10,000 for bodily injury and $5,000 for property damage—the amount of insurance in force in the 1950s was "peanuts," reflects Mr. Anderson. "But it was enough to support a training ground for the plaintiffs' bar as it learned to expand the scope of the fledgling system."

## IMPETUS FROM DETROIT

At the same time, a symbiotic relationship was evolving between the auto-insurance industry and the car manufacturers, Mr. Anderson points out. "With the growth of property-damage liability insurance, together with collision insurance, the automakers knew that adequate money would be available for the repair of the great majority of damaged cars. . . . Typically, the owner of the damaged car has not been concerned about what he was charged for repairs, as long as it was covered by insurance."

This knowledge influenced how auto manufacturers built and priced their cars. The philosophy was: "Keep the price of new cars low to encourage sales and make up the difference on repair and replacement parts," Mr. Anderson notes. "It also occurred to them that it might be in their financial interest to design cars that were easily damaged. For example, look at what Detroit has done to bumpers over the years, designing them to be more like ornaments that

provide little or no protection, thus adding substantially to repair costs."

Mr. Anderson claims that the insurance industry played a useful role in improving the construction of automobile bumpers. "It was the advertising and lobbying efforts of the insurance companies that led to state and federal laws requiring sensible bumpers rather than fragile ornaments."

## TWO CRISES

The first major crisis in the tort law/auto insurance system arose in the mid-1970s with the proposal for "no-fault" auto insurance. "In essence, it would have meant the elimination of tort law in the case of auto accidents. It would have been replaced by a 'first-party' system which would compensate the injured parties for medical expenses and economic loss, regardless of fault," the former insurance executive explains.

He recalls that the auto-insurance business was deeply divided on the no-fault issue. Proponents were mainly those carriers writing auto insurance for large corporate clients. Opponents of no-fault were the companies doing business primarily with individuals.

"Unfortunately, what finally emerged from the battle over no-fault was 'modified no-fault,' which included the poorer parts of both systems and ended up costing the public more than the old 'fault' system."

The next crisis in the system occurred with the huge growth in medical-malpractice suits. As Mr. Anderson sees it, the medical profession did "a miserable job" of policing itself. "Incompetent doctors remained at large because medical societies took little action. In those days, doctors operated under their version of the Mafia's *omerta* or 'vow of silence'—which precluded doctors from testifying against each other."

Mr. Anderson credits the plaintiffs' bar and the judicial system for cracking this "vow of silence" and turning the spotlight on the shabby performance of the medical profession—"even though its motives were hardly altruistic."

## *Cultivating the Market*

Initially, the average damage settlements were relatively small, Mr. Anderson points out. Even so, studies indicated that the insurance industry could economically provide higher amounts of coverage. And carriers jumped at the chance to tap a new market; they urged policyholders to buy higher limits on liability coverage.

Although it seemed to be in the best interests of the public, "from a systems standpoint it proved to be ill-advised," Mr. Anderson reflects. "The plaintiffs' bar reacted to the higher limits like a cat to catnip.

"Here again," he says, "it is obvious that the system that has evolved is not the best way to 'monitor' the quality of medical care. The sooner the plaintiffs' bar is removed from the picture, the better."

As Mr. Anderson sees it, the experience in the auto and medical arenas set the stage for the legal profession's pursuit of greener pastures—product liability. "It is in the area of product liability that some of the most significant precedents of tort law have been established and enhanced," he points out. The legal system has accepted new thinking on joint and several liability, punitive damages, class-action suits, and cumulative injury (due, for example, to repeated exposure to a toxic substance).

In product liability the stakes are high. Injury, and the number of people affected, can accumulate over long periods.

Mr. Anderson says the classic case may be asbestosis. "The amount of damages that corporations now have to pay are astronomically so much higher than the direct economic loss that they can bankrupt a company."

## A GLOOMY PROSPECT

As bad as the asbestos case has been, it pales in comparison with potential damage claims against companies, or even entire industries, stemming from toxic chemicals or long-term environmental degradation.

"The explosive nature of the present product-liability system is [such] that it will ultimately be beyond the capacity of the insurance business to carry it," Mr. Anderson contends. "The systems are

so out of control that our economy and society can no longer bear the cost."

Mr. Anderson believes that the public, as well as federal and state legislators, recognize that something must be done. The problem, however, transcends the issues of law, insurance, and compensation.

"In fact," he claims, "what we are dealing with is the very value structure of our society." Mr. Anderson warns that change will come slowly, because "the legal fraternity has a great vested interest in the system."

## *Solutions Coming*

But, as bleak as the situation seems today, this futurist sees a light at the end of the tunnel. A start is likely this year; Congress is expected to pass legislation to cap the amount of damages that can be awarded.

That legislation, however, will not solve the basic problem of a tort law-liability insurance system running amok. Nevertheless, Mr. Anderson believes there is reason to hope for a long-range solution. Congressional action, he predicts, will break a logjam and set into motion waves of change that will ripple through other aspects of tort law.

Organic, man-made systems have life cycles and ultimately run their course, Mr. Anderson observes. "The system of liability insurance is well into the stage of decline," he believes.

He thinks that the system of tort law is also in a state of decline. "However, the course of its future and the timing of its demise will differ greatly from that of the insurance system. Because tort law is an important part of the much broader system of civil and criminal law, its future—and its demise—will be tied to its broader parent system," he concludes.

## *Tort-Law Change*

As for tort law, the futurist makes this prediction: The two purposes served under the present system— compensating the injured persons and punishing those at fault—eventually will be served by two different systems.

"The compensation of injured people will be included under a much broader system that will compensate or cure injured persons, regardless of the cause of the injury," he anticipates.

The "punishment" purpose, Mr. Anderson predicts, will be handled under the criminal justice system. "There would be standards of performance required for the various professions; those who failed to adhere to those standards would be punished by their profession—or under criminal law."

The same would apply to manufactured products. "Standards would be established and tests would be required. Manufacturers failing to follow the standards, thereby causing injury, would be punished under criminal law."

## QUESTIONS

1. How did we "get into this mess," according to Modic? What is the mess we are in? How does Modic think we can get out of the mess?

2. How did the major crises in the tort law/auto insurance system complicate the issues of liability?

Henry Fairlie | # Fear of Living

Henry Fairlie writes for *The New Republic* magazine.

In January 1967 the first Apollo spacecraft caught fire during a test on the launchpad. Three astronauts were killed. The nation was shocked and horrified, all the more so because the screams and scrambles of the astronauts could be clearly heard. But although there was a congressional hearing, and some delay of the manned flights, the Apollo program went smartly ahead, with the full understanding and support of the nation, and within 18 months Apollo 11 landed on the moon, ahead of the deadline set by John Kennedy. The Apollo disaster was not graven on the public mind as a rebuke to America's confidence in its technology, or taken as the occasion to preach that Americans must learn the limits to their energy and power.

Nineteen years later, the space shuttle Challenger was destroyed before our eyes on television. It was a spectacular tragedy, the result of human miscalculation and technical failure, neither of which should have been present, perhaps, but both of which are understood risks in the still dangerous enterprise of space flight. Yet the prevailing mood in America so panicked NASA that it took almost three years to send up another shuttle. NASA even reached the stage, as members of its staff said, of taking so many precautions that it was in danger of enlarging, instead of diminishing, the possibility of malfunction.

In the 19 years between these tragedies, the idea that our individual lives and the nation's life can and should be risk-free has grown to be an obsession, driven far and deep into American attitudes. Indeed, the desire for a risk-free society is one of the most debilitating influences in America today, progressively enfeebling the economy with a mass of safety regulations and a widespread fear of liability rulings, and threatening to create an unbuoyant and uninventive society. As many studies show, this is strikingly an American phenomenon, one that seems to have taken root in yet another distortion of the philosophy of rights underlying the Constitution, as if the Declaration of Independence had been rewritten to include

From *The New Republic*, January 23, 1989.

freedom from risk among the self-evident rights to life, liberty, and the pursuit of happiness. This morbid aversion to risk calls into question how Americans now envision the destiny of their country.

If America's new timorousness had prevailed among the Vikings, their ships with the bold prows but frail hulls would have been declared unseaworthy. The Norsemen would have stayed home and jogged. Columbus's three tubs would not have been allowed to sail; as it was, one was left wrecked on American shores. The Vikings and Columbus were exploring what was as unknown to them then as our solar system is to us today, and it is not only the practical achievements of such venturing that are frustrated by the desire for a risk-free society. Something of the questing endeavor of the human spirit is also lost. The Vikings made sagas of their explorations, as European and English literature flowered during the great Age of Exploration. There once was, but there is not now, a promise of saga in America. Its literature has retreated into a preoccupation with private anxieties and fretting.

At Three Mile Island, the fail-safe system worked. The power station switched itself off. There was a scare, but no disaster. Yet Three Mile Island in the American mind is an emblem of catastrophe. Nuclear power in America, as in no equivalent industrial or industrializing nation, has been almost paralyzed, although it is the only sufficient, efficient, and *relatively* safe source of energy that can avoid the greater risks of pollution and the "greenhouse effect." Of course there is a risk in nuclear power, and there should be thorough inspections and safeguards. Of course, also, there is such a thing as a level of risk that is unacceptable. But in America the threshold of tolerable risk has now been set so low that the nation is refusing to pay the inevitable costs of human endeavor. Stand beneath the majesty of the Grand Coulee Dam, or gaze up at the marvel of the Brooklyn Bridge—"O Harp and Altar," as Hart Crane sang of it—and count the number of lives lost in their construction. But then feel the power, even the beauty, of both dam and bridge, and weigh the cost of lives against the benefits they have brought.

The origins of the widespread refusal to accept a sometimes high level of risk as a normal and necessary hazard of life lie in the early 1970s. As America lost heart in the prosecution of the war in Vietnam, the energy of the dissenters—the vanguard of the "Me Decade"—turned to lavish care for the environment, the snail darter, and their own exquisite, often imagined, physical and emotional well-being. The simultaneous loss of faith in American technology was part of the same phenomenon; technology, it was observed, not only fouled the environment, but had proved incapable of winning a war against guerrillas in the jungle. And beyond this, of course, has been the growth of the larger belief that science itself has somehow betrayed us, that it promises evil and not beneficence.

This loss of courage and faith has manifested itself in many ways, but it has found its most immediately dangerous expression in tort (liability) law. Tort law is not only threatening to make the economy uncompetitive, it is warping the American legal system and its judicial philosophy. As Peter W. Huber observes in *The Legal Revolution and Its Consequences*, "No other country in the world administers anything like it." Tort law was "set in place in the 1960s and 1970s by a new generation of lawyers and judges. . . . Some grew famous and more grew rich in selling their services to enforce the rights they themselves invented."

In November a court in Albany had seriously to consider a claim for $1 million in damages against New York state, brought by a woman who, while she was sunbathing on the beach in a public park on Long Island, was hit in the neck by a Frisbee being tossed between a nine-year-old boy and a 20-year-old woman. Her lawyer contended that the Frisbee was a "dangerous instrument" that should not have been allowed on the beach. (Since the idea of the Frisbee was taken from the bakery of that name where the workers whizzed pie plates to each other, rather than laboriously carry them, are we to assume that today the Occupational Safety and Health Administration would have stepped in to stop this skilled, efficient, rapid, but clearly "dangerous" method of conveyance?) At least this woman's claim was thrown out: the judge observed that she could have moved to another part of the beach if she feared injury from these alarming flying objects. Consider also the mother who sued a baseball club because her son was injured by a ball fouled back to their seats. It may well be that they had chosen seats there because her son had hopes of capturing a foul ball as a trophy, in which case the risk was known and invited by the mother; in any event, blame cannot be said to lie with the club, the hitter, or the ball. Here we see one pernicious moral effect of America's growing fear of risk: a commensurate diminution of the notion of individual responsibility for one's actions.

Claims of others' liability for our plights are, with the support of judges, lawyers, and juries, producing a "tort tax" on goods and services. They amount to a $300 billion levy on the American economy, observes Huber, that "accounts for 30 percent of the price of a stepladder and 95 percent of the price of childhood vaccines." The development of tort law has been particularly vicious in its effect because of another phenomenon peculiar to the United States—the award of huge punitive damages (as opposed to nominal damages, intended only to compensate the victim for the actual injury inflicted). The flagrant injustice of many of these awards was illustrated in a case brought against the Monsanto Company that sought damages for 65 plaintiffs for alleged personal injuries from one of the company's products used to make wood preservatives. After the longest-running trial in American history, the jury awarded each plaintiff one dollar in nominal damages, but then, "in a burst of tortured reasoning," as Monsanto Chairman Richard J. Mahoney says, awarded $16 million to the plaintiffs in punitive damages.

There is no justification for this. The Supreme Court has recently agreed to hear a case in which the constitutionality of huge punitive damages will be tested. In an earlier case, Justices Antonin Scalia and Sandra Day O'Connor observed that "this grant of wholly standardless discretion to determine the severity of punishment appears inconsistent with due process." Meanwhile, the awards further frustrate, if they are not crushing, the spirit of innovation in American business. The Conference Board in 1988 conducted a survey of chief executive officers. It showed that uncertainty over potential liability had led almost 50 percent to discontinue product lines,

and nearly 40 percent to withhold new products, including beneficial drugs. The fault lies not only with the "wholly standardless discretion" allowed to juries to determine the severity of the punishment, but with the present power of a single jury to decide what conduct is liable for punitive damages.

The result of all this, says Justice Richard Neely of the West Virginia Supreme Court, author of *The Product Liability Mess*, is that "as a state court judge much of my time is devoted to ways to make business pay for everyone else's bad luck." When the step of a stepladder breaks because it was made of defective material, the payment of reasonable damages to the injured party is just. But as anyone with any household experience knows, sometimes a broken stepladder is just a broken stepladder, the result of bad luck; and surely each of us has the individual responsibility to approach any stepladder with some circumspection. The prevailing attitude in America is that people should be safeguarded against not only negligence but bad luck; it has become all too easy for lawyers to manipulate jurors who generally are scientifically ignorant and believe that they can be guaranteed a risk-free society.

One confirmation that the obsessive American aversion to risk is a growth of the last two decades is the proliferation in that time of academic and quasi-academic literature on risk, with such titles as "Public Perceptions of Acceptable Risks as Evidence of Their Cognitive, Technical, and Social Structure." The conclusions of much of this literature were drawn together in 1982 by Mary Douglas and Aaron Wildavsky in *Risk and Culture*, their own still impressive critique of this phenomenon. Among the interesting questions asked by the authors is "Why is asbestos poisoning now seen to be more fearsome than fire," especially when asbestos was introduced and welcomed as a prevention of injury or death by fire? The question is made even more interesting by Mahoney's revelation that Monsanto "abandoned a possible substitute product for asbestos just before commercialization, not because it was unsafe or ineffective, but because a whole generation of liability lawyers had been schooled in asbestos liability theories that could possibly be turned against the substitute." In principle, Douglas and Wildavsky note, a society selects which risks it will worry, and perhaps even legislate, about in the hope of diminishing or eliminating them. But why do Americans seem to be more concerned about the risks of pollution than about the budget deficit, economic stagnation, and even war?

Who are the people who promote the intolerance of risk in contemporary America, and select which risks the society should worry about? It is reasonable and almost certainly correct to assume a link between the attitudes that have led to the slowing of such new and promising industries as space technology and nuclear power, the gross development of liability law and litigation, the concern about environmental pollution, and the finicky attention to one's bodily health, comfort, and even purity. Together they form a syndrome. The people who are environmental extremists are likely also to be exorbitantly fussy about the risks to their bodily purity from a multitude of pollutants, natural and artifical, not much concerned about the progress of the space and nuclear power industries, automatically against manufacturing companies in liability cases, and generally uninterested in creating and maintaining a productive industrial economy.

From such people are drawn the staffs and membership of the special interest groups that have sedulously promoted America's risk aversion. Douglas and Wildavsky counted some 75 national environmental groups alone, and thousands more at state and local levels. By something like sleight of hand they represent themselves as public interest groups, but in fact these risk-averse groups speak for a very clear special interest: those who work not in manufacturing industries, but in the now vast services sector, including government and corporate bureaucracies, and who manufacture nothing. In short, they do not get their hands dirty. So it is easy for them—it does not violate their "class interest"—to be indifferent to creating a productive industrial economy. It is no sweat off their backs if a manufacturer is closed down, and its workers laid off for environmental reasons. The risk-averse groups are drawn from a privileged class.

Since it is in the interest of these groups to multiply regulations and strengthen their control of

the economy, they have encouraged the growth of government bureaucracy (federal, state, and local). The federal environmental agencies have grown like a coral reef into this bureaucracy and are as indestructible. Since their bureaucrats also wish to keep their paper-shuffling jobs, they work hand in glove to promote yet more regulation of the manufacturing sector of the economy.

One of the reasons why an aversion to risk has taken hold in America is the manner in which the American political system has developed during precisely the same two decades as the growth of the movement for a risk-free society. All the influences that have been observed and analyzed—the decline of parties, the proliferation of committees and subcommittees and the undermining of seniority in Congress, and the development of the primary electoral system—have given advantage to single-issue special interest groups. Direct-mailings have provided special interest groups, as well as candidates, with direct access to the voters without having to work through the established political institutions that would have forced them to adjust their own aims to accommodate the broader national interest. Never has it been so evident that, as Macaulay wrote to his American correspondent H. S. Randall, the biographer of Jefferson, "your Constitution is all sail and no anchor." Those now filling the sails are the special interest groups, of whom the risk-averse are the most successful. European countries, in contrast, simply have not permitted the sacrifice of their political systems to the single-issue special interests. Strong parties compel these special interests to adjust to the national interests.

But these groups could not have been so destructively successful if Americans had not already suffered a loss of faith in their nation—a loss of faith in the science and technology on which American progress has been built (while paradoxically they look to science to create their version of a risk-free country); a loss of faith in America's inexhaustible possibilities, its sense of limitlessness; a loss of faith in the ever-advancing frontier, even, as Kennedy proclaimed, the exploration of the new frontier in space. And with it all, a loss of the American adventuring spirit, of the American gusto whose absence the world now laments, the gusto that, until the 1960s, blew like a fresh wind around the globe, showing what could be accomplished in so short a time by a nation that did not shrink from risk but found it a challenge.

There is something grossly at fault in the conception of the Vietnam War Memorial and the false veneration it excites. It is not, like the Iwo Jima Memorial, a monument to heroism, or even to sacrifice. It is a monument to a loss of life that is seen as wasteful and dishonorable. The feelings it excites reflect a nation that is coming to believe that even

war should be fought without risk to its fighting men or risk of defeat.

A nation should lament the deaths, and succor the survivors. But it cannot forever be counting its dead.

## QUESTIONS

1. What is the "fear of living"? Should we have it? How can we escape it?

2. What groups encourage the fear of living? Why do they do so?

---

Warren E. Burger | # Too Many Lawyers, Too Many Suits

Warren E. Burger was the Chief Justice of the U.S. Supreme Court from 1969 to 1986 and presided over several of the most important cases in recent American history.

In a speech to the American Bar Association convention in 1906, the famous legal philosopher and Harvard Law School Dean, Roscoe Pound, criticized lawyers for making litigation a "sporting contest." The A.B.A. did not like the criticism and at first refused to publish the speech. In "The Litigation Explosion," Walter K. Olson echoes and amplifies Pound's indictment of the legal profession.

Writing especially for nonlawyers, Mr. Olson, a journalist and a senior fellow at the Manhattan Institute, argues that the decline in ethics and the profession's abandonment of age-old constraints on lawyers has created the "litigation business." Lawyers, he tells us, are moving from a profession to a trade, with a corresponding decline in ethics, and they are developing many of the attitudes exhibited by used car dealers. Lawyers' behavior, Mr. Olson says, is largely responsible for the alarming

increase in the number of lawsuits in the United States in comparison to other countries that share the basic structure of our legal system. Mr. Olson adds that this rise parallels the rise in the number of law schools and lawyers—producing a kind of "chicken and egg" situation. . . .

To demonstrate that our society is drowning in litigation, one only has to look at the overworked system of justice, the delays in trials, the clogs businessmen face in commerce and a medical profession rendered overcautious for fear of malpractice suits. The litigation explosion, which developed in barely more than a decade beginning in the 1970's, has affected us at all levels, including, as Mr. Olson notes, "the most sensitive and profound relationships of human life." The consequences of the explosion have become painfully obvious. Suits against hospitals and doctors, which went up 300-fold since the 1970's, increased doctors' medical insurance premiums more than 30-fold for some. We have more lawyers per 100,000 people than any other society in the world. We have almost three times as many lawyers per capita as Britain, with whom we share the common law system.

From the *New York Times*, May 12, 1991. Reprinted with permission.

Mr. Olson notes that lawyers who got their start advertising on late-night television are moving from automobile cases into commercial litigation—or any litigation that earns fees. Another recent book, "Shark Tank," by Kim Isaac Eisler, tells the dismal tale of a mega-law firm, Finley Kumble, and reveals, among other things, the growing use of public relations consultants to tout a law firm's skills and accomplishments. The United States stands alone as the glorifier of lawyers and litigation. And who pays? All of us! Malpractice insurance (which can cost a doctor upward of $50,000 a year), higher automobile insurance rates and other such expenses are a "sales tax" paid by all of us, but one that goes into lawyers' pockets.

There was a time, Mr. Olson indicates, when litigation was viewed as undesirable and, at best, like war, a necessary evil. Strict professional standards, tough laws and social stigma discouraged shyster lawyers from the temptation to stir up litigation. Professional ethics were alive and on the minds of most attorneys. Today, however, success at the bar is measured by salaries and bonuses, while many lawyers, Mr. Olson notes, justify their new role in our litigious society by asserting that they are preserving and protecting people's rights—giving more "access to justice." In short, as he aptly puts it, lawyers want Americans to believe that "the more lawsuits there are . . . the closer to perfect the world will become."

The author says this idea—that lawsuits can be used to deter wrongdoing—is one reason for the litigation explosion. Lawsuits, he argues, have become known as assertions of "rights." Lawyers have justified a wide range of grossly unprofessional actions, like flying off to Bhopal, India, to solicit cases, or to Alaska in a chase for cases on oil spills. To those who have praised litigation as having social value per se, one is tempted to cite Judge Learned Hand: "I must say that as a litigant, I should dread a lawsuit beyond almost anything else short of sickness and death."

One way Mr. Olson documents the disintegration of professional ethics is by examining lawyer advertising on television and in print. In 1977, in *Bates v. Arizona*, the Supreme Court held 5 to 4 that such advertising was protected by the First Amendment;

prior to that time, lawyers were forbidden to advertise or to solicit clients. Apart from a handful of "ambulance chasers," only the shysters went further than sending a business card to a potential client or joining the right clubs. Clearly, the disintegration accelerated after the Bates case. But Mr. Olson's argument that the decision itself changed legal ethics attributes too much to it. The author ignores the difference between a profession, like the law, and a trade or business where advertising is more acceptable.

For centuries, the standards of the legal profession were higher than simply compliance with the law. Yet after the Bates ruling, the American Bar Association quickly relaxed its traditional Canons of Professional Ethics, leading some commentators to wonder whether the A.B.A. had become more interested in a large membership than in traditional ethical standards. Today, the ancient and hallowed concept that lawyers are officers of the court is too often treated with an indulgent smile, not only by shyster advertisers, of course, but unfortunately even by some members of the legal profession who have been entrusted with teaching law students.

Legal academia is one of Mr. Olson's frequent targets. For example, he takes on a law professor who argues that in the "contemporary social context" it may be appropriate for lawyers to sponsor and finance litigation. Mr. Olson also perceptively criticizes the tricky business of champerty, allowing a third party, a bank for instance, to finance litigation, with the attorney often agreeing to pay back that third party, or even putting up collateral. Transactions of this kind reflect what has gone on in the savings and loan and the bank scandals— and in the Ivan Boesky and Michael Milken cases. Champerty, as Mr. Olson explains, developed from another form of legal gambling, the contingency fee.

Mr. Olson would be on even sounder ground if he were to expand his discussion and say that a contingency fee is unethical and dishonest, and ought to be unlawful whenever liability is certain, as it often is, for example, in multiple-victim disasters like plane crashes or railroad collisions.

Admittedly, unless the measure of damages is fixed by statute, the *amount* of a recovery can vary, even when liability is certain. A highly experienced litigator is likely to get a larger settlement or verdict than an amateur. But if a lawyer soliciting a case is required to tell a client whenever liability is certain, that should at least rule out unconscionable contingency fees of 33 percent and 50 percent in those certain-recovery cases.

Mr. Olson contrasts lawyers' contingency fees with the ethical prohibition against doctors charging a fee contingent on the success of the treatment of a patient. The American Medical Association, unlike the American Bar Association, has not thought that the constitutional protection of advertising called for a change in medical ethics. The Hippocratic oath still prevails among doctors. Because a doctor may *constitutionally* advertise has not meant that doctors may do so *ethically*. Compare this with the A.B.A.'s tentative standard forbidding only "false and misleading" advertising. Shyster advertisers stimulate litigation with their advertisements, offering a "free" conference. This kind of advertising is reminiscent of that old poem we recited in our school days: " 'Come into my parlor,' said the spider to the fly."

There is some hope, Mr. Olson points out, of curbing the litigation explosion through third-party arbitration and other forms of "alternative dispute resolution." In 1976, the Judicial Conference of the United States and the A.B.A. sponsored a conference to celebrate the 70th anniversary of Pound's famous speech. That meeting introduced "alternative dispute resolution" into our vocabulary. With hordes of unneeded lawyers flooding the country, perhaps the surplus could be used as arbitrators and mediators.

Who, finally, is to blame for the current problem? Journalists? Lawyers? Law professors? The A.B.A.? The Supreme Court? Mr. Olson indicts all of us; and while there is much to this, those charged with legal stewardship, pre-eminently the A.B.A., can especially be called to account.

The legal and the medical professions are monopolies. Historically, each has largely regulated itself with codes and creeds. Medicine has the Hippocratic oath. Lawyers have no counterpart, but over centuries they have developed common law ethical standards. Up till now, legislative bodies and courts have left regulation to the organized bar. Will that continue? One can only hope that Mr. Olson's book will stimulate moves to control unethical lawyers.

In an era noted for corruption in business, the clergy, academia, science, the political arena— and even among Federal judges—it should not be surprising that there has been a deterioration in the standards and practices of the legal profession. More Federal judges have been found guilty of bribe-taking and tax fraud in the past decade than in the first 190 years of our history. Mr. Olson need not be totally correct in all his criticisms to make "The Litigation Explosion" a valuable contribution to the public interest. Will the legal profession, especially the A.B.A., do anything to clean its own house? It remains uncertain.

## QUESTIONS

1. Why does Justice Berger think there are too many lawyers?

2. Can you argue, against Burger, that we need more lawyers?

Mark Dowie | # Pinto Madness

Mark Dowie is a multiple award-winning journalist. He wrote this explosive piece for *Mother Jones.*

One evening in the mid-1960s, Arjay Miller was driving home from his office in Dearborn, Michigan, in the four-door Lincoln Continental that went with his job as president of the Ford Motor Company. On a crowded highway, another car struck his from the rear. The Continental spun around and burst into flames. Because he was wearing a shoulder-strap seat belt, Miller was unharmed by the crash, and because his doors didn't jam he escaped the gasoline-drenched, flaming wreck. But the accident made a vivid impression on him. Several months later, on July 15, 1965, he recounted it to a U.S. Senate subcommittee that was hearing testimony on auto safety legislation. "I still have burning in my mind the image of that gas tank on fire," Miller said. He went on to express an almost passionate interest in controlling fuel-fed fires in cars that crash or roll over. He spoke with excitement about the fabric gas tank Ford was testing at that very moment. "If it proves out," he promised the senators, "it will be a feature you will see in our standard cars."

Almost seven years after Miller's testimony, a woman, whom for legal reasons we will call Sandra Gillespie, pulled onto a Minneapolis highway in her new Ford Pinto. Riding with her was a young boy, whom we'll call Robbie Carlton. As she entered a merge lane, Sandra Gillespie's car stalled. Another car rear-ended hers at an impact speed of 28 miles per hour. The Pinto's gas tank ruptured. Vapors from it mixed quickly with the air in the passenger compartment. A spark ignited the mixture and the car exploded in a ball of fire. Sandra died in agony

a few hours later in an emergency hospital. Her passenger, 13-year-old Robbie Carlton, is still alive; he has just come home from another futile operation aimed at grafting a new ear and nose from skin on the few unscarred portions of his badly burned body. (This accident is real; the details are from police reports.)

Why did Sandra Gillespie's Ford Pinto catch fire so easily, seven years after Ford's Arjay Miller made his apparently sincere pronouncements—the same seven years that brought more safety improvements to cars than any other period in automotive history? An extensive investigation by *Mother Jones* over the past six months has found these answers:

- Fighting strong competition from Volkswagen for the lucrative small-car market, the Ford Motor Company rushed the Pinto into production in much less than the usual time.
- Ford engineers discovered in pre-production crash tests that rear-end collisions would rupture the Pinto's fuel system extremely easily.
- Because assembly-line machinery was already tooled when engineers found this defect, top Ford officials decided to manufacture the car anyway—exploding gas tank and all—*even though Ford owned the patent on a much safer gas tank.*
- For more than eight years afterwards, Ford successfully lobbied, with extraordinary vigor and some blatant lies, against a key government safety standard that would have forced the company to change the Pinto's fire-prone gas tank.

By conservative estimates Pinto crashes have caused 500 burn deaths to people who would not have been seriously injured if the car had not burst into flames. The figure could be as high as 900. Burning Pintos have become such an embarrassment to Ford that its advertising agency, J. Walter Thompson, dropped a line from the end of a radio spot that read "Pinto leaves you with that warm feeling."

Ford knows the Pinto is a firetrap, yet it has paid out millions to settle damage suits out of court, and it is prepared to spend millions more lobbying against safety standards. With a half million cars rolling off the assembly lines each year, Pinto is the biggest-selling subcompact in America, and the company's operating profit on the car is fantastic. Finally, in 1977, new Pinto models have incorporated a few minor alterations necessary to meet that federal standard Ford managed to hold off for eight years. Why did the company delay so long in making these minimal, inexpensive improvements?

- Ford waited eight years because its internal "cost-benefit analysis," *which places a dollar value on human life*, said it wasn't profitable to make the changes sooner. . . .

Cost–benefit analysis was used only occasionally in government until President Kennedy appointed Ford Motor Company President Robert McNamara to be Secretary of Defense. McNamara, originally an accountant, preached cost benefit with all the force of a Biblical zealot. Stated in its simplest terms, cost-benefit analysis says that if the cost is greater than the benefit, the project is not worth it—no matter what the benefit. Examine the cost of every action, decision, contract, part, or change, the doctrine says, then carefully evaluate the benefits (in dollars) to be certain that they exceed the cost before you begin a program or—and this is the crucial part for our story—pass a regulation.

As a management tool in a business in which profits matter over everything else, cost-benefit analysis makes a certain amount of sense. Serious problems come, however, when public officials who ought to have more than corporate profits at heart apply cost-benefit analysis to every conceivable decision. The

inevitable result is that they must place a dollar value on human life.

Ever wonder what your life is worth in dollars? Perhaps $10 million? Ford has a better idea: $200,000.

Remember, Ford had gotten the federal regulators to agree to talk auto safety in terms of cost-benefit analysis. But in order to be able to argue that various safety costs were greater than their benefits, Ford needed to have a dollar value figure for the "benefit." Rather than be so uncouth as to come up with such a price tag itself, the auto industry pressured the National Highway Traffic Safety Administration to do so. And in a 1972 report the agency decided a human life was worth $200,725. (For its reasoning, see [Table 9-1].) Inflationary forces have recently pushed the figure up to $278,000.

TABLE **9-1** What's Your Life Worth? Societal Cost Components for Fatalities, 1972 NHTSA Study

| Component | 1971 Costs |
|---|---|
| Future productivity losses | |
| Direct | $132,000 |
| Indirect | 41,300 |
| Medical costs | |
| Hospital | 700 |
| Other | 425 |
| Property damage | 1,500 |
| Insurance administration | 4,700 |
| Legal and court | 3,000 |
| Employer losses | 1,000 |
| Victim's pain and suffering | 10,000 |
| Funeral | 900 |
| Assets (lost consumption) | 5,000 |
| Miscellaneous accident costs | 200 |
| Total per fatality: | $200,725 |

*Here is a chart from a federal study showing how the National Highway Traffic Safety Administration has calculated the value of a human life. The estimate was arrived at under pressure from the auto industry. The Ford Motor Company has used it in cost–benefit analyses arguing why certain safety measures are not "worth" the savings in human lives. The calculation above is a breakdown of the estimated cost to society every time someone is killed in a car accident. We were not able to find anyone, either in the government or at Ford, who could explain how the $10,000 figure for "pain and suffering" had been arrived at.*

Furnished with this useful tool, Ford immediately went to work using it to prove why various safety improvements were too expensive to make.

Nowhere did the company argue harder that it should make no changes than in the area of ruptureprone fuel tanks. Not long after the government arrived at the $200,725-per-life figure, it surfaced, rounded off to a cleaner $200,000, in an internal Ford memorandum. This cost-benefit analysis argued that Ford should not make an $11-per-car improvement that would prevent 180 fiery deaths a year. (This minor change would have prevented gas tanks from breaking so easily both in rear-end collisions, like Sandra Gillespie's, and in rollover accidents, where the same thing tends to happen.)

Ford's cost–benefit table [Table 9-2] is buried in a seven-page company memorandum entitled "Fatalities Associated with Crash-Induced Fuel Leakage and Fires." The memo argues that there is no financial benefit in complying with proposed safety standards that would admittedly result in fewer auto fires, fewer burn deaths and fewer burn injuries. Naturally, memoranda that speak so casually of "burn deaths" and "bum injuries" are not released to the public. They are very effective, however, with

TABLE 9-2 $11 vs. a Burn Death: Benefits and Costs Relating to Fuel Leakage Associated with the Static Rollover Test Portion of FMVSS 208

*Benefits*
   *Savings*: 180 burn deaths, 180 serious bum injuries, 2,100 burned vehicles.
   *Unit cost*: $200,000 per death, $67,000 per injury, $700 per vehicle.
   *Total benefit*: 180 × ($200,000) + 180 × ($67,000) + 2,100 × ($700) = $49.5 million.

*Costs*
   *Sales*: 11 million cars, 1.5 million light trucks.
   *Unit cost*: $11 per car, $11 per truck.
   *Total cost*: 11,000,000 × ($11) + 1,500,000 × ($11) = $137 million.

*From Ford Motor Company internal memorandum: "Fatalities Associated with Crash-Induced Fuel Leakage and Fires."*

Department of Transportation officials indoctrinated in McNamarian cost-benefit analysis.

———————

The Nixon Transportation Secretaries were the kind of regulatory officials big business dreams of. They understood and loved capitalism and thought like businessmen. Yet, best of all, they came into office uninformed on technical automotive matters. And you could talk "burn injuries" and "burn deaths" with these guys, and they didn't seem to envision children crying at funerals and people hiding in their homes with melted faces. Their minds appeared to have leapt right to the bottom line—more safety meant higher prices, higher prices meant lower sales and lower sales meant lower profits.

So when J. C. Echold, Director of Automotive Safety (which means chief anti-safety lobbyist) for Ford wrote to the Department of Transportation—which he still does frequently, at great length—he felt secure attaching a memorandum that in effect says it is acceptable to kill 180 people and burn another 180 every year, *even though we have the technology that could save their lives for $11 a car.*

Furthermore, Echold attached this memo, confident, evidently, that the Secretary would question neither his low death/injury statistics nor his high cost estimates. But it turns out, on closer examination, that both these findings were misleading.

First, note that Ford's table shows an equal number of burn deaths and burn injuries. This is false. All independent experts estimate that for each person who dies by an auto fire, many more are left with charred hands, faces and limbs. Andrew McGuire of the Northern California Burn Center estimates the ratio of burn injuries to deaths at ten to one instead of the one to one Ford shows here. Even though Ford values a burn at only a piddling $67,000 instead of the $200,000 price of life, the true ratio obviously throws the company's calculations way off.

The other side of the equation, the alleged $11 cost of a fire-prevention device, is also a misleading estimation. One document that was *not* sent to Washington by Ford was a "Confidential" cost analysis *Mother Jones* has managed to obtain, showing that crash fires could be largely prevented for con- siderably *less* than $11 a car. The cheapest method involves placing a heavy rubber bladder inside the gas tank to keep the fuel from spilling if the tank ruptures. Goodyear had developed the bladder and had demonstrated it to the automotive industry. We have in our possession crash-test reports showing that the Goodyear bladder worked well. On December 2, 1970 (*two years before* Echold sent his cost–benefit memo to Washington), Ford Motor Company ran a rear-end crash test on a car with the rubber bladder in the gas tank. The tank ruptured, but no fuel leaked. On January 15, 1971, Ford again tested the bladder

and again it worked. The total purchase and instal- lation cost of the bladder would have been $5.08 per car. That $5.08 could have saved the lives of Sandra Gillespie and several hundred others.

## QUESTIONS

1. What was the fundamental moral mistake made by Ford?

2. Insurers place dollar values on human lives all the time—otherwise they would go out of business. When is it permissible to assign a cash value to a human life, and when not? What differentiates between the cases?

---

Patricia Werhane

# The Pinto Case and the Rashomon Effect

Patricia Werhane teaches business ethics at the University of Virginia and currently holds the Wicklander Chair in Business Ethics and is Director of the Institute for Business and Professional Ethics at De Paul University in Chicago. This is from her book, *Moral Imagination and Management Decision-Making.*

The Academy Award-winning 1950 Japanese movie *Rashomon* depicts an incident involving an outlaw, a rape or seduction of a woman, and a murder or suicide of her husband. A passerby, who is also the narrator, explains how the story is told to officials from four different perspectives: that of the outlaw, the woman, the husband, and himself. The four nar- ratives agree that the outlaw, wandering through the forest, came upon the woman on a horse led by her husband; the outlaw tied up the husband; the woman and the outlaw had intercourse in front of the bound husband; and the husband was found dead. The

narratives do not agree on how these events occurred or who killed the husband. The outlaw contends that consensual intercourse occurred between him and the wife, and he claims to have killed the husband. The wife depicts the sexual act as rape and claims that because of her disgrace, she killed her hus- band. The husband, through a medium, says that the sexual act began as rape and ended as consent, and that, in shame after being untied by the outlaw, he killed himself. The passerby's story confirms the husband's account of the sexual contact but claims that the bandit was initially afraid to kill the husband. The passerby depicted both men as cowards, prefer- ring to save their own lives rather than protect the wife. Eventually, however, the husband was killed by the bandit. Interestingly, because the passerby is also the narrator of the film, recounting to friends the strange contradictory reportings of this event, we tend to believe his version. But what actually took place is never resolved.

From Patricia Werhane, *Moral Imagination and Management Decision-Making* (New York: Oxford University Press, 1999), pp. 69–75.

In this chapter I examine the role of narratives and make the following claim: the ways we present or re-present a story, the narrative we employ, and the conceptual framing of that story affect its content, its moral analysis, and the subsequent evaluation. Sometimes, narratives of a particular set of events contradict each other. Other times, when one narrative becomes dominant, we appeal to that story for reinforcement of facts, assuming it represents what actually happened, even though it may have distorting effects. The result in either case is a *Rashomon* effect. Yet we seldom carefully examine the narrative we use, often unaware of the "frame" or mental model at work. If my thesis is correct, it is important, morally important, to understand the constructive nature and limits of narratives. . . .

We are at once byproducts of, characters in, and authors of, our own stories. Still, sometimes we become so embroiled in a particular set of narratives, of our own making or not, that we fail to compare with other accounts or evaluate its implications. . . .

Let us begin with some accounts of the Ford Pinto. The accounts of these cases are Mark Dowie's "Pinto Madness" from *Mother Jones*, later revised and reprinted in *Business and Society*; "Beyond Products Liability" by Michael Schmitt and William W. May from the *University of Detroit Journal of Urban Law*; Manuel Velasquez's treatment of the Pinto in his book *Business Ethics* (second edition); Dekkers L. Davidson and Kenneth Goodpaster's Harvard Business School case, "Managing Product Safety: The Ford Pinto"; Ford Motor Company's statements from its lawsuit, *State of Indiana vs. Ford Motor Company;* and Michael Hoffman's case/essay, "The Ford Pinto." Reporting on these incidents, different commentators present "independently supportable facts". In each instance, the commentator claims to be presenting facts, not assumptions, commentary, or conjecture. Yet these "facts" seem to differ. One report, Mark Dowie's, one of the earliest accounts of the case, becomes the dominant narrative despite some of its suspect claims.

The Grimshaw/Pinto case began the documentation of a series of Pinto automobile fires involving rear-end collisions, usually at low speeds, that caused the gas tanks in the Pintos to explode. There is *one* indisputable set of data upon which all commentators agree:

> On May 28, 1972 Mrs. Lily Gray was driving a six-month old Pinto on Interstate 15 near San Bernardino, California. In the car with her was Richard Grimshaw, a thirteen-year old boy. . . . Mrs. Gray stopped in San Bernardino for gasoline, got back onto the freeway (Interstate 15) and proceeded toward her destination at sixty to sixty-five miles per hour. As she approached Route 30 off-ramp, . . . the Pinto suddenly stalled and coasted to a halt in the middle lane. . . . [T]he driver of a 1962 Ford Galaxie was unable to avoid colliding with the Pinto. Before impact the Galaxie had been braked to a speed of from twenty-eight to thirty-seven miles per hour.
>
> At the moment of impact, the Pinto caught fire and its interior burst into flames. The crash had driven the Pinto's gas tank forward and punctured it against the flange on the differential housing. . . . Mrs. Gray died a few days later. . . . Grimshaw managed to survive with severe burns over 90 percent of his body.

What is the background behind the development of the Pinto? Lee Iacocca, then CEO of Ford, stated publicly that in order to meet Japanese competition, Ford decided to design a subcompact car that would weigh less than 2,000 pounds and cost less than $2,000. According to Davidson and Goodpaster, Ford began planning the Pinto in June 1967 and began producing it in September 1970. This represented a 38-month turnaround time as opposed to the industry average of 43 months for engineering and developing a new automobile. Mark Dowie claims that the development was "rushed" into 25 months; Velasquez says it occurred in "under two years"; Hoffman, claims that Ford "rushed the Pinto into production in much less than the usual time". Although the actual time of development may seem unimportant, critics of the Pinto design argue that *because* it was "rushed into production," the Pinto was not as carefully designed or as carefully checked for safety as a model created over a 43-month time span. But if it took 38 months rather than 25, perhaps the Pinto was not rushed into production after all.

The Pinto was designed so that the gas tank was placed behind the rear axle. According to Davidson and Goodpaster, "[a]t that time almost every American-made car had the fuel tank located in the same place". Dowie wonders why Ford did not place the gas tank over the rear axle, Ford's patented design for its Capri models. This placement is confirmed by Dowie, Velasquez, and some Ford engineers as the "safest place." Yet, according to Davidson and Goodpaster, other studies at Ford showed that the Capri placement actually increased the likelihood of ignition inside the automobile. Moreover, such placement reduces storage space and precludes a hatchback design. Velasquez says that "[b]ecause the Pinto was a rush project, styling preceded engineering", thus accounting for the gas tank placement. This notion may have been derived from Dowie's quotation, allegedly from a "Ford engineer, who doesn't want his name used," that "[t]his company is run by salesmen, not engineers; so the priority is styling, not safety".

Dowie claims that in addition to rushing the Pinto into production, "Ford engineers discovered in pre-production crash tests that rear-end collisions would rupture the Pinto's fuel system extremely easily." According to Dowie, Ford crash-tested the Pinto in a secret location, and in every test made at over 25 mph the fuel tank ruptured. But according to Ford, Pinto's gas tank exploded during many of its tests, because, following government guidelines, Ford had tested the car using a fixed barrier standard, wherein the vehicle is towed backwards into a fixed barrier at the speed specified in the test. Ford argued that Pinto behaved well under a less stringent moving-barrier standard, which, Ford contended, is a more realistic test.

Ford Motor Company and the commentators on this case agree that in 1971, before Ford launched the automobile, an internal study showed that a rubber bladder inner tank would improve the reliability of Pinto's gas tank placement. The bladder would cost perhaps $5.08, $5.80, or $11. The $11 figure probably refers to a design adjustment required to meet a later government rollover standard. However, the idea of this installation was discarded, according to Ford, because of the unreliability of the rubber at

cold temperatures, a conjecture not mentioned by commentators. Dowie also contends that Ford could have reduced the dangers from rear-end collisions by installing a $1 plastic baffle between the gas tank and the differential housing to reduce the likelihood of gas tank perforation. I can find no other verification of this contention.

All commentators claim that Ford did a cost/benefit analysis to determine whether it would be more costly to change the Pinto design or to assume the liability costs for burn victims, and memos to that effect were cited as evidence at the Grimshaw trial. However, according to trial evidence submitted by Ford in *Grimshaw*, this estimate was made in 1973, the year *after* the Grimshaw accident, after Ford had evaluated a proposed new government rollover standard. According to evidence presented by Ford in *Grimshaw*, Ford calculated that it would cost $11 per auto to meet the rollover requirement. Ford used government data for the cost of a life ($200,000 per person), and projected an estimate of 180 burn deaths from rollovers. The study was not applicable to rear-end collisions, as some commentators, following Dowie's story, claimed.

Many reports of this case noted the $200,000 figure as Ford's price of a human life. Dowie says, for example, "Ever wonder what your life is worth in dollars? Perhaps $10 million? Ford has a better idea: $200,000". In fact, it was the National Highway Traffic Safety Administration's 1973 figure.

How many people have died as a result of being inside a Pinto during a rear-end collision? "By conservative estimates Pinto crashes have caused 500 burn deaths to people who would not have been seriously injured had the car not burst into flames. The figure could be as high as 900," Dowie claimed. Hoffman repeats Dowie's figures, word for word. A more cautious Velasquez claims that by 1978 at least 53 people had died and "many more had been severely burnt". Schmitt and May, quoting a 1978 article in an issue of *Business and Society Review* that I could not find, estimate the number as "at least 32". Davidson and Goodpaster claim that by 1978, NHTSA estimated that 38 cases involved 27 fatalities.

In the 1978 trial that followed the Grimshaw accident, a jury awarded Grimshaw at least $125 million in punitive damages. *Auto News* printed a headline, "Ford Fights Pinto Case: Jury Gives 128 Million" on February 13, 1978. The commonly cited figure of $125 million is in the court records as the total initial punitive award. The $128 million might be the total award including punitive damages. This award was later reduced on appeal to $3.5 million, a fact that is seldom cited.

A second famous Pinto accident led Indiana to charge Ford with criminal liability. Hoffman reports the incident that led to the charges, on which all agree:

> On August 10, 1978, a tragic automobile accident occurred on US Highway 33 near Goshen, Indiana. Sisters Judy and Lynn Ulrich (ages 18 and 16, respectively) and their cousin Donna Ulrich (age 18) were struck from the rear in their, 1973 Ford Pinto by a van. The gas tank of the Pinto ruptured, the car burst into flames, and the three teenagers were burned to death.

There are two points of interest in this case that apparently led the jury to find Ford not guilty. First, in June 1978 Ford recalled 1.5 million Pintos in order to modify the fuel tank. There was some evidence that the Ulrich auto had not participated in the recall. Second, Ulrich's Pinto was hit from behind at 50 mph by a van driven by a man named Duggar. Duggar later testified that he looked down for a "smoke" and then hit the car, although, according to police reports, the Ulrich car had safety blinkers on. Found in Duggar's van were at least two empty beer bottles and an undisclosed amount of marijuana. Yet this evidence, cited in the *State of Indiana v. Ford Motor Co.* case, is seldom mentioned in the context of the Ulrich tragedy, and Duggar was never indicted.

The purpose of this exercise is not to exonerate Ford or to argue for bringing back the Pinto. Rather, it is to point out a simple phenomenon—a story can become a narrative and can be taken as fact even when other alleged equally verifiable facts contradict that story. Moreover, one narrative can dominate as *the facts*. Dowie's interesting tale of the Pinto became the prototype for Pinto cases; many authors accepted his version without going back to check whether his data were correct or to question why some of his data contradicted Ford and government claims. Dowie's reporting of Grimshaw became a prototype for the narrative of the Ulrich case as well, so that questions concerning the recall of the Ulrich auto and Duggar's performance were virtually ignored. Such omissions not only make Ford look better, they also question the integrity of these reports and cases. Thus, this set of cases illustrates pitfalls that develop when a particular narrative becomes the paradigm for data and fact.

## QUESTIONS

1. What is the "Rashomon effect?" How does it affect the Pinto case?

2. How do the stories we tell about ourselves (and to ourselves) influence our moral decisions? Do you ever see yourself as a character in a drama that you are creating? But what about when the drama becomes all too real? What about the other characters in this drama?

Judith Jarvis Thomson | # Remarks on Causation and Liability

Judith Jarvis Thomson is one of the world's leading moral philosophers.

## I

Under traditional tort law, a plaintiff had to show three things in order to win his case: that he suffered a harm or loss, that an act or omission of the defendant's caused that harm or loss, and that the defendant was at fault in so acting or refraining from acting. It is widely known by non-lawyers that liability may nowadays be imposed in many kinds of cases in which there is no showing that the third requirement is met. Strict product liability is one example. Thus if you buy a lawn mower, and are harmed when you use it, then (other things being equal) you win your suit against the manufacturer if you show that you suffered a harm when you used it, and that the harm you suffered was caused by a defect in the lawn mower—as it might be, a missing bolt. You do not need also to show the manufacturer was at fault for the defect; it is enough that the lawn mower was defective when it left his hands, and that the defect caused your harm.

What may be less widely known by non-lawyers is that there have been some recent cases which were won without plaintiff's having shown that the second requirement was met, namely, that of causation. Perhaps the most often discussed nowadays is *Sindell v. Abbott Laboratories*,[1] which was decided by the California Supreme Court in 1980. Plaintiff Sindell had brought an action against eleven drug companies that had manufactured, promoted, and marketed diethylstilbesterol (DES) between 1941 and 1971. The plaintiff's mother took DES to prevent miscarriage. The plaintiff alleged that the defendants knew or should have known that DES was ineffective as

a miscarriage-preventive, and that it would cause cancer in the daughters of the mothers who took it, and that they nevertheless continued to market the drug as a miscarriage-preventive. The plaintiff also alleged that she developed cancer as a result of the DES taken by her mother. Due to the passage of time, and to the fact that the drug was often sold under its generic name, the plaintiff was unable to identify the particular company which had manufactured the DES taken by her mother; and the trial court therefore dismissed the case. The California Supreme Court reversed. It held that if the plaintiff "joins in the action the manufacturers of a substantial share of the DES which her mother might have taken," then she need not carry the burden of showing which manufactured the quantity of DES that her mother took; rather the burden shifts to them to show they could not have manufactured it.[2] And it held also that if damages are awarded her, they should be apportioned among the defendants who cannot make such a showing in accordance with their percentage of "the appropriate market" in DES.

In short, then, the plaintiff need not show about any defendant company that it caused the harm in order to win her suit.

Was the Court's decision in *Sindell* fair? I think most people will be inclined to think it was. On the other hand, it is not easy to give principled reasons why it should be thought fair, for some strong moral intuitions get in the way of quick generalization. What I want to do is to bring out some of the sources of worry.

But the case is in fact extremely complicated, so I suggest we begin with a simpler case, *Summers v. Tice*,[3] which the same court had decided in 1948, and which the plaintiff in *Sindell* offered as a precedent.

From *Philosophy and Public Affairs* 13(2) (Spring, 1984). Reprinted with permission of Blackwell Publishing.

## II

Plaintiff Summers had gone quail hunting with the two defendants, Tice and Simonson. A quail was flushed, and the defendants fired negligently in the plaintiffs direction; one shot struck the plaintiff in the eye. The defendants were equally distant from the plaintiff, and both had an unobstructed view of him. Both were using the same kind of gun and the same kind of birdshot; and it was not possible to determine which gun the pellet in the plaintiff's eye had come from. The trial court found in the plaintiff's favor, and held both defendants "jointly and severally liable." That is, it declared the plaintiff entitled to collect damages from whichever defendant he chose. The defendants appealed, and their appeals were consolidated. The California Supreme Court affirmed the judgment.

Was the Court's decision in *Summers* fair? There are two questions to be addressed. First, why should either defendant be held liable for any of the costs? And second, why should each defendant be held liable for all of the costs—that is, why should the plaintiff be entitled to collect all of the costs from either?

Why should either defendant be held liable for any of the costs? The facts suggest that in the case of each defendant, it was only .5 probable that he caused the injury; normally, however, a plaintiff must show that it is more likely than not, and thus more than .5 probable, that the defendant caused the harm complained of if he is to win his case.

The Court's reply is this:

> When we consider the relative position of the parties and the results that would flow if plaintiff was required to pin the injury on one of the defendants only, a requirement that the burden of proof on that subject be shifted to defendants becomes manifest. They are both wrongdoers—both negligent toward plaintiff. They brought about a situation where the negligence of one of them injured the plaintiff, hence it should rest with them each to absolve himself if he can. The injured party has been placed by defendants in the unfair position of pointing to which defendant caused the harm. If one can escape the other may also and plaintiff is remediless.

The Court's argument seems to me to go as follows. The plaintiff cannot determine which defendant caused the harm. If the plaintiff has the burden of determining which defendant caused the harm, he will therefore be without remedy. But both defendants acted negligently "toward plaintiff," and the negligence of one of them caused the harm. Therefore the plaintiff should not be without remedy. Therefore it is manifest that the burden should shift to each defendant to show that he did not cause the injury; and, if neither can carry that burden, then both should be held liable.

The argument does not say merely that both defendants are wrongdoers, or that both defendants acted negligently: it says that both defendants acted negligently "toward plaintiff"—that is, both were in breach of a duty of care that they owed to the plaintiff. Suppose, for example, that the plaintiff had brought suit, not against the two hunters who were out quail hunting with him, but against three people: the two hunters, and Jones, who was driving negligently in New York that afternoon. All three members of that class of defendants were wrongdoers, all three acted negligently, and indeed one of the three caused the harm, though it is not possible to tell which. But it could hardly be thought fair for all of them, and so a fortiori, for Jones to have to carry the burden of showing that *his* negligence did not cause the harm. Perhaps he could carry that burden easily; but it would not be fair to require that he do so on pain of liability for the harm. The argument excludes Jones, however, for although he was negligent, he was not negligent toward the plaintiff.

And even that qualification is not enough—we must suppose a further qualification to lie in the background of the argument. Consider Smith, who was driving negligently in California that day, and who in fact nearly ran the plaintiff down as the plaintiff was on his way to go quail hunting. And suppose that the plaintiff had brought his suit against the following three people: the two hunters and Smith. All three were wrongdoers, all three acted negligently, and indeed negligently toward the plaintiff, and one of the three caused the harm, though it is not possible to tell which. But it could hardly be thought fair for all of them, and so a fortiori for Smith to have to carry the burden of showing that *his* negligence did not cause the harm. As it stands, the argument does not exclude Smith, for he *was* negligent toward the plaintiff. So we must suppose that the Court had in mind not merely that all the defendants were negligent toward the plaintiff, but also that their negligent acts were in a measure likely to have caused the harm for which the plaintiff sought compensation.

There lurks behind these considerations what I take to be a deep and difficult question, namely: Why does it matter to us whose negligent act caused the harm in deciding who is to compensate the victim?

## III

It will help to focus on a hypothetical variant of the case, which I shall call *Summers II*. Same plaintiff, same defendants, same negligence, same injury as in *Summers;* but *Summers II* differs in that during the course of the trial, evidence suddenly becomes available which makes it as certain as empirical matters ever get to be, that the pellet lodged in plaintiff Summers' eye came from defendant Tice's gun. Tort law being what it is, defendant Simonson is straightway dismissed from the case. And isn't that the right outcome? Don't we feel that Tice alone should be held liable in *Summers II?* We do not feel that Simonson should be dismissed with a blessing: he acted very badly indeed. So did Tice act badly. But Tice also caused the harm, and (other things being equal) fairness requires that he pay for it.[4] But why? After all, both defendants acted equally negligently toward Summers in shooting as they did; and it was simple good luck for Simonson that, as things turned out, he did not cause the harm to Summers.

It is arguable that there is no principled stopping place other than Tice.[5] Consider, for example, a rule which says: Liability is to be shared among the actual harm-causer and anyone else (if there is anyone else) who acted as negligently toward the victim, and who nearly caused him a harm of the same kind as the actual harm-causer did. Under this rule, liability should presumably be shared between Tice and

Simonson in *Summers II*. But only presumably, since what, after all, counts for these purposes as a "harm of the same kind"? (Compare Smith of the preceding section.) And by what principle should liability be shared only among those who acted negligently toward the victim? (Compare Jones of the preceding section.)

Moreover, even if there is no principled stopping place *other than* Tice, it would remain to be answered what is the principle behind a rule which stops liability *at* Tice.

It pays to begin by asking: What if Tice has an insurance policy that covers him for the costs of harms he causes? We would not feel it unfair for the insurance company to pay Summers off for Tice.

Nor do we feel there would be any unfairness if a friendly philanthropist paid Summers off for Tice.

But the insurance company could simply be living up to its contract with Tice to pay what Tice would have had to pay if he had had no such contract; and the philanthropist would simply be making a gift to Tice—paying a debt for Tice which Tice would otherwise have had to pay himself.

Nevertheless these considerations do bring out that paying Summers' costs is not something we wish to impose on Tice by way of retribution or punishment for his act. If imposing this were a punishment, we would not regard it as acceptable that a third party (insurance company, friendly philanthropist) suffer it as a surrogate for Tice.[6]

What we are concerned with here is not blame, but only who is to be out of pocket for the costs. More precisely, why it is Tice who is to be out of pocket for the costs. It pays to take note of what lies on the other side of this coin. You and your neighbor work equally hard, and equally imaginatively, on a cure for the common cold. Nature then smiles on you: a sudden gust of wind blows your test tubes together, and rattles your chemicals, and lo, there you have it. Both of you acted well; but who is to be in pocket for the profits? You are. Why? That is as deep and difficult a question as the one we are attending to. I think that the considerations I shall appeal to for an answer to our question could also be helpfully appealed to for an answer to this one, but I shall not try to show how.

There is something quite general at work here. "*B* is responsible for the damage to *A*'s fence; so *B* should repair it." "The mess on *A*'s floor is *B*'s fault; so *B* should clean it up." Or anyway, *B* should have the fence repaired, the mess cleaned up. The step is common, familiar, entirely natural. But what warrants taking it?

It is a plausible first idea that the answer lies in the concept "enrichment." Suppose I steal your coffee mug. I am thereby enriched, and at your expense. Fairness calls for return for the good: I must return the coffee mug.

That model is oversimple, of course: it cannot be brought to bear directly. For only I can return the coffee mug, whereas by contrast, anyone can pay the costs of having the fence repaired or the mess cleaned up, either in his own time and effort, or in whatever it takes to get someone else to do these things.

Well, fairness needn't call for the return of the very coffee mug I took, and surely can't call for this if I have now smashed it. Replacement costs might do just as well. Or perhaps something more than replacement costs, to cover your misery while thinking you'd lost your mug. In any case, anyone can pay those costs. But I must pay them to you because I was the person enriched by the theft of the mug, and at your expense. So similarly, perhaps we can say that *B* must pay the costs of having the fence repaired because *B* was the person who enriched himself, and at *A*'s expense, by the doing of whatever it was he did by the doing of which he damaged the fence.

Enrichment? Perhaps so: *B* might literally have made a profit by doing whatever it was he did by the doing of which he made a mess on *A*'s floor (e.g., mudpie-making for profit). Or anyway, he might have greatly enjoyed himself (e.g., mudpie-making for fun). Perhaps he made the mess out of negligence? Then he at least made a saving: he saved the expense in time or effort or whatever he would have had to expend to take due care. And he made that saving at *A*'s expense.

But this cannot really be the answer—it certainly cannot be the whole answer. For consider Tice and Simonson again. They fired their guns negligently in Summers' direction, and Tice's bullet hit Summers. Why should Tice pay Summers' costs? Are we to say that that is because Tice enriched himself at Summers' expense? Or anyway, that Tice made a saving at Summers' expense—a saving in time or effort or whatever he would have had to expend to take due care? Well, Simonson saved the same as Tice did, for they acted equally negligently.[7] It would have to be said "Ah, but Tice's saving was a saving *at Summers' expense*—and Simonson's was not." But what made Tice's saving *be* a saving at Summers' expense? Plainly not the fact that his negligence was negligence "toward" Summers, for as the Court said, Tice and Simonson were both "negligent toward plaintiff." If it is said that what made Tice's saving be a saving at Summers' expense is the fact that it was Tice's negligence that caused Summers' injury, then we are back where we were: for what we began with was why that fact should make the difference.

Drawing attention to cases in which two are equally enriched also brings out more clearly a problem which is already present when only one is. Why is it *B* who must pay the costs of having the mess on *A*'s floor cleaned up, when it is *B* who caused it to be there? Because in doing what he did which caused it to be there he enriched himself (or made a saving) at *A*'s expense. But if what made the enrichment be *at A's expense* is the fact that his act caused the mess to be there, then the question has not been answered: we have merely been offered new language in which to ask it.

Perhaps it pays to set aside the concept "enrichment" and attend, instead, to what we have in mind when we characterize a person as "responsible." Consider again: "*B* is responsible for the damage to *A*'s fence; so *B* should repair it." Doesn't the responsible *person* pay the costs of damage he or she is responsible *for*? And don't we place a high value on being a responsible person?

Similarly, the responsible person pays the costs of damage which is his or her fault.

This is surely right; but what lies behind it? *Why* do we think it a good trait in a man that he pays the costs of damage he is responsible for? Why do we expect him to?

I hazard a guess that the, or anyway an, answer may be found in the value we place on freedom of action, by which I mean to include freedom to plan on action in the future, for such ends as one chooses for oneself. We take it that people are entitled to a certain "moral space" in which to assess possible ends, make choices, and then work for the means to reach those ends. Freedom of action is obviously not the only thing we value; but let us attend only to considerations of freedom of action, and bring out how they bear on the question in hand.

If *A* is injured, his planning is disrupted: he will have to take assets he meant to devote to such and such chosen purpose, and use them to pay the costs of his injury. Or that is so unless he is entitled to call on the assets of another, or others, to pay the costs for him. His moral space would be considerably larger if he were entitled to have such costs paid for him.

But who is to pay *A*'s costs? On whose assets is it to be thought he is entitled to call? Whose plans may *he* disrupt?

*A* might say to the rest of us, "Look, you share my costs with me now, and I'll share with you when you are injured later." And we might then agree to adopt a cost-spreading arrangement under which the costs of all (or some) of our injuries are shared; indeed, we might the better secure freedom of action for all of us if we did agree to such an arrangement. The question which needs answering, however, is whether *A* may call on this or that person's assets in the absence of agreement.

One thing *A* is not entitled to do is to choose a person *X* at random, and call on *X*'s assets to pay his costs. That seems right; but I think it is not easy to say exactly why. That is, it will not suffice to say that if all we know about *X* is that *X* is a person chosen at random, then we know of no reason to think that a world in which *X* pays *A*'s costs is better than a world in which *A* pays *A*'s costs. That is surely true. But by the same token, if all we know about *X* is that *X* is a person chosen at random, then we know of no reason to think that a world in which *A* pays *A*'s costs is better than a world in which *X* pays *A*'s costs. So far, it looks as if flipping a coin would be in order.

What I think we should do is to look at *A*'s situation *before* any costs have been incurred. *A* has been injured. Now he wants to be "made whole": he wants the world changed in such a way as to make him be as nearly as possible what he would have been had he not been injured. That is what he needs money for. But the freedom of action of other people lends weight to the following: If *A* wants the world changed in that (or any other) way, then—other things being equal—*A* has to pay the costs, in money, time, energy, whatever is needed, unless he can get the voluntary agreement of those others to contribute to those costs. Again, *A*'s wanting the world changed in that (or any other) way is not by itself a reason to think he may call on another person to supply him with what he needs to change it. It follows that *A* is not entitled to call on a person unless that person has a feature other than just that of being a person, which marks *his* pockets as open to *A*. *A* cannot, then, choose a person *X* at random, and call on *X* to pay the costs—on pain of infringing *X*'s freedom of action.

And it could hardly be thought that while *A* is not entitled to call on *X*'s assets before *A* has spent anything, *A* becomes entitled to call on *X*'s assets the moment he has.

So *A* is not entitled to choose a person *X* at random, and call on *X*'s assets to pay his costs.

Well, here is *B*, who is considerably richer than *A*. Perhaps some people will feel that that does entitle *A* to call on *B*. I want to set this aside. As I said, freedom of action is not the only thing we value, but I want to bring out *its* bearing on the question in hand; so I shall sidestep this issue by inviting you to imagine that no one is any richer than anyone else.

*A* is injured. Let us supply his injury with a certain history. Suppose, first, that *A* himself caused it—freely and wittingly, for purposes of his own. And suppose, second, that it is not also true of any other person *X* that *X* caused it, or even that *X* in any way causally contributed to it. Thus:

(I) *A* caused *A*'s injury, freely, wittingly, for purposes of his own; and no one other than *A* caused it, or even causally contributed to it.

We can easily construct examples of injuries which consist in loss or damage to property which have histories of this kind—for example, A might have broken up one of his chairs, to use as kindling to light a fire to get the pleasure of looking at a fire. It is harder to construct examples of injuries which consist in physical harm which have histories of this kind. But it is possible—for example, A might have cut off a gangrenous toe to save his life. A might have cut off his nose to spite his face.

Suppose now that having caused himself the injury, A wants for one or another reason to be made whole again. That will cost him something. Here is B. Since (I) is true of A's injury, B's freedom of action protects him against A: A is not entitled to call on B's assets for the purpose—A is not entitled to disrupt B's planning to reverse an outcome wholly of his own planning which he now finds unsatisfactory.

That seems right. And it seems right whatever we imagine true of B. B may be vicious or virtuous, fat or thin, tall or short; none of this gives A a right to call on B's assets. Again, B might have been acting very badly indeed contemporaneously with A's taking the steps he took to cause his own injury: B might even have been imposing risks of very serious injuries on A concurrently with A's act—for example, B might have been playing Russian roulette on A, or throwing bricks at him. No matter: if A's injury has the history I described in (I), then B's freedom of action protects him against the costs of it.

If that is right, then the answer to our question falls out easily enough. Let us suppose that A is injured, and that B did not cause the injury, indeed, that he in no way causally contributed to A's injury. Then whatever did in fact cause A's injury—whether it was A himself who caused his injury, or whether his injury was due entirely to natural causes, or whether C or D caused it—there is nothing true of B which rules out that A's injury had the history described in (I), and therefore nothing true of B which rules out that A should bear his own costs. Everything true of B is compatible with its being the case that A's costs should lie where they fell. So there is no feature of B which marks his pockets as open to A—A is no more entitled to call on B than he is entitled to call on any person X chosen at random.

Causality matters to us, then, because if B did not cause (or even causally contribute to) A's injury, then

B's freedom of action protects him against liability for A's costs. And in particular, it is Simonson's freedom of action which protects him against liability for Summers' costs in *Summers II*, for in that case it was discovered that Tice had caused the injury.

I have been saying that freedom of action is not the only thing we value, and that is certainly true. But if I am right that it is freedom of action which lies behind our inclination to think causality matters—and in particular, our inclination to think it right that Simonson be dismissed once it has been discovered that he did not cause Summers' injury—then these considerations by themselves show we place a very high value on it, for those inclinations are very strong.

## NOTES

1. 26 Cal. 3d 588, 163 Cal. Rptr. 132, 607 P. 2d 924 (1980).

2. One defendant had already been dismissed from the action on the ground that it had not manufactured DES until after the plaintiff was born.

3. 33 Cal. 2d 8o, 199 P. 2d I (1948).

4. Some people feel that Summers himself should share in the costs, in the thought that Summers assumed a risk in going out quail hunting with Tice and Simonson. I do not myself share that intuition. Anyone who does is invited to imagine, instead, that Summers is a farmer, who was passing by, on his way to market.

5. See Wex S. Malone, "Ruminations on Cause-In-Fact," *Stanford Law Review* 9 (December 1956): 66.

6. A number of people have drawn attention to the general point at work here. See, for example, Jules Coleman, "On the Moral Argument for the Fault System," *The Journal of Philosophy* 71, no. 14 (15 August 1974).

7. The general point I illustrate here was made by Jules Coleman, in "Corrective Justice and Wrongful Gain," *The Journal of Legal Studies* 11, no. 2 (June 1982).

## QUESTIONS

1. What is the connection Thomson sees between causation and liability?

2. How should we decide who pays the costs for an injured party? Why is the issue more complex than it initially appears?

Bob Sullivan

# Annoying Fine Print May Not Even Be Legal

Bob Sullivan is an award-winning author and investigative journalist.

Can the New York Yankees change the First Amendment and make their fans agree to the change? They tried recently.

Anyone who's been to the Bronx recently probably wouldn't fault an attempt to make it more family friendly, but can a baseball team change the Constitution and force you to accept it?

Welcome to the world of "boilerplate" language—also known as mouseprint, standard form contracts, fine-print fraud, shrink-wrap contracts, etc.

U.S. consumers rarely engage in any kind of transaction today without clicking or signing away a wide swath of their rights. Cellphone contracts, software purchases, baseball tickets, credit card applications—all include lengthy tomes full of ominous warning that most of us ignore.

Regular readers of this column know I am a collector of fine print and its absurdities, such as school waiver forms asking parents to sign away their kids' right to "enjoy life."

Consumers hate fine print, but emotions rarely carry the day in courtrooms. So corporations have been having a field day with barely readable terms and conditions for some time. In fact, fine-print writers have been emboldened by a recent Supreme Court decision in which the court took their side.

But in a new book titled *Boilerplate*, author and lawyer Margaret Jane Radin is taking aim at the intellectual and legal basis of fine print, trying to put a serious dent in the legal argument behind it.

"I don't think there's a contract, ever, when something is just dropped on us," Radin said, "especially when there is no option to vote with your feet as a consumer, when there are no alternatives."

Radin's point is that contracts, by definition, involve two equal parties that negotiate terms, while fine print is issued on a "take-it-or-leave-it" basis. (Just try to negotiate a lower early termination fee or strike out any clause when you sign a cellphone agreement.) In layman's terms, fine print is merely a list of bad things that can happen to you, the consumer. You might get hit with a penalty fee; your service might be terminated; your right to join a class-action lawsuit is surrendered.

Some lawyers would call these take-it-or-leave-it agreements "contracts of adhesion," a special class of contracts that can be ruled unenforceable if the consumer persuades a judge that the provisions are "unconscionable." As you might imagine, that's a high bar—it means generally that such provisions would be shocking to a normal person's conscience as excessively unfair. Such a legal battle also involves an excessive amount of legal fees, so it's not a realistic option for an aggrieved cellphone holder.

Radin wades into this confusing situation with a fairly radical idea. Trying to shove fine-print agreements into contract law, she argues, is like trying to shove a round peg into a square hole. She calls it "legal gerrymandering." Instead, courts need to adopt a brand-new way of looking at fine print, she says.

Her view is simple: Interactions between consumers and companies are more like brief encounters with strangers than negotiated bargains between equal parties. As such, they fall into the realm of tort law, rather than contract law, Radin argues.

That change would have dramatic implications for fine-print haters everywhere. Were these agreements viewed as torts, angry cellphone owners would retain the right to sue for damages, including pain

From NBCNews.com.

and suffering, if they believe a company has violated their rights, by making an unauthorized withdrawal from the consumer's checking account, for instance.

Generally, the argument in favor of fine print has been economic. Industry groups have repeatedly argued that standard-form agreements are essential because no one wants every consumer negotiating their own terms and conditions for every transaction. The logic runs like this: Form agreements save companies money, particularly when they limit liability and the potential for costly lawsuits, and that savings is passed on to consumers.

But some rights can't be signed away, Radin argues, even if a consumer seemingly agrees to that. Even if it saves them money.

"Important rights can't be canceled by a private party just because they pay the value," she said. "For example . . . you can't sell food with *E. coli* just because it's cheaper. . . . You can't say we haven't maintained our airplanes, but our prices are cheaper, so you assume the risk if we fall out of the sky."

Fine print that limits liability or complicates consumer costs is everywhere—on coffee cups, on dog bone packaging. It's flashed for a brief moment on TV mortgage ads, it's read at record-breaking speed on radio ads for car leases. Falling under the general term "disclosure," its absurdity and ineffectiveness is hard to debate.

"Disclosure doesn't work. We don't understand it, even if it's in large print. We don't read it, even lawyers," Radin said. "That's why we have to start evaluating these disclosures a different way. They aren't contracts."

When consumers talk about fine print, they usually focus on hidden language that imposes punishing late fees, doubles prices after some unknown trial period, or springs other tricks and traps that ding their wallets. But when consumer lawyers talk about fine print, they are usually complaining about something a bit more theoretical—common provisions within agreements that indicate that consumers waive their rights to sue the company if something goes wrong or join in a class-action lawsuit. Instead, consumers are forced into a process known as binding mandatory arbitration. Most consumer agreements with banks, cellphone companies, credit card issuers, television subscription services, and other service providers include arbitration clauses.

Consumer groups and class-action lawyers despise such provisions and have been fighting them in courtrooms around the country for some time, arguing that waiver of jury trial rights is "unconscionable."

After compiling a mixed legal record, the fight was dealt a devastating blow last year, when the U.S. Supreme Court sided with AT&T in a case involving a consumer who sued to have a class-action lawsuit waiver thrown out of a cellphone contract. Within months, similar waivers began appearing in nearly all consumer agreements, dealing a blow to the entire class-action system.

Consumer lawyers argue that waiving a right to a jury trial in order to buy a car or baseball ticket is similar to waiving the right to free speech.

Anyone who's ever received a 50-cent coupon because of an old class-action lawsuit that earned lawyers millions knows that lawsuits are hardly a panacea for the problem of misbehaving companies or those that impose overreaching terms and conditions. But neither is a free market, argues Radin, unless it is truly a thriving market with informed consumers.

In many markets, consumers have few or no choices. Most cellphone firms have the same early termination fees and arbitration clauses, for example. Meanwhile, if fine print is too small to read or too arcane to understand, there won't even be a handful of ace consumers who can provide a watchdog effect. What happens next is called a "lemon's equilibrium," a term first coined in the 1970s by economist George Akerlof.

"If there is a lot of competition in a marketplace, and at least some consumers are very well informed, then market forces can have a positive impact on fine print," Radin explained. "But even if there's a lot of competition, but not enough people in the market know what's going on, there's a race to the bottom. Everybody just buys the cheaper product . . . and everyone gets a lemon."

Radin's argument is broader than a need to protect consumers from $480 satellite dish early termination fees or to preserve their right to sue. She thinks that industry's reliance on sweeping rights clauses in every consumer agreement, and the courts' compliance with that, has created an alternate legal system in America—one that voters never agreed to.

"This is creating a mockery of state legislatures. We elect legislators, they decide something is important and debate it, then vote on a law, then it becomes law," she said. "Then corporations write rules and they effectively become law, contradicting what the legislature did. What we think of as a contract is really important to our conception of social order.

Think of how many people are affected by boilerplate language. If it is thousands or millions of people, that's letting a firm create a new legal universe. That undermines our rule of law."

## QUESTIONS

1. Are consumers required to adhere to the terms of the contracts they sign, even if they have not read them?

2. Is there anything a manufacturer couldn't put into fine print? Think of three examples.

# CASES

## CASE 9.1
## The Skateboard Scare
William H. Shaw and Vincent Barry

Colin Brewster, owner of Brewster's Bicycle Shop, had to admit that skateboard sales had salvaged his business now that interest in the bicycle seemed to have peaked. In fact, skateboard business was so brisk that Brewster could hardly keep them in stock. But the picture was far from rosy.

Just last week a concerned consumer group visited his shop. They informed Brewster that they had ample evidence to prove that skateboards present a real and immediate hazard to consumer safety. Brewster conceded that the group surely provided enough statistical support; the number of broken bones and concussions that had resulted directly and indirectly from accidents involving skateboards was shocking. But he thought the group's position was fundamentally unsound because, as he told them, "It's not the skateboards that are unsafe but how people use them."

Committee members weren't impressed with Brewster's distinction. They likened it to saying

automobile manufacturers shouldn't be conscious of consumer safety because it's not the automobiles that are unsafe but how we drive them. Brewster objected that automobiles present an entirely different problem, because a number of things could be done to ensure their safe use. "But what can you do about a skateboard?" he asked them. "Besides, I don't manufacture them, I just sell them."

The committee pointed out that other groups were attacking the problem on the manufacturing level. What they expected of Brewster was some responsible management of the problem at the local retail level. They pointed out that recently Brewster had run a series of local television ads portraying young but accomplished skateboarders performing fancy flips and turns. The ad implied that anyone could easily accomplish such feats. Only yesterday one parent had told the committee of her child's breaking an arm attempting such gymnastics

From William H. Shaw and Vincent Barry, *Moral Issues in Business*, 5th ed. (Belmont, CA: Wadsworth, 1996).

after having purchased a Brewster skateboard. "Obviously," Brewster countered, "the woman has an irresponsible kid whose activities she should monitor, not me." He pointed out that his ad was not intended to imply anyone could or should do those tricks, no more than an ad showing a car traveling at high speeds while doing stunt tricks implies that you should drive that way.

The committee disagreed. They said Brewster not only should discontinue such misleading advertising but also should actively publicize the potential dangers of skateboarding. Specifically, the committee wanted him to display prominently beside his skateboard stock the statistical data testifying to its hazards. Furthermore, he should make sure anyone buying a skateboard reads this material before purchase.

Brewster argued that the committee's demands were unreasonable. "Do you have any idea what effect that would have on sales?" he asked them.

Committee members readily admitted that they were less interested in his sales than in their children's safety. Brewster told them that in this matter their children's safety was their responsibility, not his. But the committee was adamant. Members told Brewster that they'd be back in a week to find out what positive steps, if any, he'd taken to correct the problem. In the event he'd done nothing, they indicated they were prepared to picket his shop.

## QUESTIONS

1. With whom do you agree—Brewster or the committee? Why?

2. Would you criticize Brewster's advertisements? Do you think the demand that he publicize the dangers of skateboarding is reasonable?

3. What responsibilities, if any, do retailers have to ensure consumer safety? Compare the responsibilities of manufacturers, skateboarders, and parents.

## CASE 9.2

## Aspartame: Miracle Sweetener or Dangerous Substance?

William H. Shaw and Vincent Barry

Diet Coke stands alone as the greatest overnight success in the marketplace. But when you quaff a Diet Coke on a hot summer's day, you may be doing more than quenching your thirst. You could be inviting a headache, depression, seizure, aggressive behavior, visual impairment, or menstrual disturbances. You might even be loading your tissues with a carcinogen. The reason, say most nutritionists and medical scientists, is that soft drinks like Diet Coke—and a host of other products—contain the low-calorie sweetener aspartame, which goes by the name NutraSweet.

In 1983 the Reagan administration's commissioner of the Food and Drug Administration, Dr. Arthur Hull

Hayes, Jr., approved the use of aspartame in carbonated beverages. In one stroke, he seemed to end the prolonged controversy over the safety of the artificial sweetener. That controversy erupted in 1974, when the FDA first approved aspartame as a food additive.

No sooner had aspartame's manufacturer, G. D. Searle & Co., begun to celebrate the FDA's initial approval of its profits-promising sweetener than things turned sour. Largely as a result of the rancorous protests of lawyer James Turner, author of a book about food additives, the FDA suspended its approval. Armed with the results of animal experiments conducted at Washington University, Turner

William H. Shaw and Vincent Barry, *Moral Issues in Business* 5th ed. (Belmont, CA: Wadsworth, 1996).

insisted that aspartame could damage the brain, especially in infants and children. Searle pooh-poohed the charges, citing experiments of its own that, it said, established the safety of its chemical sweetener. Unconvinced, Dr. Alexander M. Schmidt, then FDA commissioner, appointed a task force of six scientists to examine Searle's experiments.

The task force's findings did not corroborate Searle's rosy assurances of safety. In fact, it concluded that Searle had distorted the safety data to win FDA approval of aspartame. According to the task force's 1976 report, "Searle made a number of deliberate decisions which seemingly were calculated to minimize the chances of discovering toxicity and/or to allay FDA concern." Schmidt not only endorsed the task force's findings but told Congress in April 1976 that he saw in Searle's experiments "a pattern of conduct which compromises the scientific integrity of the studies." He added: "At the heart of the FDA's regulatory process is the ability to rely upon the integrity of the basic safety data submitted by the sponsors of regulated products. Our investigation clearly demonstrates that, in the G. D. Searle Co., we have no basis for such reliance now." Specifically addressing the tests of aspartame, the commissioner and other FDA officials reported such irregularities as test animals recorded as dead on one date and alive on another and autopsies on rats conducted a year after the rodents had died during a feeding experiment. Schmidt further branded Searle's animal studies as "poorly conceived, carelessly executed, or inaccurately analyzed or reported."

Understandably, Searle wasn't about to allow these broadsides to pass unanswered. In a May 1976 letter to Schmidt, the firm's executive vice president, James Buzard, asserted that the FDA task force investigators "totally failed to find fraud, totally failed to find concrete evidence of an intent to deceive or mislead the agency or any advisory committee, or a failure to make any required report."

Sticking to his opinions, Schmidt asked the Justice Department to investigate the possibility that Searle had deliberately misled the FDA. After looking into the matter, a grand jury brought no indictment against the company. Nevertheless, under FDA pressure Searle enlisted the services of Universities Associated for Research and Education in Pathology (UAREP), a private group of fifteen universities that work under contracts and grants for paying clients. UAREP was to scrutinize eight of the fifteen as yet unreviewed aspartame studies to check Searle's conclusions. Under the terms of its agreement with Searle, UAREP would submit its findings to the company before submitting them to the FDA. Searle said that procedure was necessary to ensure accuracy. But Adrian Gross, a task force member and senior FDA scientist, expressed misgivings about the arrangement to his superiors. The report that UAREP submitted, Gross argued, "may well be interpreted as nothing short of an improper whitewash."

Despite Gross's concern, the UAREP body proceeded, focusing solely on the microscopic slides produced by Searle in its animal experiments. In the end, the consortium could find nothing improper in Searle's interpretation of the slides. But James Turner complained that the review was unacceptably narrow and incomplete because it had failed to consider either the design or execution of Searle's experiments. He was assured in writing that these and other relevant matters would be taken up by a public board of inquiry.

That board, made up of three independent scientists, had plenty to do. By January 1980, when the panel convened, the FDA had amassed 140 volumes of data on aspartame. Unable to deal with the mountain of information, the board concentrated on the same studies UAREP had examined. On September 30, 1980, the panel recommended that the FDA withdraw approval of aspartame. In making its recommendation, the board said it couldn't exclude the possibility that aspartame causes cancer in rats.

It thus appeared that the FDA would keep aspartame off the market for good. But in November 1980 the country elected a new president, and within a few short months, the chemical would be sweetening a multitude of products and making millions of dollars for its manufacturer.

The day after Ronald Reagan was inaugurated president of the United States, Searle repetitioned the FDA to approve the sale of aspartame. It based its appeal on the same data it had previously submitted. Six months later, on July 24, 1981, the new FDA commissioner, Dr. Hayes, approved the sale of aspartame as a "tabletop sweetener and ingredient of dry foods."

In approving the product for sale, Hayes discounted the possible cancer connection. He cited a study done in 1981 by Ajinomoto, a Japanese chemical firm. Its study found that, while rats fed with aspartame did develop more brain tumors than untreated rats, the increase was not statistically significant. The commissioner took the results as breaking the tie between two similar experiments conducted earlier by Searle, which had produced differing results.

Some scientists immediately discredited the Ajinomoto experiments, claiming that they used a strain of rat different from the one used in earlier Searle studies. In reply, Searle insisted that all three rat studies demonstrated that aspartame was noncarcinogenic.

In 1983 Searle successfully petitioned the FDA to permit aspartame to be used in carbonated beverages. Hayes gave FDA approval on July 8, 1983.

Worldwide sales of aspartame the next year were estimated at $600 million.

One month after granting Searle permission to use aspartame in soft drinks, Dr. Hayes resigned from the FDA to become dean of New York Medical College. Three months later, in November 1983, he also took a job as senior scientific consultant to Burson Marsteller, the public relations firm that has Searle's account for aspartame.

## QUESTIONS

1. Does the aspartame controversy tend to support or belie the assumption that regulatory agencies are sufficient to ensure consumer safety?

2. Who do you think should have primary responsibility for ensuring product safety—manufacturer or government agency?

3. Does requiring a label warning consumers that a food or beverage contains carcinogenic chemicals sufficiently discharge a government agency's obligation to protect the public? Or should such products be banned? What if the product contains a substance that is only possibly carcinogenic?

# CASE 9.3
# Children and Reasonably Safe Products
Joseph R. Desjardins and John J. McCall

When children are involved, how safe need a "reasonably safe" product be? How vigilant should manufacturers be in forseeing misuse? Consider two cases.

In *Ritter v. Narragansett Electric Co.*, a four-year-old girl was injured when she used an oven door as a stepstool to stand on so that she could peak into a pot on the top of the stove. Her weight caused the stove to tip over, causing serious injury to the child. The first question concerns a possible defective design.

Was the stove defective because it could not support thirty pounds on the oven door without tipping? A foreseeable use of the stove could involve placing a heavy roasting pan on the oven door while checking food during preparation. If the stove tipped over and injured the cook during this use, it is very likely that a court would rule against the manufacturer on the grounds of a design defect. The manufacturer should have foreseen the use of the door as a shelf.

From Joseph R. Desjardins and John J. McCall, *Contemporary Issues in Business Ethics*, 2nd ed. (Belmont, CA: Wadsworth, 1990).

Could the manufacturer foresee the use of the door as a step-stool? Should it matter, since the product was defective in this regard anyway?

*Vincer v. Esther Williams Swimming Pool Co.* concerned a two-year-old boy who climbed the ladder of an above-ground swimming pool at his grandparents' house and fell into the pool. He remained under water for some time before being rescued. As a result, he suffered severe and permanent brain damage. His family sued the manufacturer, claiming that the pool should have had a self-closing gate and/or an automatically retractable ladder. Knowing that children are attracted to swimming pools and knowing that many children drown each year because of

such accidents, should the manufacturer have foreseen this possibility? Was it "unreasonable" not to include protections against such an accident in the design of the swimming pool?

## QUESTIONS

1. Courts ruled against the manufacturer in *Ritter*, and in favor of the manufacturer in *Vincer*. Do you agree? Why or why not?

2. Does your determination of "reasonably safe product" depend on the person who is using it? If so, are any products "reasonably safe" where children are concerned? If so, who decides what is "reasonable"?

# CASE 9.4
# Living and Dying with Asbestos
## William H. Shaw and Vincent Barry

Asbestos is a fibrous mineral used for fireproofing, electrical insulation, building materials, brake linings, and chemical filters. If exposed long enough to asbestos particles—usually ten or more years—people can develop a chronic lung inflammation called asbestosis, which makes breathing difficult and infection easy. Also linked to asbestos exposure is mesothelioma, a cancer of the chest lining that sometimes doesn't develop until forty years after the first exposure. Although the first major scientific conference on the dangers of asbestos was not held until 1964, the asbestos industry knew of its hazards more than sixty years ago.

As early as 1932, the British documented the occupational hazards of asbestos dust inhalation. Indeed, on September 25, 1935, the editors of the trade journal *Asbestos* wrote to Summer Simpson, president of Raybestos-Manhattan, a leading

asbestos company, asking permission to publish an article on the dangers of asbestos. Simpson refused and later praised the magazine for not printing the article. In a letter to Vandivar Brown, secretary of Johns-Manville, another asbestos manufacturer, Simpson observed: "The less said about asbestosis the better off we are." Brown agreed, adding that any article on asbestosis should reflect American, not English, data.

In fact, American data were available, and Brown, as one of the editors of the journal, knew it. Working on behalf of Raybestos-Manhattan and Johns-Manville and their insurance carrier, Metropolitan Life Insurance Company, Anthony Lanza had conducted research between 1929 and 1931 on 126 workers with three or more years of asbestos exposure. But Brown and others were not pleased with the paper Lanza submitted to them for

William H. Shaw and Vincent Barry, *Moral Issues in Business*, 9th ed., (Belmont, CA: Wadsworth, 2004). Notes were deleted from this text.

editorial review. Lanza, said Brown, had failed to portray asbestosis as milder than silicosis, a lung disease caused by longterm inhalation of silica dust and resulting in chronic shortness of breath. Under the then-pending Workmen's Compensation law, silicosis was categorized as a compensable disease. If asbestosis was worse than silicosis or indistinguishable from it, then it, too, would have to be covered. Apparently Brown didn't want this and thus requested that Lanza depict asbestosis as less serious than silicosis. Lanza complied and also omitted from his published report the fact that more than half the workers examined—67 of 126—were suffering from asbestosis.

Meanwhile, Summer Simpson was writing F. H. Schulter, president of Thermoid Rubber Company, to suggest that several manufacturers sponsor additional asbestos experiments. The sponsors, said Simpson, could exercise oversight prerogatives; they "could determine from time to time after the findings are made whether we wish any publication or not." Added Simpson: "It would be a good idea to distribute the information to the medical fraternity, providing it is of the right type and would not injure our companies." Lest there be any question about the arbiter of publication, Brown wrote to officials at the laboratory conducting the tests:

> It is our further understanding that the results obtained will be considered the property of those who are advancing the required funds, who will determine whether, to what extent and in what manner they shall be made public. In the event it is deemed desirable that the results be made public, the manuscript of your study will be submitted to us for approval prior to publication [Brown].

Industry officials were concerned with more than controlling public information flow. They also sought to deny workers early evidence of their asbestosis. Dr. Kenneth Smith, medical director of a Johns-Manville plant in Canada, explained why seven workers he found to have asbestosis should not be informed of their disease:

> It must be remembered that although these men have the X-ray evidence of asbestosis, they are working today and definitely are not disabled from

asbestosis. They have not been told of this diagnosis, for it is felt that as long as the man feels well, is happy at home and at work, and his physical condition remains good, nothing should be said. When he becomes disabled and sick, then the diagnosis should be made and the claim submitted *by the Company*. The fibrosis of this disease is irreversible and permanent so that eventually compensation will be paid to each of these men. But as long as the man is not disabled, it is felt that he should not be told of his condition so that he can live and work in peace and the Company can benefit by his many years of experience. Should the man be told of his condition today there is a very definite possibility that he would become mentally and physically ill, simply through the knowledge that he has asbestosis.

When lawsuits filed by asbestos workers who had developed cancer reached the industry in the 1950s, Dr. Smith suggested that the industry retain the Industrial Health Foundation to conduct a cancer study that would, in effect, squelch the asbestos-cancer connection. The asbestos companies refused, claiming that such a study would only bring further unfavorable publicity to the industry and that there wasn't enough evidence linking asbestos and cancer industrywide to warrant it.

Shortly before his death in 1977, Dr. Smith was asked whether he had ever recommended to Johns-Manville officials that warning labels be placed on insulation products containing asbestos. He testified as follows:

> The reasons why the caution labels were not implemented immediately, it was a business decision as far as I could understand. Here was a recommendation, the corporation is in business to make, to provide jobs for people and make money for stockholders and they had to take into consideration the effects of everything they did, and if the application of a caution label identifying a product as hazardous would cut out sales, there would be serious financial implications. And the powers that be had to make some effort to judge the necessity of the label vs. the consequences of placing the label on the product.

Dr. Smith's testimony and related documents have figured prominently in hundreds of asbestos-related lawsuits. In the 1980s these lawsuits swamped Manville (as Johns-Manville is now called) and forced the company into bankruptcy. A trust fund valued at $2.5 billion was set up to pay Manville's asbestos claimants. To fund the trust, shareholders were required to surrender half the value of their stock, and the company had to give up much of its projected earnings over the next twenty-five years. Claims, however, soon over-whelmed the trust, which ran out of money in 1990. After various legal delays, the trust fund's stake in Manville was increased to 80 percent, and Manville was required to pay it an additional $300 million in dividends. The trust fund itself was restructured to pay the most seriously ill victims first, but average payments to victims were lowered significantly—from $145,000 to $43,000.

Meanwhile, in 1997 the U.S. Supreme Court struck down a landmark $1.3-billion class-action settlement between some twenty former asbestos producers and their injured workers. A few years earlier, the companies involved had approached the workers' lawyers and agreed to settle thousands of existing health complaints, in a deal that netted the lawyers millions of dollars in fees. Then the lawyers and companies devised a settlement agreement involving people who had not filed claims against the company by a specified date. It was this aspect of the settlement that was the main sticking point. Although a lower court had praised the settlement for "forging a solution to a major social problem," the Supreme Court balked at the fact that future claimants were not allowed to opt out of the agreement. A class-action agreement, the Court said, was not the best way to resolve thousands of different claims involving different factual and legal issues. In 1999, the Court rejected a second proposed settlement. As a result, thousands of lawsuits that would have been settled by the agreements continue to clog federal dockets.

The situation is made worse by the fact that in the last few years asbestos-related litigation has expanded exponentially—spun out of control, some would say—as workers who did not make asbestos, but only handled it every now and then or worked in the vicinity of those who did, are suing companies that never made the stuff but only used it. Altogether more than 200,000 cases are pending nationwide against more than 1,000 companies. In fact, of the 91,000 cases filed in 2001, only 6 percent of the plaintiffs have actually suffered from asbestos-related diseases. Almost all of the other claimants are seeking compensation for anxiety they have experienced over the risk that they might have asbestosis.

## QUESTIONS

1. Hand-of-government proponents would say that it's the responsibility of government, not the asbestos industry, to ensure health and safety with respect to asbestos—that in the absence of appropriate government regulations, asbestos manufacturers have no responsibility other than to operate efficiently and profitably. Do you agree?

2. What responsibilities do asbestos manufacturers now have to their injured workers? How should society respond to these workers' claims for restitution? Is our legal system adequate for handling this problem? Should the asbestos companies be punished in some way, or is their liability to civil lawsuits sufficient?

3. Do you see any parallels between this case and the tobacco industry's response to the health risks of smoking?

# CASE 9.5
## Merck and Vioxx
Kenneth B. Moll and Associates

On October 5, 2004, Kenneth B. Moll & Associates, Ltd. filed the first worldwide class action lawsuit against Merck, on behalf of all persons who were prescribed the potentially deadly arthritis drug rofecoxib, also known as Vioxx (Ceoxx outside the United States).

The law firm has already received inquiries from persons who believe they were injured by Vioxx in over 14 countries (China, South Africa, Italy, Canada, Iceland, Israel, Chile, United Kingdom, New Zealand, Brazil, The Netherlands, Singapore, the United States, and other countries). Merck estimates that over 24 million patients have been prescribed the drug worldwide.

The lawsuit, known as the "VIOXX Class Action," was filed in the Federal District Court for the Northern District of Illinois.

On September 30, 2004, Merck officially announced a voluntary withdraw of Vioxx from all markets worldwide in light of unequivocal results from a clinical trial demonstrating that Vioxx almost triples the risk of heart attack and stroke for those who take the product long term. The company's decision is based on three-year data from a prospective, randomized, placebo-controlled clinical trial, the APPROVe (Adenomatous Polyp Prevention on VIOXX) trial.

The APPROVe study followed the 1999 VIGOR (Vioxx Gastrointestinal Outcomes Research Study) study. In the VIGOR study, analysis of the cardiovascular data by the Safety Monitoring Board focused on "the excess deaths and cardiovascular adverse experiences in [the Vioxx group] compared to [the Naproxen group]."

Attorney Kenneth Moll said, "a primary goal of the Vioxx Class Action is to inform consumers and physicians worldwide of the potentially deadly side effects of Vioxx." Mr. Moll said he is concerned that thousands of people have been injured by the drug and are not aware of their injuries. According to our experts, a person is susceptible to a Vioxx injury beginning from the initial dosage, up to and including a week after discontinuing use of the drug.

The lawsuit will request that a medical monitoring fund be established to enable people who have taken Vioxx to monitor the existence of dangerous side effects.

IMPORTANT: Injuries from Vioxx may occur days after usage.

Our offices are working in conjunction with attorneys around the world to address the enormous public health issue created by Merck in its manufacture, marketing and distribution of the prescription drug Vioxx (marketed as Ceoxx outside of the United States). The drug has been marketed around the world since 1999 and has been prescribed tens of millions of times. In light of the millions of patients around the world who were taking Vioxx, even if a fraction of a percent of patients experience cardiovascular events, that would translate into thousands of affected people. The Italian consumer protection group, ADUC, has addressed the health concerns surrounding Vioxx and has issued a press release.

## QUESTIONS

1. What duties does Merck have in the Vioxx case?
2. Should attorneys always be the ones to "solve" liability problems? Why or why not?

Source: Kenneth B. Moll and Associates. Reprinted by permission of Kenneth B. Moll and Associates.

## CASE 9.6
# The Top 10 Most Dangerous Toys of All Time
Claude Wyle

As concerned consumers we trust that the toys we buy for our children are safe and won't cause any harm from use, but that is not always the case. In the heat of the Holiday Season, the Consumer Product Safety Commission works tirelessly to recall millions of harmful toys each year, yet they cannot guard against all potential dangers. Below are some of the most dangerous toys that slipped through the cracks.

1. **CSI—Fingerprint Examination Kit.** Based on the hit TV show, the powder given to investigate fingerprints was found to contain asbestos. (2007)
2. **Magnetix.** A magnet building set, which could easily be broken, spilling the small magnets from inside. These magnets were incredibly harmful if swallowed, as they would reconnect through tissue walls causing digestive complications and even death within a short period of time. (2008)
3. **Inflatable baby boats.** Prone to tearing, these boats were intended to make pool time fun for toddlers, but instead made it a potentially deadly experience. (2009)
4. **Hannah Montana Pop Star Card Game.** Lab tests revealed that the card game contained at least 75 times the recommended amount of arsenic for children's toys. It slipped through the cracks as it was made of vinyl, and not paint, allowing it to remain uncovered by regulations. (2007)
5. **Aquadots.** A more popular toy, allowed children to arrange beads into different shapes and fuse them together with water. However, it was found that the beads contained GHB, the date rape drug. Eventually 4.2 million kits were recalled. (2007)

6. **Snacktime Cabbage Patch Doll.** A must-have doll was intended to "eat" only the packaged provided fake snacks, but when it couldn't tell the difference and contained no off switch, ended up eating children's fingers and hair. (1996)
7. **Mini Hammocks.** The children's hammocks had over three million hammocks made, resulting in at least twelve children's deaths, with many more injured. (1985–96)
8. **Lawn Darts.** A toy with missile shaped weighted skewers for children to throw across the yard? It is fairly obvious why these began being banned by the CPSC. (1990–2009)
9. **The Austin Magic Pistol.** This gun delivered gas powered combustion, in the form of calcium carbide, a hazardous material that exploded when mixed with water. (1950)
10. **The Gilbert U-238 Atomic Energy Lab.** Including uranium in a children's toy is just asking for it to get pulled from the shelves. (1950)

### QUESTIONS

1. Are product manufacturers responsible for injuries incurred while using their products?
2. How might we legally define the point at which manufacturers become responsible?

From *The Legal Examiner*, Friday, December 28, 2012.

## CASE 9.7

# Ten More Deaths Blamed on Plavix

Jack Bouboushian

CHICAGO (CN)—Ten people died from the block-buster blood-thinner Plavix, which is no better than aspirin against stroke but costs 100 times more, dozens of family members claim in two complaints.

Bristol-Myers Squibb and Sanofi-Aventis reaped annual U.S. sales of $3.8 billion from Plavix, pushing the drug in TV, magazine, and Internet ads, while they "knew or should have known that when taking Plavix, the risk of suffering a heart attack, stroke, internal bleeding, blood disorder, or death far outweigh any potential benefit," lead plaintiff Geraldine Jackson says.

At least 561 lawsuits have been filed over Plavix, according to the Courthouse News database. Rose Creighton is the lead plaintiff in the other most recently filed case. Both were filed in Cook County Court.

Quotations in this article are from Jackson's lawsuit, though the dozens of plaintiffs make similar claims in both cases—that Bristol-Myers and Sanofi-Aventis deceived the public by misrepresenting the risks of Plavix, which they knew about from their own studies.

"Plavix was heavily marketed directly to consumers through television, magazine, and Internet advertising," the complaint states. "It was touted as a "super-aspirin" that would give a person even greater cardiovascular benefits than a much less expensive, daily aspirin while being safer and easier on a person's stomach than aspirin. Those assertions have proven to be false.

"The truth is that BMS and Sanofi always knew—or, if they had paid attention to the findings of their own studies, should have known—that Plavix was not more efficacious than aspirin to prevent heart attacks and strokes. More importantly though, defendants knew or should have known that when taking Plavix, the risk of suffering a heart attack,

stroke, internal bleeding, blood disorder, or death far outweigh any potential benefit."

Plavix is the sixth best-selling drug in the United States, with annual sales of $3.8 billion, although it works no better than aspirin in many cases, according to the complaint. A dose of Plavix costs $4, 100 times more than aspirin, at 4 cents a dose.

"Defendants' nearly eight-year run of lying to physicians and to the public about the safety and efficacy of Plavix for the sole purpose of increasing corporate profits has now been uncovered by scientific studies that reveal that not only is Plavix not worth its high price—it is dangerous," the complaint states.

A recent study "uncovered another truth about Plavix," the complaint adds. "It found that Plavix plus aspirin (dual therapy) is only minimally more effective than aspirin plus placebo at preventing atherothrombotic events. But more importantly, it found that in patients who do not have peripheral arterial disease (PAD) or acute coronary syndrome (ACS), Plavix plus aspirin (dual therapy) poses a 20 percent increased risk to the patient of suffering bleeding injuries, heart attacks, stroke and death. In other words, in those patients without ACS or PAD, dual therapy with aspirin and Plavix does more harm than good.

"Despite a growing body of scientific knowledge that the four-dollar ($4.00) Plavix pill was not much better than a four-cent-a-day aspirin, Defendants kept promoting it to the public and to physicians, using hyperbole and outright falsification in the process."

Three people died because they took Plavix, according to Jackson's lawsuit. Creighton's lawsuit, filed the same day, claims that seven people died from the drug.

"Defendants failed to fully, truthfully, and accurately communicate the safety and efficacy of

From Courthouse News Service, January 2, 2013.

Plavix drug products and intentionally and fraudulently misled the medical community, physicians, plaintiffs' physicians, and ingesting plaintiffs and decedents about the risks associated with Plavix," Jackson's complaint states.

The families seek punitive damages for products liability, manufacturing defect, failure to warn, negligence, loss of consortium, and wrongful death.

All plaintiffs are represented by Steven Aroesty with Nafoli, Bern, Ripka, and Shkolnik, of Edwardsville, Illinois.

Plavix has been prescribed to prevent stroke after operations, which may be caused by blood clots breaking loose and traveling toward the brain. It has been a drug of choice for conditions such as those being suffered by Secretary of State Hillary Clinton

## QUESTIONS

1. How do Plavix and aspirin differ?
2. How can Bristol-Meyers Squibb compensate the 561 patients who died due to Plavix?

# CHAPTER QUESTIONS

1. When should producers be responsible for harms that are caused by their products? What moral responsibilities do producers have? What are the responsibilities of consumers? Where (and how) do we draw the line?

2. Is life becoming more dangerous? Is greater fear one of the costs of greater convenience and greater luxury? How can we regulate business—if we should—to manage the escalating risks created by mushrooming production?

# 10

# "You Know How to Whistle, Don't You?"

## *Whistle-Blowing, Company Loyalty, and Employee Responsibility*

## Introduction

One of the wise-guy employees of a local, particularly vicious, crime family, let's call them the Baritones, finds himself increasingly repulsed by some of his assignments, which involve, among other things, the breaking of various bones and the noncosmetic rearrangement of unresponsive clients' faces. He starts to feel sorry for his victims, most of whom are perfectly law-abiding citizens who just happen to have small businesses in Baritone territory and find themselves unable to make the extortion payments that have been demanded of them. Eventually, his conscience gets the better of him, and he has a change of heart. He gets in touch with the FBI (though he by no means feels all that good about doing so) and offers to testify ("rat," in his lexicon) on his bosses. There is no doubt that they have been doing wrong (to put it mildly). There is no doubt that their activities have been both destructive of the community and corrupting to the real free enterprise system (which, as Adam Smith warned years ago, can be ruined by "Force and Fraud"). But this guy took an oath, a blood oath, in fact, to keep his secrets and not betray his employers, who have come to seem to him, over the years, like a literal family. And the question that bugs him, over and over, is how he can justify violating that oath, however evil his "family" may be.

Whatever our affection for fictional crime families may be—indeed, whatever misplaced affection we may have for real-life criminals in the news—we recognize or should recognize evil for what it is, evil. We're not talking here about bending the law or cutting corners. We're not talking about wrongdoers who deserve one another. We're talking about terrorizing and ruining the lives of hardworking, innocent people. But even so, we can understand the turmoil of the wise guy, torn between his belated recognition of evil and his sense of loyalty. And if that is so, we should be all the more sympathetic toward those who see less than evil—shoddy business practices, dangerous situations for employees, pollution or destruction of the environment, the violation of tax laws, and the systematic misleading of investors—and are moved to say something about it. Whistle-blowing, as it has come to be called, is always a painful

# Martin Luther King on Silence

*Our lives begin to end the day we become silent about things
that matter.*

*—From an Enron Company notepad*

and desperate course of action. But sometimes it is heroic and necessary. And that becomes a question for all of us. Most of us will, at some time in our lives, work for a corporation or an institution with flaws. At what point might we feel justified, indeed even compelled, to speak out, first, of course, with a more or less polite internal memo. But if that memo gets no results, are we ever justified in violating our own sense of loyalty—and others' expectations of loyalty—to go outside the company? This, of course, has been the dilemma of several high-placed whistle-blowers in recent years. Erin Brockovich became a national heroine (and had superstar Julia Roberts depict her in a movie) for blowing the whistle on corporate polluters. Jeffrey Wigand went through utter Hell exposing the lethal lies told by his employers in the tobacco industry, but he also emerged a hero (played by Russell Crowe in the movie *The Insider)* for daring to risk his life and career for the sake of the truth and public safety. More recently, Sherron Watkins (along with Cynthia Cooper of WorldCom and Coleen Rowley of the FBI) made the cover of *Time* magazine for writing a now-famous memo to Enron CEO Kenneth Lay, warning of an "implosion" if Enron's accounting practices ever came to light, and then testified against her superiors in the much-awaited criminal cases that followed.

Most of us will never find ourselves in such a difficult position, but we all need to keep that possibility in mind. First of all, we all need to have some sense of what lines we will not cross, what sorts of things we would refuse to do, what sorts of activities we will not tolerate, even if we ourselves are not direct participants but only observers (and therefore nonetheless complicit). And second, we need to keep in mind how painful such a dilemma must be for those who are so involved, rather than simply retreat to the knee-jerk (or perhaps just jerk) reaction that "they should not have gotten themselves into that situation in the first place" or "I would never rat on my employer." (No? Never? No matter what?) What's more, the opposition is not always (or usually) the company versus the public, but the very existence of the company. An early whistleblower (especially if he or she is heeded *within* the company) can prevent the massive Enron-type collapse and bankruptcy. Not only the ethics but the health of the free enterprise system depends on the freedom of everyone in it to speak up and to criticize or expose wrongdoing. This is not to say that speaking up is easy or that all criticism is warranted criticism. But unless we acknowledge and even celebrate those who are willing to act as correctives when our market system goes wrong, we are in danger of finding ourselves in a world that is no longer free or a true market but, as wrongdoing tends to find its imitators, what Smith warned us about, a system of Force and Fraud.

Sissela Bok offers a general characterization of the ethical foundations of whistle-blowing in her "Whistleblowing and Professional Responsibility." Michael Davis explains the many tensions and difficulties in an adequate characterization of the moral obligation to blow the whistle in his "Some Paradoxes of Whistleblowing." Ronald Duska emphasizes the particular difficulties posed by the conflict between loyalty and a moral obligation to blow the whistle in his "Whistleblowing and Employee Loyalty." David E. Soles offers a comprehensive analysis of the ethical foundations of employee loyalty in his "Four Concepts of Loyalty." George D. Randels expands the idea of loyalty to include loyalties between employees and corporations, corporations and communities, and corporations to employees in his "Loyalty, Corporations, and Community." Finally, Kim Zetter interviews economist, psychologist and philosopher Dan Ariely on "why we cheat."

Sissela Bok

# Whistleblowing and Professional Responsibility

Sissela Bok is a member of the American Academy of Political and Social Science and is an Eleanor Roosevelt Fellow. She was formerly professor of philosophy at Brandeis University.

"Whistleblowing" is a new label generated by our increased awareness of the ethical conflicts encountered at work. Whistleblowers sound an alarm from within the very organization in which they work, aiming to spotlight neglect or abuses that threaten the public interest.

The stakes in whistleblowing are high. Take the nurse who alleges that physicians enrich themselves in her hospital through unnecessary surgery; the engineer who discloses safety defects in the braking systems of a fleet of new rapid-transit vehicles; the Defense Department official who alerts Congress to military graft and overspending: all know that they pose a threat to those whom they denounce and that their own careers may be at risk. . . .

## NATURE OF WHISTLEBLOWING

Three elements, each jarring, and triply jarring when conjoined, lend acts of whistleblowing special

urgency and bitterness: dissent, breach of loyalty, and accusation.

Like all dissent, whistleblowing makes public a disagreement with an authority or a majority view. But whereas dissent can concern all forms of disagreement with, for instance, religious dogma or government policy or court decisions, whistleblowing has the narrower aim of shedding light on negligence or abuse, or alerting to a risk, and of assigning responsibility for this risk.

Would-be whistleblowers confront the conflict inherent in all dissent: between conforming and sticking their necks out. The more repressive the authority they challenge, the greater the personal risk they take in speaking out. At exceptional times, as in times of war, even ordinarily tolerant authorities may come to regard dissent as unacceptable and even disloyal.

Furthermore, the whistleblower hopes to stop the game; but since he is neither referee nor coach, and since he blows the whistle on his own team, his act is seen as a violation of loyalty. In holding his position, he has assumed certain obligations to his colleagues and clients. He may even have subscribed to a loyalty oath or a promise of confidentiality. Loyalty to

From Sissela Bok, "Whistleblowing and Professional Responsibility," *New York University Education Quarterly*, 11 (Summer 1980): 2–7. Reprinted with permission.

colleagues and to clients comes to be pitted against loyalty to the public interest, to those who may be injured unless the revelation is made.

Not only is loyalty violated in whistleblowing, hierarchy as well is often opposed, since the whistle-blower is not only a colleague but a subordinate. Though aware of the risks inherent in such disobedience, he often hopes to keep his job. At times, however, he plans his alarm to coincide with leaving the institution. If he is highly placed, or joined by others, resigning in protest may effectively direct public attention to the wrongdoing at issue. Still another alternative, often chosen by those who wish to be safe from retaliation, is to leave the institution quietly, to secure another post, then to blow the whistle. In this way, it is possible to speak with the authority and knowledge of an insider without having the vulnerability of that position.

It is the element of accusation, of calling a "foul," that arouses the strongest reactions on the part of the hierarchy. The accusation may be of neglect, of willfully concealed dangers, or of outright abuse on the part of colleagues or superiors. It singles out specific persons or groups as responsible for threats to the public interest. If no one could be held responsible—as in the case of an impending avalanche—the warning would not constitute whistleblowing.

The accusation of the whistleblower, moreover, concerns a present or an imminent threat. Past errors or misdeeds occasion such an alarm only if they still affect current practices. And risks far in the future lack the immediacy needed to make the alarm a compelling one, as well as the close connection to particular individuals that would justify actual accusations. Thus an alarm can be sounded about safety defects in a rapid-transit system that threaten or will shortly threaten passengers, but the revelation of safety defects in a system no longer in use, while of historical interest, would not constitute whistleblowing. Nor would the revelation of potential problems in a system not yet fully designed and far from implemented.

Not only immediacy, but also specificity, is needed for there to be an alarm capable of pinpointing responsibility. A concrete risk must be at issue rather than a vague foreboding or a somber prediction. The act of whistle-blowing differs in this

respect from the lamentation or the dire prophecy. An immediate and specific threat would normally be acted upon by those at risk. The whistleblower assumes that his message will alert listeners to something they do not know, or whose significance they have not grasped because it has been kept secret.

The desire for openness inheres in the temptation to reveal any secret, sometimes joined to an urge for self-aggrandizement and publicity and the hope for revenge for past slights or injustices. There can be pleasure, too—righteous or malicious—in laying bare the secrets of co-workers and in setting the record straight at last. Colleagues of the whistleblower often suspect his motives: they may regard him as a crank, as publicity-hungry, wrong about the facts, eager for scandal and discord, and driven to indiscretion by his personal biases and shortcomings.

For whistleblowing to be effective, it must arouse its audience. Inarticulate whistleblowers are likely to fail from the outset. When they are greeted by apathy, their message dissipates. When they are greeted by disbelief, they elicit no response at all. And when the audience is not free to receive or to act on the information—when censorship or fear of retribution stifles response—then the message rebounds to injure the whistleblower. Whistleblowing also requires the possibility of concerted public response: the idea of whistleblowing in an anarchy is therefore merely quixotic.

Such characteristics of whistleblowing and strategic considerations for achieving an impact are common to the noblest warnings, the most vicious personal attacks, and the delusions of the paranoid. How can one distinguish the many acts of sounding an alarm that are genuinely in the public interest from all the petty, biased, or lurid revelations that pervade our querulous and gossip-ridden society? Can we draw distinctions between different whistleblowers, different messages, different methods?

We clearly can, in a number of cases. Whistleblowing may be starkly inappropriate when in malice or error, or when it lays bare legitimately private matters having to do, for instance, with political belief or sexual life. It can, just as clearly, be the only way to shed light on an ongoing unjust practice such as drugging political prisoners or subjecting them to electroshock treatment. It can be the last resort for alerting the public to an impending disaster. Taking such clear-cut cases as benchmarks, and reflecting on what it is about them that weighs so heavily for or against speaking out, we can work our way toward the admittedly more complex cases in which whistleblowing is not so clearly the right or wrong choice, or where different points of view exist regarding its legitimacy—cases where there are moral reasons both for concealment and for disclosure and where judgments conflict. Consider the following cases[1]:

A. As a construction inspector for a federal agency, John Samuels (not his real name) had personal knowledge of shoddy and deficient construction practices by private contractors. He knew his superiors received free vacations and entertainment, had their homes remodeled and found jobs for their relatives—all courtesy of a private contractor. These superiors later approved a multimillion no-bid contract with the same "generous" firm.

Samuels also had evidence that other firms were hiring nonunion laborers at a low wage while receiving substantially higher payments from the government for labor costs. A former superior, unaware of an office dictaphone, had incautiously instructed Samuels on how to accept bribes for overlooking sub-par performance.

As he prepared to volunteer this information to various members of Congress, he became tense and uneasy. His family was scared and the fears were valid. It might cost Samuels thousands of dollars to protect his job. Those who had freely provided Samuels with information would probably recant or withdraw their friendship. A number of people might object to his using a dictaphone to gather information. His agency would start covering up and vent its collective wrath upon him. As for reporters and writers, they would gather for a few days, then move on to the next story. He would be left without a job, with fewer friends, with massive battles looming, and without the financial means of fighting them. Samuels decided to remain silent.

B. Engineers of Company "A" prepared plans and specifications for machinery to be used in a manufacturing process and Company "A" turned them over to Company "B" for production. The engineers of Company "B," in reviewing the plans and specifications, came to the conclusion that they included certain miscalculations and technical deficiencies of a nature that the final product might be unsuitable for the purposes of the ultimate users, and that the equipment, if built according to the original plans and specifications, might endanger the lives of persons in proximity to it. The engineers of Company "B" called the matter to the attention of appropriate officials of their employer who, in turn, advised Company "A." Company "A" replied that its engineers felt that the design and specifications for the equipment were adequate and safe and that Company "B" should proceed to build the equipment as designed and specified. The officials of Company "B" instructed its engineers to proceed with the work.

C. A recently hired assistant director of admissions in a state university begins to wonder whether

---

To: You
From: The Philosopher
Subject: "Ralph Nader on Whistle-Blowing"

The key question is, at what point should an employee resolve that allegiance to society (e.g., the public safety) must supersede allegiance to the organization's policies (e.g., the corporate profit) and then act on that resolve by informing outsiders or legal authorities? It is a question that involves basic issues of individual freedom, concentration of power, and information flow to the public.

transcripts of some applicants accurately reflect their accomplishments. He knows that it matters to many in the university community, including alumni, that the football team continue its winning tradition. He has heard rumors that surrogates may be available to take tests for a fee, signing the names of designated applicants for admission, and that some of the transcripts may have been altered. But he has no hard facts. When he brings the question up with the director of admissions, he is told that the rumors are unfounded and is asked not to inquire further into the matter.

## INDIVIDUAL MORAL CHOICE

What questions might those who consider sounding an alarm in public ask themselves? How might they articulate the problem they see and weigh its injustice before deciding whether or not to reveal it? How can they best try to make sure their choice is the right one? In thinking about these questions it helps to keep in mind the three elements mentioned earlier: dissent, breach of loyalty, and accusation. They impose certain requirements—of accuracy and judgment in dissent; of exploring alternative ways to cope with improprieties that minimize the breach of loyalty; and of fairness in accusation. For each, careful articulation and testing of arguments are needed to limit error and bias.

Dissent by whistleblowers, first of all, is expressly claimed to be intended to benefit the public. It carries with it, as a result, an obligation to consider the nature of this benefit and to consider also the possible harm that may come from speaking out: harm to persons or institutions and, ultimately, to the public interest itself. Whistleblowers must, therefore, begin by making every effort to consider the effects of speaking out versus those of remaining silent. They must assure themselves of the accuracy of their reports, checking and rechecking the facts before speaking out; specify the degree to which there is genuine impropriety; consider how imminent is the threat they see, how serious, and how closely linked to those accused of neglect and abuse.

If the facts warrant whistleblowing, how can the second element—breach of loyalty—be minimized? The most important question here is whether the

existing avenues for change within the organization have been explored. It is a waste of time for the public as well as harmful to the institution to sound the loudest alarm first. Whistleblowing has to remain a last alternative because of its destructive side effects: it must be chosen only when other alternatives have been considered and rejected. They may be rejected if they simply do not apply to the problem at hand, or when there is not time to go through routine channels or when the institution is so corrupt or coercive that steps will be taken to silence the whistleblower should he try the regular channels first.

What weight should an oath or a promise of silence have in the conflict of loyalties? One sworn to silence is doubtless under a stronger obligation because of the oath he has taken. He has bound himself, assumed specific obligations beyond those assumed in merely taking a new position. But even such promises can be overridden when the public interest at issue is strong enough. They can be overridden if they were obtained under duress or through deceit. They can be overridden, too, if they promise something that is in itself wrong or unlawful. The fact that one has promised silence is no excuse for complicity in covering up a crime or a violation of the public's trust.

The third element in whistleblowing—accusation—raises equally serious ethical concerns. They are concerns of fairness to the persons accused of impropriety. Is the message one to which the public is entitled in the first place? Or does it infringe on personal and private matters that one has no right to invade? Here, the very notion of what is in the public's best "interest" is at issue: "accusations" regarding an official's unusual sexual or religious experiences may well appeal to the public's interest without being information relevant to "the public interest."

Great conflicts arise here. We have witnessed excessive claims to executive privilege and to secrecy by government officials during the Watergate scandal in order to cover up for abuses the public had every right to discover. Conversely, those hoping to profit from prying into private matters have become adept at invoking "the public's right to know." Some even regard such private matters as threats to the public: they voice their own religious and political prejudices in the language of accusation. Such a danger is never stronger than when the accusation is delivered surreptitiously. The anonymous accusations made during the McCarthy period regarding political beliefs and associations often injured persons who' did not even know their accusers or the exact nature of the accusations.

From the public's point of view, accusations that are openly made by identifiable individuals are more likely to be taken seriously. And in fairness to those criticized, openly accepted responsibility for blowing the whistle should be preferred to the denunciation or the leaked rumor. What is openly stated can more easily be checked, its source's motives challenged, and the underlying information examined. Those under attack may otherwise be hard put to defend themselves against nameless adversaries. Often they do not even know that they are threatened until it is too late to respond. The anonymous denunciation, moreover, common to so many regimes, places the burden of investigation on government agencies that may thereby gain the power of a secret police.

From the point of view of the whistleblower, on the other hand, the anonymous message is safer in situations where retaliation is likely. But it is also often less likely to be taken seriously. Unless the message is accompanied by indications of how the evidence can be checked, its anonymity, however safe for the source, speaks against it.

During the process of weighing the legitimacy of speaking out, the method used, and the degree of fairness needed, whistleblowers must try to compensate for the strong possibility of bias on their part. They should be scrupulously aware of any motive that might skew their message: a desire for self-defense in a difficult bureaucratic situation, perhaps, or the urge to seek revenge, or inflated expectations regarding the effect their message will have on the situation. (Needless to say, bias affects the silent as well as the outspoken. The motive for holding back important information about abuses and injustice ought to give similar cause for soul-searching.)

Likewise, the possibility of personal gain from sounding the alarm ought to give pause. Once again there is then greater risk of a biased message. Even if the whistleblower regards himself as incorruptible, his profiting from revelations of neglect or abuse will lead others to question his motives and to put less credence in his charges. If, for example, a government employee stands to make large profits from a book exposing the iniquities in his agency, there is danger that he will, perhaps even unconsciously, slant his report in order to cause more of a sensation.

A special problem arises when there is a high risk that the civil servant who speaks out will have to go through costly litigation. Might he not justifiably try to make enough money on his public revelations—say, through books or public speaking—to offset his losses? In so doing he will not strictly speaking have *profited* from his revelations: he merely avoids being financially crushed by their sequels. He will nevertheless still be suspected at the time of revelation, and his message will therefore seem more questionable.

Reducing bias and error in moral choice often requires consultation, even open debate: methods that force articulation of the moral arguments at stake and challenge privately held assumptions. But acts of whistleblowing present special problems when it comes to open consultation. On the one hand, once the whistleblower sounds his alarm publicly, his arguments will be subjected to open scrutiny; he will have to articulate his reasons for speaking out and substantiate his charges. On the other hand, it will then be too late to retract the alarm or to combat its harmful effects, should his choice to speak out have been ill-advised.

For this reason, the whistleblower owes it to all involved to make sure of two things: that he has sought as much and as objective advice regarding his choice as he can *before* going public; and that he is aware of the arguments for and against the practice of whistleblowing in general, so that he can see his own choice against as richly detailed and coherently structured a background as possible. Satisfying these two requirements once again has special problems because of the very nature of whistleblowing: the more corrupt the circumstances, the more dangerous it may be to seek consultation before speaking out. And yet, since the whistleblower himself may have a biased view of the state of affairs, he may choose not to consult others when in fact it would be not only safe but advantageous to do so; he may see corruption and conspiracy where none exists.

## NOTE

1. Case A is adapted from Louis Clark, "The Sound of Professional Suicide," *Barrister*, Summer 1978, p. 10; Case B is Case 5 in Robert J. Baum and Albert Flores, eds., *Ethical Problems of Engineering* (Troy, NY: Rensselaer Polytechnic Institute, 1978), p. 186.

## QUESTIONS

1. When and why do we have a duty to blow the whistle, according to Bok?
2. What are the constraints that govern whistleblowers?

Michael Davis

# Some Paradoxes of Whistleblowing

Michael Davis is a Senior Fellow at the Illinois Institute of Technology Center for Study of Ethics in the Professions and a professor of philosophy.

Most acts, though permitted or required by morality, need no justification. There is no reason to think them wrong. Their justification is too plain for words. Why then is whistleblowing so problematic that we need *theories* of its justification? What reason do we have to think whistleblowing might be morally wrong?

Whistleblowing always involves revealing information that would not ordinarily be revealed. But there is nothing morally problematic about that; after all, revealing information not ordinarily revealed is one function of science. Whistleblowing always involves, in addition, an actual (or at least declared) intention to prevent something bad that would otherwise occur. There is nothing morally problematic in that either. That may well be the chief use of information.

What seems to make whistleblowing morally problematic is its organizational context. A mere individual cannot blow the whistle (in any interesting sense); only a member of an organization, whether a current or a former member, can do so. Indeed, he can only blow the whistle on his own organization (or some part of it). . . .

The whistleblower cannot blow the whistle using just any information obtained in virtue of membership in the organization. A clerk in Accounts who, happening upon evidence of serious wrongdoing while visiting a friend in Quality Control, is not a whistleblower just because she passes the information to a friend at the *Tribune*. She is more like a self-appointed spy. She seems to differ from the whistleblower, or at least from clear cases of the whistleblower, precisely in her relation to the information in question. To be a whistleblower is to reveal information with which one is *entrusted*.

But it is more than that. The whistleblower does not reveal the information to save his own skin (for example, to avoid perjury under oath). He has no excuse for revealing what his organization does not want revealed. Instead, he claims to be doing what he should be doing. If he cannot honestly make that claim—if, that is, he does not have that intention—his revelation is not whistleblowing (and so, not justified as whistleblowing), but something analogous, much as pulling a child from the water is not a rescue, even if it saves the child's life, when the "rescuer" merely believes herself to be salvaging old clothes. What makes whistleblowing morally problematic, if anything does, is this high-minded but unexcused misuse of one's position in a generally law-abiding, morally decent organization, an organization that *prima facie*

From *Business and Professional Ethics Journal* 15 (Spring 1996). Reprinted by permission of the author.

deserves the whistleblower's loyalty (as a burglary ring does not).

The whistleblower must reveal information the organization does not want revealed. But, in any actual organization, "what the organization wants" will be contested, with various individuals or groups asking to be taken as speaking for the organization. Who, for example, did what Thiokol wanted the night before the *Challenger* exploded? In retrospect, it is obvious that the three vice presidents, Lund, Kilminster, and Mason, did not do what Thiokol wanted—or, at least, what it would have wanted. At the time, however, they had authority to speak for the company—the conglomerate Morton-Thiokol headquartered in Chicago—while the protesting engineers, including Boisjoly, did not. Yet, even before the explosion, was it obvious that the three were doing what the company wanted? To be a whistleblower, one must, I think, at least temporarily lose an argument about what the organization wants. The whistleblower is disloyal only in a sense—the sense the winners of the internal argument get to dictate. What can justify such disloyalty?

## THE STANDARD THEORY

According to the theory now more or less standard,[1] such disloyalty is morally permissible when:

(S1) The organization to which the would-be whistleblower belongs will, through its product or policy, do serious considerable harm to the public (whether to users of its product, to innocent bystanders, or to the public at large);

(S2) The would-be whistleblower has identified that threat of harm, reported it to her immediate superior, making clear both the threat itself and the objection to it, and concluded that the superior will do nothing effective; and

(S3) The would-be whistleblower has exhausted other internal procedures within the organization (for example, by going up the organizational ladder as far as allowed)—or at least made use of as many internal

procedures as the danger to others and her own safety make reasonable.

Whistleblowing is morally required (according to the standard theory) when, in addition:

(S4) The would-be whistleblower has (or has accessible) evidence that would convince a reasonable, impartial observer that her view of the threat is correct; and

(S5) The would-be whistleblower has good reason to believe that revealing the threat will (probably) prevent the harm at reasonable cost (all things considered).

Why is whistleblowing morally required when these five conditions are met? According to the standard theory, whistleblowing is morally required, when it is required at all, because "people have a moral obligation to prevent serious harm to others if they can do so with little cost to themselves."[2] In other words, whistleblowing meeting all five conditions is a form of "minimally decent Samaritanism" (a doing of what morality requires) rather than "good Samaritanism" (going well beyond the moral minimum). . . .

## THREE PARADOXES

That's the standard theory—where are the paradoxes? The first paradox I want to call attention to concerns a commonplace of the whistleblowing literature. Whistleblowers are not minimally decent Samaritans. If they are Samaritans at all, they are good Samaritans. They always act at considerable risk to career, and generally, at considerable risk to their financial security and personal relations.

In this respect, as in many others, Roger Boisjoly is typical. Boisjoly blew the whistle on his employer, Thiokol; he volunteered information, in public testimony before the Rogers Commission, that Thioko did not want him to volunteer. As often happens, both his employer and many who relied on it for employment reacted hostilely. Boisjoly had to say goodbye to the company town, to old friends and neighbors, and to building rockets; he had to start a new career at an age when most people are preparing for retirement.

Since whistleblowing is generally costly to the whistleblower in some large way as this, the standard theory's minimally decent Samaritanism provides *no* justification for the central cases of whistleblowing. That is the first paradox, what we might call "the paradox of burden."

The second paradox concerns the prevention of "harm." On the standard theory, the would-be whistleblower must seek to prevent "serious and considerable harm" in order for the whistleblowing to be even morally permissible. There seems to be a good deal of play in the term *harm*. The harm in question can be physical (such as death or disease), financial (such as loss of or damage to property), and perhaps even psychological (such as fear or mental illness). But there is a limit to how much the standard theory can stretch "harm." Beyond that limit are "harms" like injustice, deception, and waste. As morally important as injustice, deception, and waste can be, they do not seem to constitute the "serious and considerable harm" that can require someone to become even a minimally decent Samaritan.

Yet, many cases of whistleblowing, perhaps most, are not about preventing serious and considerable physical, financial, or psychological harm. For example, when Boisjoly spoke up the evening before the *Challenger* exploded, the lives of seven astronauts sat in the balance. Speaking up then was about preventing serious and considerable physical, financial, and psychological harm—but it was not whistleblowing. Boisjoly was then serving his employer, not betraying a trust (even on the employer's understanding of that trust); he was calling his superiors' attention to what he thought they should take into account in their decision and not publicly revealing confidential information. The whistleblowing came after the explosion, in testimony before the Rogers Commission. By then, the seven astronauts were beyond help, the shuttle program was suspended, and any further threat of physical, financial, or psychological harm to the "public" was—after discounting for time—negligible. Boisjoly had little reason to believe his testimony would make a significant difference in the booster's redesign, in safety procedures in the shuttle program, or even in reawakening concern for safety among NASA employees and contractors. The

*Challenger*'s explosion was much more likely to do that than anything Boisjoly could do. What Boisjoly could do in his testimony, what I think he tried to do, was prevent falsification of the record.

Falsification of the record is, of course, harm in a sense, especially a record as historically important as that which the Rogers Commission was to produce. But falsification is harm only in a sense that almost empties "harm" of its distinctive meaning, leaving it more or less equivalent to "moral wrong." The proponents of the standard theory mean more by "harm" than that De George, for example, explicitly says that a threat justifying whistleblowing must be to "life or health."[3] The standard theory is strikingly more narrow in its grounds of justification than many examples of justified whistleblowing suggest it should be. That is the second paradox, the "paradox of missing harm."

The third paradox is related to the second. Insofar as whistleblowers are understood as people out to prevent harm, not just to prevent moral wrong, their chances of success are not good. Whistleblowers generally do not prevent much harm. In this too, Boisjoly is typical. As he has said many times, the situation at Thiokol is now much as it was before the disaster. Insofar as we can identify cause and effect, even now we have little reason to believe that—whatever his actual intention—Boisjoly's testimony actually prevented any harm (beyond the moral harm of falsification). So, if whistleblowers must have, as the standard theory says (S5), (beyond the moral wrong of falsification) "good reason to believe that revealing the threat will (probably) prevent the harm," then the history of whistleblowing virtually rules out the moral justification of whistleblowing. That is certainly paradoxical in a theory purporting to state sufficient conditions for the central cases of justified whistleblowing. Let us call this "the paradox of failure."

## A COMPLICITY THEORY

As I look down the roll of whistleblowers, I do not see anyone who, like the clerk from Accounts, just happened upon key documents in a cover-up. Few, if any, whistleblowers are mere third-parties like the good Samaritan. They are generally deeply involved in the activity they reveal. This involvement suggests that we might better understand what justifies (most) whistleblowing if we understand the whistleblower's obligation to derive from *complicity* in wrongdoing rather than from the ability to prevent harm.

Any complicity theory of justified whistleblowing has two obvious advantages over the standard theory. One is that (moral) complicity itself presupposes (moral) wrongdoing, not harm. So, a complicity justification automatically avoids the paradox of missing harm, fitting the facts of whistleblowing better than a theory which, like the standard one, emphasizes prevention of harm.

That is one obvious advantage of a complicity theory. The second advantage is that complicity invokes a more demanding obligation than the ability to prevent harm does. We are morally obliged to avoid doing moral wrongs. When, despite our best efforts, we nonetheless find ourselves engaged in some wrong, we have an obligation to do what we reasonably can to set things right. If, for example, I cause a traffic accident, I have a moral (and legal) obligation to call for help, stay at the scene until help arrives, and render first aid (if I know how), even at substantial cost to myself and those to whom I owe my time, and even with little likelihood that anything I do will help much. Just as a complicity theory avoids the paradox of missing harm, it also avoids the paradox of burden.

What about the third paradox, the paradox of failure? I shall come to that, but only after remedying one disadvantage of the complicity theory. That disadvantage is obvious—we do not yet have such a theory, not even a sketch. Here, then, is the place to offer a sketch of such a theory.

## Complicity Theory

You are morally required to reveal what you know to the public (or to a suitable agent or representative of it) when:

**(C1)** what you will reveal derives from your work for an organization;

**(C2)** you are a voluntary member of that organization;

**(C3)** you believe that the organization, though legitimate, is engaged in serious moral wrong doing;

**(C4)** you believe that your work for that organization will contribute (more or less directly) to the wrong if (but *not* only if) you do not publicly reveal what you know;

**(C5)** you are justified in beliefs C3 and C4; and

**(C6)** beliefs C3 and C4 are true.

The complicity theory differs from the standard theory in several ways worth pointing out here. The first is that, according to C1, what the whistleblower reveals must derive from his work for the organization. This condition distinguishes the whistleblower from the spy (and the clerk in Accounts). The spy seeks out information in order to reveal it; the whistleblower learns it as a proper part of doing the job the organization has assigned him. The standard theory, in contrast, has nothing to say about how the whistleblower comes to know of the threat she reveals (S2). For the standard theory, spies are just another kind of whistleblower.

A second way in which the complicity theory differs from the standard theory is that the complicity theory (C2) explicitly requires the whistleblower to be a *voluntary* participant in the organization in question. Whistleblowing is not—according to the complicity theory—an activity in which slaves, prisoners, or other involuntary participants in an organization engage. . . .

A third way in which the complicity theory differs from the standard theory is that the complicity theory (C3) requires moral wrong, not harm, for justification. The wrong need not be a new event (as a harm must be if it is to be *prevented*). It might, for example, consist in no more than silence about facts necessary to correct a serious injustice.

The complicity theory (C3) does, however, follow the standard theory in requiring that the predicate of whistleblowing be "serious." Under the complicity theory, minor wrongdoing can no more justify whistleblowing than can minor harm under the standard theory. While organizational loyalty cannot forbid whistleblowing, it does forbid "tattling," that is, revealing minor wrongdoing.

A fourth way in which the complicity theory differs from the standard theory, the most important, is that the complicity theory (C4) requires that the whistleblower believe that her work will have contributed to the wrong in question if she does nothing, but it does *not* require that she believe that her revelation will prevent (or undo) the wrong. The complicity theory does not require any belief about what the whistleblowing can accomplish (beyond ending complicity in the wrong in question). The whistleblower reveals what she knows in order to prevent complicity in the wrong, not to prevent the wrong as such. She can prevent complicity (if there is any to prevent) simply by publicly revealing what she knows. The revelation itself breaks the bond of complicity, the secret partnership in wrongdoing, that makes her an accomplice in her organization's wrongdoing. The complicity theory thus avoids the third paradox, the paradox of failure, just as it avoided the other two.

The fifth difference between the complicity theory and the standard theory is closely related to the fourth. Because publicly revealing what one knows breaks the bond of complicity, the complicity theory does not require the whistleblower to have enough evidence to convince others of the wrong in question. Convincing others, or just being able to convince them, is not, as such, an element in the justification of whistleblowing.

The complicity theory does, however, require (C5) that the whistleblower be (epistemically) justified in believing both that his organization is engaged in wrongdoing and that he will contribute to that wrong unless he blows the whistle. Such (epistemic) justification may require substantial physical evidence (as the standard theory says) or just a good sense of how things work. The complicity theory does not share the standard theory's substantial evidential demand (S4).

In one respect, however, the complicity theory clearly requires more of the whistleblower than the standard theory does. The complicity theory's C6—combined with C5—requires not only that the whistleblower be *justified* in her beliefs about the organization's wrongdoing and her part in it, but also that she be *right* about them. If she is wrong about

either the wrongdoing or her complicity, her revelation will not be justified whistleblowing. . . .

The complicity theory says nothing on at least one matter about which the standard theory says much—going through channels before publicly revealing what one knows. But the two theories do not differ as much as this difference in emphasis suggests. If going through channels would suffice to prevent (or undo) the wrong, then it cannot be true (as C4 and C6 together require) that the would-be whistleblower's work will contribute to the wrong if she does not publicly reveal what she knows. Where, however, going through channels would *not* prevent (or undo) the wrong, there is no need to go through channels. Condition C4's if-clause will be satisfied. For the complicity theory, going through channels is a way of finding out what the organization will do, not an independent requirement of justification. That, I think, is also how the standard theory understands it.

## TESTING THE THEORY

Let us now test the theory against Boisjoly's testimony before the Rogers Commission. Recall that under the standard theory any justification of that testimony seemed to fail for at least three reasons: First, Boisjoly could not testify without substantial cost to himself and Thiokol (to whom he owned loyalty). Second, there was no serious and substantial harm his testimony could prevent. And, third, he had little reason to believe that, even if he could identify a serious and considerable harm to prevent, his testimony had a significant chance of preventing it.

Since few doubt that Boisjoly's testimony before the Rogers Commission constitutes justified whistleblowing, if anything does, we should welcome a theory that—unlike the standard one—justifies that testimony as whistleblowing. The complicity theory sketched above does that:

(C1) Boisjoly's testimony consisted almost entirely of information derived from his work on booster rockets at Thiokol.

**(C2)** Boisjoly was a voluntary member of Thiokol.

**(C3)** Boisjoly believed Thiokol, a legitimate organization, was attempting to mislead its client, the government, about the causes of a deadly accident. Attempting to do that certainly seems a serious moral wrong.

**(C4)** On the evening before the *Challenger* exploded, Boisjoly gave up objecting to the launch once his superiors, including the three Thiokol vice presidents, had made it clear that they were no longer willing to listen to him. He also had a part in preparing those superiors to testify intelligently before the Rogers Commission concerning the booster's fatal field joint. Boisjoly believed that Thiokol would use his failure to offer his own interpretation of his retreat into silence the night before the launch, and the knowledge that he had imparted to his superiors, to contribute to the attempt to mislead Thiokol's client.

**(C5)** The evidence justifying beliefs C3 and C4 consisted of comments of various officers of Thiokol, what Boisjoly had seen at Thiokol over the years, and what he learned about the rocket business over a long career. I find this evidence sufficient to justify his belief both that his organization was engaged in wrongdoing and that his work was implicated.

**(C6)** Here we reach a paradox of *knowledge*. Since belief is knowledge if, but only if, it is *both* justified *and* true, we cannot *show* that we know anything. All we can show is that a belief is now justified and that we have no reason to expect anything to turn up later to prove it false. The evidence now available still justifies Boisjoly's belief both about what Thiokol was attempting and about what would have been his part in the attempt. Since new evidence is unlikely, his testimony seems to satisfy C6 just as it satisfied the complicity theory's other five conditions.

Since the complicity theory explains why Boisjoly's testimony before the Rogers Commission was morally required whistleblowing, it has passed its first test, a test the standard theory failed.

## NOTES

1. Throughout this essay, I take the standard theory to be Richard T. De George's version in *Business Ethics*, 3rd Edition (New York: Macmillan, 1990), pp. 200–214 (amended only insofar as necessary to include nonbusinesses as well as businesses). Why treat De George's theory as standard? There are two reasons: first, it seems the most commonly cited; and second, people offering alternatives generally treat it as the one to be replaced. The only obvious competitor, Norman Bowie's account, is distinguishable from De George's on no point relevant here. See Bowie's *Business Ethics* (Englewood Cliffs, NJ: Prentice Hall, 1982), p. 143.

2. De George, op. cit.

3. De George, p. 210: "The notion of *serious* harm might be expanded to include serious financial harm, and kinds of harm other than death and serious threats to health and body. But as we noted earlier, we shall restrict ourselves here to products and practices that produce or threaten serious harm or danger to life and health."

## QUESTIONS

1. What are the paradoxes of whistle-blowing?

2. What is Davis's "complicity theory" of the morality of whistle-blowing? How does it avoid the failures of the standard theory?

Ronald Duska | # Whistleblowing and Employee Loyalty

Ronald Duska is Charles F. Lamont Post Chair of Ethics and the Professions Professor of Ethics at the American College.

There are proponents on both sides of the issue—those who praise whistleblowers as civic heroes and those who condemn them as "finks." Maxwell Glen and Cody Shearer, who wrote about the whistleblowers at Three Mile Island say, "Without the *courageous* breed of assorted company insiders known as whistleblowers—workers who often risk their livelihoods to disclose information about construction and design flaws—the Nuclear Regulatory Commission itself would be nearly as idle as Three Mile Island. . . . That whistle-blowers deserve both gratitude and protection is beyond disagreement."[1]

Still, while Glen and Shearer praise whistleblowers, others vociferously condemn them. For example, in a now infamous quote, James Roche, the former president of General Motors said:

> Some critics are now busy eroding another support of free enterprise—the loyalty of a management team, with its unifying values and cooperative work. Some of the enemies of business now encourage an employee to be *disloyal* to the enterprise. They want to create suspicion and disharmony, and pry into the proprietary interests of the business. However this is labeled—industrial espionage, whistle blowing, or professional responsibility—it is another tactic for spreading disunity and creating conflict.[2]

From Roche's point of view, not only is whistleblowing not "courageous" and not deserving of gratitude and protection" as Glen and Shearer would have it, it is corrosive and impermissible.

Discussions of whistleblowing generally revolve around three topics: (1) attempts to define whistleblowing more precisely, (2) debates about whether and when whistleblowing is permissible, and (3) debates about whether and when one has an obligation to blow the whistle.

In this paper I want to focus on the second problem, because I find it somewhat disconcerting that there is a problem at all. When I first looked into the ethics of whistleblowing it seemed to me that whistleblowing was a good thing, and yet I found in the literature claim after claim that it was in need of defense, that there was something wrong with it, namely that it was an act of disloyalty.

If whistleblowing is a disloyal act, it deserves disapproval, and ultimately any action of whistleblowing needs justification. This disturbs me. It is as if the act of a good Samaritan is being condemned as an act of interference, as if the prevention of a suicide needs to be justified.

In his book *Business Ethics*, Norman Bowie claims that "whistleblowing . . . violate(s) a *prima facie* duty of loyalty to one's employer." According to Bowie, there is a duty of loyalty that prohibits one from reporting his employer or company. Bowie, of course, recognizes that this is only a *prima facie* duty, that is, one that can be overridden by a higher duty to the public good. Nevertheless, the axiom that whistleblowing is disloyal is Bowie's starting point.[3]

Bowie is not alone. Sissela Bok sees "whistleblowing" as an instance of disloyalty:

> The whistleblower hopes to stop the game; but since he is neither referee nor coach, and since he blows the whistle on his own team, his act is seen as a *violation of loyalty*. In holding his position, he has assumed certain obligations to his colleagues and clients. He may even have subscribed to a loyalty oath or a promise of confidentiality. . . . Loyalty to colleagues and to clients comes to be pitted against loyalty to the public interest, to those who may be injured unless the revelation is made.[4]

From Tom L. Beauchamp and Norman E. Bowie, *Ethical Theory and Business* (Englewood Cliffs, NJ: Prentice Hall, 2001). Reprinted by permission of the author.

Bowie and Bok end up defending whistleblowing in certain contexts, so I don't necessarily disagree with their conclusions. However, I fail to see how one has an obligation of loyalty to one's company, so I disagree with their perception of the problem and their starting point. I want to argue that one does not have an obligation of loyalty to a company, even a prima facie one, because companies are not the kind of things that are properly objects of loyalty. To make them objects of loyalty gives them a moral status they do not deserve and in raising their status, one lowers the status of the individuals who work for the companies. Thus, the difference in perception is important because those who think employees have an obligation of loyalty to a company fail to take into account a relevant moral difference between persons and corporations.

But why aren't companies the kind of things that can be objects of loyalty? To answer that we have to ask what are proper objects of loyalty. John Ladd states the problem this way, "Granted that loyalty is the wholehearted devotion to an object of some kind, what kind of thing is the object? Is it an abstract entity, such as an idea or a collective being? Or is it a person or group of persons?"[5] Philosophers fall into three camps on the question. On one side are the idealists who hold that loyalty is devotion to something more than persons, to some cause or abstract entity. On the other side are what Ladd calls "social atomists," and these include empiricists and utilitarians, who think that at most one can only be loyal to individuals and that loyalty can ultimately be explained away as some other obligation that holds between two people. Finally, there is a moderate position that holds that although idealists go too far in postulating some super-personal entity as an object of loyalty, loyalty is still an important and real relation that holds between people, one that cannot be dismissed by reducing it to some other relation.

There does seem to be a view of loyalty that is not extreme. According to Ladd, " 'loyalty' is taken to refer to a relationship between persons—for instance, between a lord and his vassal, between a parent and his children, or between friends. Thus the object of loyalty is ordinarily taken to be a person or a group of persons."[6]

But this raises a problem that Ladd glosses over. There is a difference between a person or a group of persons, and aside from instances of loyalty that relate two people such as lord/vassal, parent/child, or friend/friend, there are instances of loyalty relating a person to a group, such as a person to his family, a person to this team, and a person to his country. Families, countries, and teams are presumably groups of persons. They are certainly ordinarily construed as objects of loyalty.

But to what am I loyal in such a group? In being loyal to the group am I being loyal to the whole group or to its members? It is easy to see the object of loyalty in the case of an individual person. It is simply the individual. But to whom am I loyal in a group? To whom am I loyal in a family? Am I loyal to each and every individual or to something larger, and if to something larger, what is it? We are tempted to think of a group as an entity of its own, an individual in its own right, having an identity of its own.

To avoid the problem of individuals existing for the sake of the group, the atomists insist that a group is nothing more than the individuals who comprise it, nothing other than a mental fiction by which we refer to a group of individuals. It is certainly not a reality or entity over and above the sum of its parts, and consequently is not a proper object of loyalty. Under such a position, of course, no loyalty would be owed to a company because a company is a mere mental fiction, since it is a group. One would have obligations to the individual members of the company, but one could never be justified in overriding those obligations for the sake of the "group" taken collectively. A company has no moral status except in terms of the individual members who comprise it. It is not a proper object of loyalty. But the atomists go too far. Some groups, such as a family, do have a reality of their own, whereas groups of people walking down the street do not. From Ladd's point of view the social atomist is wrong because he fails to recognize the kinds of groups that are held together by "the ties that bind." The atomist tries to reduce these groups to simple sets of individuals bound together by some externally imposed criteria. This seems wrong.

There do seem to be groups in which the relationships and interactions create a new force or entity. A group takes on an identity and a reality of its own that is determined by its purpose, and this purpose defines the various relationships and roles set up within the group. There is a division of labor into roles necessary for the fulfillment of the purposes of the group. The membership, then, is not of individuals who are the same but of individuals who have specific relationships to one another determined by the aim of the group. Thus we get specific relationships like parent/child, coach/player, and so on, that don't occur in other groups. It seems then that an atomist account of loyalty that restricts loyalty merely to individuals and does not include loyalty to groups might be inadequate.

But once I have admitted that we can have loyalty to a group, do I not open myself up to criticism from the proponent of loyalty to the company? Might not the proponent of loyalty to business say: "Very well. I agree with you. The atomists are short-sighted. Groups have some sort of reality and they can be proper objects of loyalty. But companies are groups. Therefore companies are proper objects of loyalty."

The point seems well taken, except for the fact that the kinds of relationships that loyalty requires are just the kind that one does not find in business. As Ladd says, "The ties that bind the persons together provide the basis of loyalty." But all sorts of ties bind people together. I am a member of a group of fans if I go to a ball game. I am a member of a group if I merely walk down the street. What binds people together in a business is not sufficient to require loyalty.

A business or corporation does two things in the free enterprise system: It produces a good or service and it makes a profit. The making of a profit, however, is the primary function of a business as a business, for if the production of the good or service is not profitable, the business would be out of business. Thus nonprofitable goods or services are a means to an end. People bound together in a business are bound together not for mutual fulfillment and support, but to divide labor or make a profit. Thus, while we can jokingly refer to a family as a place where "they have to take you in no matter what," we cannot refer to a company in that way. If a worker does not produce in a company or if cheaper laborers are available, the company—in order to fulfill its purpose—should get rid of the worker. A company feels no obligation of loyalty. The saying "You can't buy loyalty" is true. Loyalty depends on ties that demand self-sacrifice with no expectation of reward. Business functions on the basis of enlightened self-interest. I am devoted to a company not because it is like a parent to me; it is not. Attempts of some companies to create "one big happy family" ought to be looked on with suspicion. I am not devoted to it at all, nor should I be. I work for it because it pays me. I am not in a family to get paid, I am in a company to get paid.

The cold hard truth is that the goal of profit is what gives birth to a company and forms that

# On Secrecy and Disclosure
Joseph Pulitzer

There is not a crime, there is not a dodge, there is not a trick, there is not a swindle, there is not a vice which does not live by secrecy. Get these things out in the open, describe them, attack them, ridicule them in the press, and sooner or later public opinion will sweep them away. Publicity may not be the only thing that is needed, but it is the one thing without which all other agencies will fail.

particular group. Money is what ties the group together. But in such a commercialized venture, with such a goal, there is no loyalty, or at least none need be expected. An employer will release an employee and an employee will walk away from an employer when it is profitable for either one to do so.

Not only is loyalty to a corporation not required, it more than likely is misguided. There is nothing as pathetic as the story of the loyal employee who, having given above and beyond the call of duty, is let go in the restructuring of the company. He feels betrayed because he mistakenly viewed the company as an object of his loyalty. Getting rid of such foolish romanticism and coming to grips with this hard but accurate assessment should ultimately benefit everyone.

To think we owe a company or corporation loyalty requires us to think of that company as a person or as a group with a goal of human fulfillment. If we think of it in this way we can be loyal. But this is the wrong way to think. A company is not a person. A company is an instrument, and an instrument with a specific purpose, the making of profit. To treat an instrument as an end in itself, like a person, may not be as bad as treating an end as an instrument, but it does give the instrument a moral status it does not deserve; and by elevating the instrument we lower the end. All things, instruments and ends, become alike.

Remember that Roche refers to the "management team" and Bok sees the name "whistleblowing" coming from the instance of a referee blowing a whistle in the presence of a foul. What is perceived as bad about whistleblowing in business from this perspective is that one blows the whistle on one's own team, thereby violating team loyalty. If the company can get its employees to view it as a team they belong to, it is easier to demand loyalty. Then the rules governing teamwork and team loyalty will apply. One reason the appeal to a team and team loyalty works so well in business is that businesses are in competition with one another. Effective motivation turns business practices into a game and instills teamwork.

But businesses differ from teams in very important respects, which makes the analogy between business and a team dangerous. Loyalty to a team is loyalty within the context of sport or a competition.

Teamwork and team loyalty require that in the circumscribed activity of the game I cooperate with my fellow players, so that pulling all together, we may win. The object of (most) sports is victory. But winning in sports is a social convention, divorced from the usual goings on of society. Such a winning is most times a harmless, morally neutral diversion.

But the fact that this victory in sports, within the rules enforced by a referee (whistleblower), is a socially developed convention taking place within a larger social context makes it quite different from competition in business, which, rather than being defined by a context, permeates the whole of society in its influence. Competition leads not only to victory but to losers. One can lose at sport with precious few consequences. The consequences of losing at business are much larger. Further, the losers in business can be those who are not in the game voluntarily (we are all forced to participate) but who are still affected by business decisions. People cannot choose to participate in business. It permeates everyone's lives.

The team model, then, fits very well with the model of the free market system, because there competition is said to be the name of the game. Rival companies compete and their object is to win. To call a foul on one's own teammate is to jeopardize one's chances of winning and is viewed as disloyalty.

But isn't it time to stop viewing corporate machinations as games? These games are not controlled and are not ended after a specific time. The activities of business affect the lives of everyone, not just the game players. The analogy of the corporation to a team and the consequent appeal to team loyalty, although understandable, is seriously misleading, at least in the moral sphere where competition is not the prevailing virtue.

If my analysis is correct, the issue of the permissibility of whistleblowing is not a real issue since there is no obligation of loyalty to a company. Whistleblowing is not only permissible but expected when a company is harming society. The issue is not one of disloyalty to the company, but of whether the whistleblower has an obligation to society if blowing the whistle will bring him retaliation.

# The Upside of Whistle-Blowing
## Jim Yardley

The nightclub sparkled under a strobe light, as dancers gyrated to "Play That Funky Music" and Court TV's guest of honor, Sherron S. Watkins, sipped wine from a glow-in-the-dark glass. The music stopped so Ms. Watkins could accept the cable channel's Scales of Justice award.

It was not quite the Nobel Prize ceremony. "Let's rock-n-roll and have a few drinks!" exclaimed Court TV's chairman, Henry Schleiff, after handing Ms. Watkins a bronze statuette. The D.J. obeyed and blasted "Shaft," as the 1970's-theme publicity party roared on.

For Ms. Watkins, the Enron vice president whose blunt-spoken warning about the company's accounting practices made her an instant celebrity, the Court TV party in New Orleans on Sunday was only one weird scene from her surreal new life. The day before, Sam Donaldson introduced her to President Bush at the White House Correspondent's Association dinner in Washington.

And this week in Houston, she has continued to do what some consider the unlikeliest thing of all—work at Enron, whose improprieties she sought to expose in the memo, now famous, she wrote to the former chairman, Kenneth L. Lay, months before the company filed for bankruptcy.

"Generally, people are surprised that she is still there," said Philip H. Hilder, Ms. Watkins's lawyer. "Some people think she has been fired. Some people thought that just on her own she had moved on."

For now, while she remains at Enron, the 42-year-old Ms. Watkins is also tip-toeing toward a public life. Her persona as an upscale Erin Brockovich has brought her book and movie deals. She is in demand on the lecture circuit, and next week she is scheduled to be the keynote speaker at a San Francisco conference that is being sponsored by Steve Forbes.

*The New York Times*, May 10, 2002.

## NOTES

1. Maxwell Glen and Cody Shearer, "Going After the Whistle-blowers," *Philadelphia Inquirer*, Tuesday, August 2, 1983, Op-ed page, p. 11A.

2. James M. Roche, "The Competitive System, to Work, to Preserve, and to Protect," *Vital Speeches of the Day* (May 1971): 445.

3. Norman Bowie, *Business Ethics* (Englewood Cliffs, NJ: Prentice Hall, 1982), pp. 140–143.

4. Sissela Bok, "Whistleblowing and Professional Responsibilities," *New York University Education Quarterly* 2 (1980): 3.

5. John Ladd, "Loyalty," *The Encyclopedia of Philosophy* 5: 97.

6. Ibid.

## QUESTIONS

1. Whether and when is whistle-blowing permissible, according to Duska? What moral constraints do whistle-blowers have?

2. What is the "team model"? How does it solve the problem of whistle-blowing?

David E. Soles | # Four Concepts of Loyalty

David E. Soles is an author and a philosopher.

## THE IDEALIST ACCOUNT

The first view of loyalty may be called an idealist account because of the close resemblance it bears to the position developed by the American idealist, Josiah Royce. According to Royce, loyalty is

> [t]he willing and practical and thorough-going devotion of a person to a cause. A man is loyal when, first, he has some cause to which he is loyal; secondly, he willingly and thoroughly devotes himself to this cause; and when, thirdly, he expresses his devotion in some sustained and practical way, by acting steadily in the service of his cause. Instances of loyalty are: The devotion of a patriot to his country, when this devotion leads him to actually live and perhaps to die for his country; the devotion of a martyr to his religion; the devotion of a ship's captain to the requirements of his office when, after a disaster, he works steadily for his ship and for the saving of the ship's company until the last possible service is accomplished, so that he is the last man to leave the ship, and is ready if need be to go down with his ship.[1]

As Royce realizes, each of the aspects of his analysis requires further elucidation. To begin with the object of loyalty: that to which one is loyal must be something objective, external to the individual, and possessed of its own inherent value; "[i]t does not get its value merely from your being pleased with it. You believe, on the contrary, that you love it just because of its own value, which it has by itself, even if you die" (19).

By saying that loyalty requires willing devotion, Royce is maintaining that loyalty must be freely given; while obedience can be demanded, loyalty cannot. In part, this follows from Royce's thesis that loyalty entails devotion: devotion is a mental state not reducible to behavior, and while behavior can be demanded, mental states cannot. But while loyalty may entail devotion, devotion is never sufficient for loyalty: "[l]oyalty is never mere emotion. Adoration and affection may go with loyalty, but can never alone constitute loyalty" (18).

This follows from the claim that loyalty is practical—to be loyal is to serve a cause. Furthermore, this service is thorough-going and sustained; a loyal person does whatever is necessary to promote the cause, "ready to live or die as the cause directs" (18).

This idealist conception of loyalty is germane to discussions of business ethics in the following way. If this is the accepted conception of loyalty and if it can be established that employees ought to be loyal to their employers, then the stringent obligations sometimes placed upon employees in the name of loyalty would be perfectly justified. A loyal employee would be one thoroughly dedicated to serving the interests of his principal, ready to live or die as directed, and to say that employees should be loyal would be to advocate such dedication. It is instructive to consider some examples of the sorts of obligations this conception of loyalty could require of a loyal employee. A loyal employee would always be willing to place the interests of the principal before purely private interests, even in matters unrelated to employment; a loyal employee would be willing to sacrifice the interests of uninvolved third parties or even society at large, if doing so served the employer's interest; a loyal employee would never advocate or vote for social policies or legislation that might damage the interests of the employer; a loyal employee would never publicly criticize or oppose the actions of the employer; a loyal employee would never consider leaving the employer. That something akin to the idealist conception of loyalty is operative in some quarters is evidenced by the frequent endorsements of these claims.

Reprinted by permission of the author from *The International Journal of Applied Philosophy* 8 (Summer 1993).

Lest it be thought that I am constructing a straw man here; consider the following case which Marcia Baron discusses in *The Moral Status of Loyalty*.

> In a 1973 CBS report on Phillips Petroleum, Inc., one of its chief executives was asked to describe what sort of qualities his company looks for in prospective employees. He responded without hesitation that above all else, what Phillips wants and needs is loyalty on the part of its employees. A loyal employee, he elaborated, would buy only Phillips products. . . . Moreover, a loyal employee would vote in local, state, and national elections in whatever way was most conducive to the growth and flourishing of Phillips. And, of course, a loyal employee would never leave Phillips unless it was absolutely unavoidable. To reduce the likelihood of that happening, prospective employees were screened to make sure their respective wives did not have careers which might conflict with lifelong loyalty to Phillips.[2]

Is it true that employees have an obligation to so thoroughly dedicate themselves to the interests of their employers and, if so, what are the grounds of that obligation? . . .

It is morally irresponsible to be willing to perform any conceivable action that would further the interests of one's chosen cause; one must always reserve the option of saying that one can no longer serve a cause if it requires the performance of certain sorts of actions. . . .

If loyalty requires such total, thorough-going dedication to a cause, there are very few things worthy of loyalty; furthermore, since the interests of any two causes could conceivably come into conflict, one can be loyal to only one object. Therefore, it is incumbent upon each person to ensure that the object of his loyalty is of the highest inherent worth.

It is very unlikely that business institutions qualify as objects of the most inherent worth. To begin with, business institutions are instrumentally, not inherently, valuable; they are valued because they are means for providing goods and services which are valued. If we no longer cared for those goods and services or if we found better ways to obtain them, the institutions which provide them would lose much of their value. Furthermore, not all business institutions possess instrumental value: some produce more

harm than good by manufacturing dangerous, inferior products, polluting the environment, engaging in illegal business practices, etc. But whether instrumentally good or evil, a business institution is not the sort of thing worthy of loyalty in the idealist sense.

In summary, if the idealist conception of loyalty were accepted as our working notion of loyalty, and if it could be established that employees ought to be loyal to their employers, then the demands placed upon employees in the name of loyalty would be justified: employees would have an obligation to place the interests of their employers before all other interests. However, it is not clear that we should accept this as our working conception of loyalty and, more importantly, even if we did, we must conclude that business institutions could not be appropriate objects of loyalty.

## THE COMMON SENSE CONCEPTION

The common sense view of loyalty more satisfactorily captures the everyday conception of loyalty with which most of us are familiar. Most of us are untroubled by statements to the effect that someone is a loyal fan of the Kansas City Royals, a loyal member of the Republican party, or loyal to her alma mater, and when we hear such claims we are not inclined to suppose that the person is totally dedicated to the cause, "willing to live or die as the cause directs."

A version of the common sense view of loyalty has been formulated by Andrew Oldenquist in "Loyalties."[3] According to Oldenquist,

> . . . [w]hen I have a loyalty to something I have somehow come to view it as *mine*. It is an object of non-instrumental value to me in virtue (but not only in virtue) of its being mine, and I am disposed to feel pride when it prospers, shame when it declines, and anger or indignation when it is harmed. In general, people care about the objects of their loyalties, and they acknowledge obligations that they would not acknowledge were it not for their loyalties. (175)
> . . . [L]oyalty is positive and is primarily characterized by esteem and concern for the common good of one's group. (177)

On this view, there are three essential features of loyalty. First, loyalty entails having a positive attitude towards the objects of one's loyalty; a loyalty is to "an object of non-instrumental value," people "care about" the objects of their loyalties. Second, loyalty entails a disposition to serve the interests of the object to which one is loyal; loyal persons "acknowledge obligations that they would not acknowledge were it not for their loyalties." Third, both the concern and the obligations are rooted in the individual's belief that he stands in some personal relationship to the object of his loyalty; to have a loyalty to something is to somehow come to view it as one's own.

The first thing to note about this conception of loyalty is that it is not sufficient to distinguish loyalty from many other virtues.[4] While caring, acknowledging obligations, and feeling a personal relationship may be necessary features of loyalty, they also are necessary features of virtues such as love and friendship and may even characterize the relationship between some professionals and their patients, clients, students, etc. Many dedicated teachers consider their students to be objects of non-instrumental value, care about them, acknowledge supererogatory obligations, and both the concern and the obligations stem from the fact that these students are their students. Similar remarks may be made about doctors, nurses, lawyers, social workers, etc. To characterize their attitude as one of loyalty seems to be stretching the common sense notion of loyalty too far. . . .

In conflating loyalty with other, distinct, virtues, Oldenquist has failed to provide the promised analysis of loyalty. Nevertheless, while this common sense account should not be construed as providing a definition of "loyalty" in terms of necessary and sufficient conditions, it may be acceptable as a rough characterization of some essential features of loyalty. Loyalty, like friendship, love, and professional interest, entails concern, obligations, and a feeling of personal identification with the object of one's loyalty. The questions that need to be asked, then, are: (1) does one have any obligation to have such attitudes to one's employer, and (2) does the having of such attitudes justify always acting in the interests of the object of one's loyalty?

Beginning with the first question, on the common sense account, the mere fact that one happens to have been born in a particular country, happens to have attended a particular school, or happens to work for a particular institution is not sufficient for saying that one should be loyal to it. Oldenquist makes this point in maintaining that ". . . a loyalist doesn't value something simply because it is his. It must have features which make it worth having, and it could deteriorate to the extent that shame ultimately kills his loyalty" (178). On this conception of loyalty, one should bestow one's loyalty only on those objects which are worthy of it and loyalty bestowed upon some nations, schools or institutions would be misguided.

Furthermore, if this is our working conception of loyalty, no one has an obligation to be loyal to anything; to suppose that one has an obligation to be loyal to anything is to make a fundamental category mistake. On this view, being loyal entails having certain sorts of attitudes; to be loyal to an object one must care about it. But while persons can have moral obligations to perform certain actions and while certain attitudes may be morally desirable or indesirable, we do not have moral obligations to have certain attitudes and beliefs. Just as no one has an obligation to have feelings of love or friendship to another, no one has an obligation to have feelings of loyalty to anything. Thus, one can have no obligation to be loyal to her nation, school, or employer even if they are worthy of loyalty.

Turning to the second question, does loyalty require one to always act in the interest of that to which one is loyal? It is often suggested that loyalty is inconsistent with certain sorts of actions, for example, whistleblowing is alleged to be incompatible with loyalty. Sissela Bok, for instance, sets up the dichotomy this way:

> . . . [T]he whistleblower hopes to stop the game; but since he is neither referee nor coach, and since he blows the whistle on his own team, his act is seen as a violation of loyalty. In holding his position, he has assumed certain obligations to his colleagues and clients. He may even have subscribed to a loyalty oath or a promise of confidentiality. Loyalty to colleagues and clients comes to be pitted against loyalty to the public interest, to those who may be injured unless the revelation is made.
> *Not only is loyalty violated in whistleblowing*, hierarchy as well is often opposed. . . . If the facts warrant whistleblowing, how can the second element— *breach of loyalty*—be minimized?[5] (my italics)

106

---

# Blind to Earned Loyalty
## Robert C. Solomon and Clancy Martin

The concept of loyalty has changed from one of "blind and obligated" to one of "insightful and earned." Several generations ago, if a person worked hard and kept his nose to the grindstone, he could pretty well be assured of work for a lifetime. People were loyal to organizations because they believed organizations would be loyal to them.

The passage of "good old loyalty" may be lamented by many, but there is some good news. It has been replaced by a strong new type—namely, earned loyalty.

So, rather than lament the loss of "good old loyalty," let's focus on a loyalty that may well provide a stronger motivational force for both management and the managed. I have identified five basic elements of the new loyalty.

1. Values and Standards. Loyalty tends to be more easily earned in those organizations that have clearly-defined values and challenging standards. People are likely to be loyal to values that lead to outstanding achievements in products, services, and relationships.
2. Clear Expectations. A willingness to be specific and forthright in terms of expected behaviors does a great deal toward developing a feeling of loyalty on the part of those who will follow. It is easier for people to be loyal to what they clearly understand.
3. Frequent Feedback. People need to know where they stand and how well or poorly they have performed when evaluated against the expectations, standards, and values. People need to hear good news as well as bad. Frequent feedback is a way of increasing meaningful involvement.
4. Respect for the Individual. The new loyalty will have to be earned on the basis of respect for the individual. Respect requires trust, based on consistency in personal and interpersonal relationships; a willingness to be open with expectations and requirements; to really listen and engage in honest exchange.
5. Long-Term Commitments. This last element is probably most difficult to achieve. In what appears to many to be an atmosphere of layoffs, terminations, forced resignations, and retirements, it is difficult to convince people that long-term commitments are realistic or possible.

—From *Above the Bottom Line*

---

On the common sense conception, this is a very misleading way of presenting the problem for it implies that whistleblowing is a breach of loyalty, that one cannot both be loyal to an institution and blow the whistle on it. But, on the common sense view, this is surely wrong; one can view an institution as one's own, care deeply about it, assume obligations towards it, and still publicly and strenuously oppose what one takes to be unethical or illegal actions on its part. This is a feature of loyalty explicitly recognized in British politics as "the loyal opposition."

Setting up a dichotomy between loyalty and whistleblowing is not merely a misleading way to present the problem of whistleblowing, it is dangerous. Loyalty is generally perceived as a virtue and disloyalty is perceived as a vice. To say that loyalty demands a certain action is to give a prima facie reason for performing that action and to label a particular action as disloyal is to give a prima facie reason for not performing that action. Under those conditions, potential whistleblowers are encouraged to construe themselves as choosing between performing a wrong act themselves (being disloyal) or remaining silent about the performance of wrongs committed by others. When presented this way, it is not surprising that many individuals choose silence. But if whistleblowing is not construed as an instance of disloyalty, the whole complexion of the problem changes. If loyalty does not require acquiescence in wrong doing, the refusal to remain silent about known wrongs cannot be construed as an ipso facto instance of disloyalty.

Acceptance of the common sense view of loyalty, thus, would justify two conclusions both of which are anathema to many discussions of business and professional ethics. First, it is simply a mistake to suppose that individuals have an obligation to be loyal to their employers and second, loyalty is compatible with strenuously opposing actions of one's employer.

## LOYALTIES AS NORMS

While he does not appear to be aware that he is doing so, Oldenquist formulates a second conception of loyalty radically different from his common sense account. According to this second view, "loyalties are norms that define the domains within which we accept the moral machinery of universalizable reasons and relevant differences" (182); alternatively, "loyalties define moral communities or domains within which we are willing to universalize moral judgments, treat equals equally, protect the common good, and in other ways adopt the familiar machinery of impersonal morality. . . .A loyalty defines a moral community in terms of a conception of a common good and a special commitment to the

members of the group who share this good" (177). This seems to be incompatible with the common sense account Oldenquist formulates. Attitudes, definitions and norms are different sorts of things. If loyalty is an attitude as the common sense account maintains, then it is neither a norm nor a definition.

Perhaps the confusion here is merely verbal. Perhaps Oldenquist's claim is something like this: the class of objects to which one is loyal is delineated by, or co-extensive with, the moral communities or domains "within which we are willing to universalize moral judgments, treat equals equally, protect the common good, and in other ways adopt the familiar machinery of impersonal morality." On this reading, loyalty is not literally a norm which defines a moral community; rather, one has attitudes of loyalty towards the moral community determined by the norms.

There are two ways of interpreting this talk of loyalty to the moral community: (1) we might have feelings of loyalty to each of the members of the community defined by the norm, or (2) we might have feelings of loyalty to the community, but not necessarily to each of its members. Either alternative faces serious difficulties.

Beginning with the first interpretation, if loyalty is characterized by positive feelings of esteem and concern, a disposition to feel pride when the object of loyalty prospers, shame when it declines, and anger or hurt when it is harmed, then the moral community defined by the norms and the objects of one's loyalty might not be co-extensive. One might, for instance, define the moral community as rational, sentient beings; this would define the domain within which we are willing to universalize moral judgments, etc. One might not, however, have positive feelings of concern, esteem, etc. for all the members of this community. In that case, the community of objects to which one is loyal would not be coextensive with the moral community.

The second interpretation would avoid this conclusion by arguing that on the above example one is loyal to the class of rational sentient beings, not individual rational sentient beings; that communities and not individuals are the proper objects of loyalty. . . .

If any moral norm to which one is committed defines a moral community to which one is loyal, then loyalty can never come into conflict with any other moral standard. Suppose that I am loyal to the institution where I am employed; it is a community towards which I have positive attitudes, I have assumed special obligations to promote its interests, I treat the members of that community according to the procedures of impersonal morality, recognizing universalizable reasons, and relevant differences, etc. Suppose that I am also committed to the principle that rational beings should always be treated as ends in themselves. Suppose, finally, that I come to perceive certain policies pursued by my institution as being grossly exploitive and am torn between a desire to protect the institution and an obligation to act on my moral principles. In choosing what course of action to pursue, it would be natural to describe myself as choosing between considerations of loyalty to the institution and some other principle of morality.

On Oldenquist's view, however, the choice is merely one between a wide and a narrow loyalty; on the one hand I am loyal to the institution and on the other hand I am loyal to the moral community defined by the norm. If any moral standard which I accept defines a moral community to which I am loyal, then loyalty can never come into conflict with any other moral standard, there can only be conflicts between wide and narrow loyalties. At precisely that point loyalty becomes a vacuous, trivial moral notion.

Furthermore, to say that loyalty is a norm does not answer any ethical questions nor provide moral guidance. . . . In particular, characterizing loyalties as norms which define moral communities provides no guidance in ascertaining whether we should be loyal to our employers nor does it provide any insight into what loyalty would demand should we decide that loyalty is appropriate. Consequently, such an analysis is useless for deciding the interesting questions about loyalty that arise in the context of business and professional ethics.

## THE MINIMALIST ACCOUNT

There is a fourth conception of loyalty which maintains that a loyal individual is one who meets reasonable expectations of trust; to be loyal just is to discharge one's obligations and responsibilities conscientiously. Such an attenuated view of loyalty does not demand positive feelings of affection, devotion, or respect nor does it expect one to perform supererogatory actions in promoting the interests of the object of one's loyalty. At most, loyalty demands that one act in a way that does not betray reasonable expectations of trust.

The Restatement of the Law of Agency is subject to a minimalist interpretation.[6] That Restatement maintains that a loyal agent has a duty ". . . to act solely for the benefit of the principal in all matters connected with his agency" (387). This claim that the agent is to act solely for the benefit of the principal is qualified in several important respects by the Restatement. First, an agent may act against the interests of his principal when doing so is necessary for the protection of his own interests or those of others (387b). Second, an agent has no obligation to perform acts which are illegal or unethical and ". . . in determining whether or not the orders of the principal are reasonable . . . business or professional ethics . . . are considered" (385-1a). Third, an agent is not "prevented from acting in good faith outside his employment in a manner which injuriously affects his principal's business" (387b). Finally, "[a]n agent is privileged to reveal information confidentially acquired . . . in the protection of a superior interest of himself or of a third person. Thus, if the confidential information is to the effect that the principal is committing or is about to commit a crime, the agent is under no duty not to reveal it" (395f).

Like most documents, the Restatement of Agency is subject to competing interpretations. As Blumberg has noted, the Restatement

. . . is drafted in terms of economic activity, economic motivation, and economic advantage and formulates duties of loyalty and obedience for the agent to prevent the agent's own economic interest from impairing his judgment, zeal, or single-minded devotion to the furtherance of his principal's economic interests. The reference in section 395, Comment permitting the agent to disclose confidential information concerning a criminal act committed or planned by the principal is the sole exception to a system of analysis that is otherwise exclusively concerned with matters relating to the economic position of the parties.[7] . . .

As Blumberg rightly emphasizes, the Restatement is concerned almost exclusively with conflicts of economic interests; nevertheless, if interpreted liberally, the Restatement can be quite useful in responding to the broader issues. The discussion of criminal activity at 395f could be treated as an example of a case where the revelation of confidential material is justified by the need to protect a superior interest; it need not be read as limiting the revelation of confidential material to cases involving criminal activity. By the same token, 387b could be interpreted as maintaining that an agent is justified in acting against the interests of the principal when doing so is necessary to protect important noneconomic interests of himself or others. Interpreted thusly, either 395f or 387b could be appealed to in justifying the claim that loyalty is consistent with acting against the interests of one's employer.

On the minimalist account, loyalty would not entail a willingness to participate in, condone or remain silent about illegal activities. It would not entail willingness to participate in unethical conduct if doing so promoted the interests of one's principal. It would be compatible with acting against the interests of one's employer, even revealing confidential information, if doing so were necessary to protect important interests of the public. Finally, contrary to the opinion of the Phillips executive, loyalty would be compatible with voting in ways not conducive to the growth and flourishing of one's principal and even compatible with seeking employment elsewhere. In this minimalist sense, simply meeting reasonable expectations of trust is sufficient for loyalty.

This, of course, raises the issue of what responsibilities it is reasonable for employers to entrust to employees. Many of these are defined and clearly stipulated in job descriptions, contracts, and codes of professional ethics and many more are informally recognized as standard acceptable practices within a profession; and, while there are bound to be grey areas and points of disagreement, there are some activities which loyalty does not enjoin.

If the minimalist conception of loyalty is accepted, it seems clear that employees ought to be loyal to their employers. That, however, merely amounts to the claim that they ought to meet reasonable, legitimate expectations of trust; it does not impose upon them the sorts of obligations that often are urged in the name of loyalty.

## CONCLUSION

Much of the confusion and disagreement infecting discussions of the role of loyalty in business and professional ethics has been engendered by equivocation and ambiguity in the concept itself. This essay has briefly considered four different conceptions of loyalty and examined some of the implications of each. If the idealist conception of loyalty is accepted, loyalty to one's employer would demand the sort of behavior sometimes advocated in its name. It is not clear, however, that this account should be accepted and, if we do accept it, employers would not be appropriate objects of loyalty. If the common sense conception of loyalty is accepted, two conclusions follow: first, since loyalty is supererogatory, no one has an obligation to feel loyal to anything; second, loyalty, in this sense, does not entail placing the interests of one's principal before all other considerations and, in fact, is compatible with opposing some of the interests of one's principal. The third conception, which maintains that the adoption of any norm regulating conduct generates a loyalty, trivializes the notion of loyalty to the point where it is useless for guiding conduct. Finally, on the minimalist conception, one can justify saying that employees ought to be loyal to their employers; the minimalist view is sufficiently attenuated, however, that such a claim does not amount to much.

## NOTES

1. Josiah Royce, *The Philosophy of Loyalty*, The MacMillan Co., New York, 1916, pp. 16–17. Subsequent references to this work are provided as page numbers in the text.

2. Marcia Baron, *The Moral Status of Loyalty*, Kendal Hunt, Dubuque, Iowa, 1984, p. 1.

3. Andrew Oldenquist, "Loyalties," *The Journal of Philosophy*, April, 1982, pp. 173–193. Subsequent references to this work are provided as page numbers in the text.

4. This should not be construed as a criticism of Oldenquist. His objective seems to be to advocate loyalty, not explicate the conception.

5. Sissela Bok, "Whistleblowing and Professional Responsibility," *New York University Education Quarterly*, Vol. II, 4 (1980), 2–7. Reprinted in Beauchamp and Bowie, *Ethical Theory and Business*, 2nd ed., Prentice Hall, Inc., Englewood Cliffs, New Jersey, pp. 261–269.

6. *Restatement of the Law, Second, Agency*, Vol. 2, American Law Institute Publishers, St. Paul, Minnesota, 1958.

7. Phillip J. Blumberg, "Corporate Responsibility and the Employee's Duty of Loyalty and Obedience," in Beauchamp and Bowie, *Ethical Theory and Business*, Prentice Hall, Inc., Englewood Cliffs, New Jersey, 1979, pp. 309–310.

## QUESTIONS

1. What are the four concepts of loyalty? How do they disagree with one another?

2. What remains of loyalty after Soles concludes his analysis? What concept of loyalty do you subscribe to? Can you offer your own, original concept of loyalty?

---

George D. Randels

# Loyalty, Corporations, and Community

George D. Randels, Jr., is associate professor of social ethics in the Religious Studies Department of the University of the Pacific.

The man in the gray flannel suit. The organization man. When it comes to loyalty, American business is not without images, flawed though they may be. But these are the ghosts of business past. In spite of their hard work, long hours, and important sacrifices, they have been downsized. It is yesterday's news that this type of devotion is not necessarily rewarded, nor does such devotion necessarily indicate loyalty to a company as opposed to the company being a mere instrument for personal advantage. Three *New Yorker* cartoons reflect current trends. In one, the downsized employee is pictured as that paradigm of loyalty, the dog. "Of *course* the company appreciates your years of loyalty," says the manager to the teary-eyed employee (destined for the Humane Society?). In another, the manager's consolation includes some positive spin: "Yes, and

the fact that you've been an outstanding employee for twenty-five years is going to look great on your résumé." The third cartoon's setting is the interview rather than the layoff. Here the personnel manager's statement depicts both sides of the coin: "We expect little loyalty. In return we offer little security." In the context that these cartoons portray, the "Why be moral?" question often associated with discussions of business ethics becomes "Why be loyal?" There seems to be no benefit, unless loyalty is somehow its own reward. . . .

## LOYALTY, DUTY, AND VIRTUE

Loyalty is often characterized as a duty that an employee owes to a corporation, or as a virtue of a good employee, but loyalty is not a duty or a virtue. It is, however, linked to both of these concepts in that loyal persons will perform certain duties and possess certain virtues. Loyalty involves a complex of

From *Business Ethics Quarterly*, 11, No. 1. © 2001. *Business Ethics Quarterly*, 11:1. ISSN 1052–1064. Notes were deleted from the text.

passions and character traits such as commitment, with outward actions springing from them. It is thus more readily identified by character-based ethics, but is not itself an individual virtue. . . .

## WHAT IS LOYALTY?

. . . Loyalty is a passion. But contrary to traditional thinking, there is not necessarily a one-to-one correspondence between passions and virtues (or vices). Loyalty seems to be the type of passion that can contribute to multiple virtues (and vices) and obviously to a multitude of ends. Ewin apparently finds loyalty so central, however, that it is the sole passion at work. He suggests that "loyalty is the emotional setting for the virtues and vices; it is not itself a virtue or a vice, but is the raw material for them."[1] Because loyalty extends beyond the self to some object, it is a social passion, and Robert Solomon likely is correct to suggest that it is a type of love.[2] But even as a type of love, loyalty is not the sole passion for the virtues, not even the moral virtues. There are, after all, other types of love, and other passions, such as fear, daring, pleasure, anger, joy, pity, pride, shame, and hope. These other loves and passions are not readily reducible to loyalty, and also provide "raw material" for virtues and vices.

Loyalty is a social passion, a type of love that extends beyond the self to some object of loyalty. As loyalty develops, this object becomes no longer strictly external, but is linked to one's self-identity and helps to provide meaning for one's life. Solomon and Fletcher both claim that it is through our loyalties that we define our sense of self, and this seems quite right.[3] Harvard or Yale, Duke or Carolina, Cubs or Sox, Catholic or Protestant, Macy's or Gimble's, Microsoft or Netscape. While loyalties often do not involve binary choices like these or an "us v. them" mentality, they clearly do define us and link us not only to the object of loyalty but perhaps also to a group of other people who share that loyalty with us. . . .

The link between self and others is key to loyalty, and relationship is the source of this link and serves as an important conceptual tool. But relationship would need to move from the literal to the metaphorical to provide a general understanding of loyalty (as opposed to a particular type of loyalty), and even then the metaphor breaks down. When venturing beyond interpersonal loyalties, the nature of relationships will differ dramatically, and it is difficult to maintain that mutuality or reciprocity is required for all forms of loyalty as it is in the friendship relation. Just as there can be unrequited love, there can be unrequited loyalty. A person can be loyal without a literal relationship to the object of loyalty. It is possible to be a loyal Cub fan without having a relationship with Sammy Sosa, or even having his autograph or ever having seen a game at Wrigley Field. Likewise, it is possible to be a loyal customer by continuing to use a product without any contact with any person from the company (e.g., Coke or Pepsi). And one can be loyal to certain ideals regardless of the support of like-minded persons.

In the corporate context, relationship works quite well for understanding interpersonal loyalties between co-workers, loyalty to one's boss, and so on. The concept presents difficulties, however, when thinking about the prospects for loyalty to an organization. Fletcher partially addresses this concern by noting that in group loyalty, membership rather than relationship provides the basis. "Membership makes one an insider; it confers identity within a matrix of relationships both to other members and to the leadership of the organization." Entry into the group and subsequent identification with it are the two key aspects of membership. Loyalties arise from this identification.[4] Membership defined in this way is a good vehicle for characterizing loyalty to an organization like a corporation. To be loyal, an employee or manager would need to feel like a part of the organization through a matrix of relationships and identify himself or herself with the organization, typically with a positive association. A sense of membership minimizes the compartmentalization or segmentation of oneself that often happens between the workplace and the rest of one's life. There are, of course, different possible levels of membership in terms of commitment and identification (not necessarily in terms of job status), and the degree of loyalty would vary with them.

Loyalty in the corporate context would have to be based on relationships and a sense of membership. This analysis necessarily cuts against traditional business/economic theory about individualism, self-interest, and the corporation. In the next section, I will discuss loyalty in relation to this standard account of business, and then move on to discuss an alternative account in the last section.

## LOYALTY AND THE STANDARD ACCOUNT OF BUSINESS

The standard account of business presents serious barriers for loyalty's prospects in the business context with its focus on the individual and self-interest in pursuit of wealth. The "spirit of capitalism," the economic mind-set, would seem to preclude loyalties except perhaps as instrumental for one's own gain. Ewin nicely presents the contrast between loyalty and the standard account of business. "A really loyal person subjugates (at least to some extent) his or her private interests to those of the object of loyalty, and that is quite different from being an entirely independent item entering a commercial relationship. Loyalty involves emotional ties and not merely commercial ties." Loyalty runs counter to commercial judgment because the latter would require one to take a better job offer from a rival company rather than stay put. Loyalty proves difficult in the business context because it would necessarily involve a "willingness *not* to follow good [commercial] judgment, at least some of the time."[5]

One must then choose between loyalty and self-interest, and in the standard account, there really could not be a choice at all. Self-interest would be the only option. There would be a very limited sense—if any—of relationship or membership, which serve as the grounding of loyalty. This is why Duska rejects a duty of loyalty in the business context, because "the kinds of relationships that loyalty requires are just the kind that one does not find in business." The common pursuit of personal

financial gain is insufficient to establish the bonds necessary for loyalty. "Loyalty depends on ties that demand self-sacrifice with no expectation of reward. Business functions on the basis of enlightened self-interest. . . . Attempts of some companies to create 'one big happy family' ought to be looked upon with suspicion. I am not devoted to it at all, nor should I be. I work for it because it pays me. I am not in a family to get paid, I am in a company to get paid." Money, not love, keeps the company together. Duska holds that loyalty to a corporation is not only not required, but is likely to be misguided when it exists. A corporation is concerned with profit, not human fulfillment. We should thus get rid of foolish romanticism about corporations. Accepting this harsh reality benefits us all, especially those loyal workers who wind up feeling betrayed. Corporate loyalty should not exist, and is a mistake when it does.[6]

. . . Insofar as a corporation operates for the sole purpose of profit making, then Duska is exactly right that such an organization does not deserve loyalty. Neither would individuals like co-workers and bosses if they were strictly rational maximizers of their own self-interest. Furthermore, if financial gain is all *I* want, then I could not be loyal anyway, whether the organization, boss, or co-workers deserve my loyalty or not. I would view it (and them) strictly in instrumental terms, even as it (and they) may also view me the same way. The grounds for loyalty would not exist.

Although Duska follows most accounts of loyalty in emphasizing self-sacrifice—and clearly loyal people sacrifice various interests, their time, and sometimes even their lives—loyalty is not strictly altruistic. The loyal person's self-interest is tied up with that of the object of loyalty. There is an important link between the self and the object of loyalty. It is not just in the company's interest or the boss's interest or my co-workers' interests that the product succeed, but *my* interest. It is not strictly a matter of sacrifice for others, although I may make sacrifices. I have invested myself and thus have a stake in the object of loyalty. In many respects, its interests *are* my interests. The necessary dichotomy between loyalty and self-interest is a false one. The standard account mistakenly assumes that they cannot co-exist in the business world.

## CORPORATE LOYALTY IN THE POSTMODERN BUSINESS WORLD

What is a proper object of loyalty? Why not loyalty to a corporation, co-worker, boss, project, team, or profession? Of course, corporate loyalty might not be prudential, as the downsizing phenomenon has shown.[7] Moreover, as Duska indicates, "A company is an instrument, and an instrument with a specific purpose, the making of profit. To treat an instrument as an end in itself . . . give[s] the instrument a moral status it does not deserve."[8]

Duska is correct that a corporation is indeed an instrument, and insofar as that is all a corporation is, then his conclusion is correct. But a corporation can also be much more, . . . Robert Solomon claims that corporations are indeed much more—they are communities. The "relationships of reciprocity and cooperation . . . consist, first of all, in a shared sense of belonging, a shared sense of mission or, at least, a shared sense of mutual interest."[9] . . .

For a corporation to be a community, it would have to be more than an instrument for financial gain. It would have to contribute to human fulfillment. This is not to say, however, that a corporation needs to become the center of its employees' lives to be a community. . . . A corporation or any group need not include all of one's social relationships, values, and interests in order to be a community. Instead, a community involves "a framework of shared beliefs, interests, and commitments unit[ing] a set of *varied* groups and activities . . . that establish a common faith or fate, a personal identity, a sense of belonging, and a supportive structure of activities and relationships." For a group like a corporation, *"the emergence of community depends on the opportunity for, and impulse toward, comprehensive interaction, commitment, and responsibility."*[10]

. . . Rather than viewing corporations strictly as instruments because they are not comprehensive communities, they can be seen as existing along a community continuum. While I would not want to see corporations all the way at the comprehensive end of

the continuum, the closer they move in that direction, the greater the sharing of values, sense of membership, and identification of the self with the whole. To the extent that corporations are communities, loyalty not only is possible, but can be very much appropriate.

Whether loyalty is appropriate is a crucial question, but can receive only a cursory reply here. Good judgment is necessary to determine if and when to invest loyalty and hence oneself in an organization. The presence of community is a necessary but insufficient condition for doing so. One must consider the ideals and goals of organization and their worthiness. Do they match with my own aspirations, or do I want to modify my own to fit with its? Furthermore, are the goals and ideals adhered to, and if so, are ethically acceptable means used to attain them?

Assuming loyalty is appropriate in a corporation, as a community it involves whole persons rather than strictly their segmented interests. Unlike the organization man's singleness of purpose, however, this involvement of the whole person does not exclude loyalties to other communities and to individuals with whom we have relationships. . . . Loyalties to family, friends, religion, town, country, and corporation, among others, may happily co-exist with one another, but likely will compete from time to time. When they do compete, as Alan Wolfe indicates, "the choice is not between loyalty and disloyalty but between competing ways of being loyal. . . . The question is how we balance them, not how we choose between them."[11]

Integrity, a personal sense of wholeness, is important to the task of balancing one's loyalties. This sense of wholeness involves not an isolated self, but includes connectedness with these various others. It involves not a return to singleness of purpose, but balance. That is not to say that all loyalties are equal and so must receive identical treatment; some undoubtedly are more important than others. Corporate loyalty should be less than some loyalties, but perhaps more than some others. This balancing must be worked out in concrete cases, however, and can only be suggested in the abstract.

While the need for such balancing may cause one to question the desirability of corporate loyalty, the inability to have loyalty to a corporation itself can damage one's integrity. The impossibility of loyalty makes for a divided self and potentially compromises one's other loyalties to religion, family, friends, etc., as one engages in tasks for a purely instrumental entity. It would be far better to establish a Connection Thesis that acknowledges the legitimacy of loyalty to corporate communities.

## NOTES

1. R. E. Ewin, "Loyalty and Virtues," *The Philosophical Quarterly* 42 (1992): 418.

2. Robert C. Solomon, *A Passion for Justice: Emotions and the Origins of the Social Contract* (Reading, Mass.: Addison-Wesley Publishing Co., 1990), p. 288.

3. Solomon, p. 289; George P. Fletcher, *Loyalty: An Essay on the Morality of Relationships* (New York: Oxford University Press, 1993), pp. 8–9.

4. Fletcher, pp. 33–34.

5. Ewin, pp. 410–412 (emphasis original), p. 554.

6. Ronald Duska, "Whistleblowing and Employee Loyalty," *Contemporary Issues in Business Ethics*, 2nd ed., ed. Joseph R. Des Jardins and John J. McCall (Belmont, Calif.: Wadsworth, 1990); reprinted in *Business Ethics: A Philosophical Reader*, ed. Thomas I. White (New York: Macmillan, 1993), p. 554.

7. *The Economist* contends that for prudential reasons employees should avoid loyalty to a corporation. Given the shrinking life expectancy of a Fortune 500 company and downsizing, employees might find a better focus than companies for their feelings of loyalty. "Two Cheers for Loyalty," *The Economist*, 6 Jan. 1996, p. 49.

8. Duska, p. 554.

9. Robert C. Solomon, "The Corporation as Community: A Reply to Ed Hartman." *Business Ethics Quarterly* 4 (1994): 277.

10. Philip Selznick, *The Moral Commonwealth: Social Theory and the Promise of Community* (Berkeley: University of California Press, 1992), pp. 358–359 (emphasis original).

11. Alan Wolfe, "On Loyalty," *Wilson Quarterly* 21 (1997): 52.

## QUESTIONS

1. How is a corporation like a community? How do they differ?

2. Does a corporation always deserve my loyalty? A community? Why or why not? When and when not?

Kim Zetter | # Why We Cheat

Kim Zetter is a freelance journalist.

Dan Ariely is a people hacker. A professor of behavioral economics at Duke University and MIT as well as director of MIT's Center for Advanced Hindsight, Ariely deconstructs human behavior to find the hidden ways we deceive ourselves about the things we do and to construct better ways of resolving some of life's issues.

In his research, Ariely gave test subjects twenty math problems to solve and told them they'd be paid cash for each correct answer. The subjects were given only five minutes to do the exam, ensuring that no one would complete it. When the time was up, the control subjects were told to count their correct answers and collect their pay. The test group, however, was told to shred their exams before reporting their totals, to see if they'd fudge the number if no one could confirm their claim. Not surprisingly, many people in the latter group cheated. But they cheated by only a small amount. And the amount by which they cheated didn't change when they

From *Wired* (February 7, 2009): Reprinted with permission.

were offered more money per question. It also didn't change when they were told to pay themselves from a bowl of money.

Conventional wisdom assumes people cheat based on whether they think they'll get caught and the level of punishment they'll receive. But Ariely says other factors come into play.

WIRED: What did your tests tell you about the ways people cheat and why they do it?

DAN ARIELY: We came up with this idea of a fudge factor, which means that people have two goals: We have a goal to look at ourselves in the mirror and feel good about ourselves, and we have a goal to cheat and benefit from cheating. And we find that there's a balance between these two goals. That is, we cheat up to the level that we would find it comfortable [to still feel good about ourselves]. Now if we have this fudge factor, we thought that we should be able to increase it or shrink it [to affect the amount of cheating someone does]. So we tried to shrink it by getting people to recite the Ten Commandments before they took the test. And it turns out that it shrinks the fudge factor completely. It eliminates it. And it's not as if the people who are more religious or who remember more commandments cheat less. In fact, even when we get atheists to swear on the Bible, they don't cheat afterwards. So it's not about fear of God; it's about reminding people of their own moral standards. That was the first thing we discovered. Then we said let's try to increase the fudge factor [to make people cheat more]. So I distributed Cokes in refrigerators in the dorm, and I found out that people very quickly took these Cokes that did not belong to them. But when I distributed plates with $1 bills on them, nobody ever took the money.

WIRED: Why would someone take a Coke but not money?

DA: When you take money, you can't help but think you're stealing. When you take a pencil, for example from work, there's all kinds of stories you can tell yourself. You can say this is something everybody does. Or, if I take a pencil home, it's actually good for work because I can work more. It's the same thing with the Coke. You can say to yourself, Maybe somebody left it on purpose, or somebody took mine once so it's okay for me to take this.

We did the [math problem] experiment with tokens instead of money to see if it would change the cheating and it did. The idea was we get people one step away from money [and they cheat more]. As we deal with things that are more distant [from] money, the easier it is to cheat and not to think of yourself as a bad person. I think we're moving to a society where things are getting more and more removed from cash. Executives backdating stock options [can think] it's not cash, it's stock options.

WIRED: What are the implications of these findings?

DA: The idea is, what are the points at which we're tempted, and can we reduce the issues at the point of temptation? When we got people to contemplate on their morality, they reduced their cheating. So the issue is, how in society we can get people to contemplate morality more when it matters? I really think that people have good moral standards, but it's just the case that you don't go around all day asking yourself am I moral. And when you don't ask yourself am I moral, you can do all kinds of little things that don't seem to be engaging your moral compass.

WIRED: So it's a matter of putting a mirror in front of people. Posting rules above the copier machine, things like that.

DA: That's right. It's basically about the mirror that reminds us who we are at the point where it matters. Now I don't want to say this is the only factor that's going on. Take what happened in Enron. There was partly a social norm that was emerging there. Somebody started cheating a little bit, and then it became more and more a part of the social norm. You see somebody behaving in a bit more extreme way, and you adopt that way. If you stopped and thought about [what you were doing] it would be clear it was crazy, but at the moment you just accept that social standard. The second thing that happened at Enron is that it wasn't clear what was the right social norm to apply to this particular emerging energy market. They could basically define it anyway they wanted. And, finally, they were dealing with stuff that was really very removed from money, which allowed them to [cheat].

WIRED: What's the difference between the person who goes along with the standard and the whistleblower who says enough?

DA: It's a very good question, but I haven't done stuff with whistleblowers and I don't really know what makes them decide to stand up. My guess is that at some point they get sufficiently exposed to other forces from outside of the organization and that gets them to think differently, but I don't really know. Think about this CEO of Merrill Lynch who just apologized for refurbishing his bathroom for $1.2 million. I think that when he was in the midst of those things, if he thought about it, he would realize it is crazy. But he wasn't thinking about it, and nobody around him was thinking about it either. They wanted to see the world in a certain way and wanted to get these incredible bonuses. So the moment you're surrounded by all these people who think the same way, it's very hard to think differently.

WIRED: What are you hoping to convey to the TED audience?

DA: That people don't predict correctly what will drive our behavior and, as a consequence, we need to be more careful. What happens is you have intuitions and axioms about the world, and you assume they are perfectly correct. I think we should just start doubting our assumptions more regularly and submitting them to empirical tests. We understand cheating is bad, but we don't really understand where it's really coming from and how we can reduce it. The common theory says that all we need to do is to make sure we don't have bad apples and that the punishment is sufficiently severe. I think that's not the right approach. I think we need to realize that most people are not bad apples—we find very, very few people who really cheat in a big way—but a lot of people are cheating just by a little bit. [Bernard] Madoff's . . . cheating is substantially lower than everything else that was happening in the market. The market for cheating is unbelievably big. It's estimated by some people to be about $600 billion a year—just internal fraud and theft within companies. The market for blue-collar criminals is tiny in comparison.

## QUESTIONS

1. What does Ariely teach us about why cheating might take place at the highest levels of the corporation?

2. How does Ariely's explanation of cheating complicate the role of the whistleblower? Could whistle blowers be the best way we have of "looking at ourselves in the mirror"?

# CASES

## CASE 10.1

## The Once Successful Business Model

Sherron Watkins

Before the catastrophic collapse of Enron, the company congratulated itself for having "the one successful business model" in the world. This piece is excerpted from whistle-blower Sherron Watkins' book, *Power Failure*.

At 7:40 the next morning, Ken Lay, founder and longtime CEO of Enron, gave the formal welcome. Even though he, too, was dressed casually, his casual—pressed jeans and a crisp white button-down shirt—was still a little starchy, an ensemble from another time. He was fifty-eight, which was nearly elderly at Enron, and his audience treated him that way—respectfully, but just a little restively. Lay had been playing the gentle sage to Skilling's samurai for years; a balding, somewhat jowly man of average build, he spoke with a sharp midwestern twang and lately had sometimes seemed too folksy for the sleek, sharklike company he had created. Maybe he knew that, because for the last few months Lay had been orchestrating his exit. Clinton was leaving the White House, and Lay's enormous, long-term investment in the Bush family was about to pay off again. (Lay didn't wonder, in November 2000, who really won the presidential election. He was an indefatigable optimist, and a major donor to the Republican party.)

Lay had succeeded beyond his wildest dreams. He was worshiped in Houston both as a political kingmaker and for his philanthropy. His was the classic American success story: He had triumphed over childhood poverty, a bad stutter, an antiquated, regulated business, and enough financial setbacks

to kill most companies. And now, in late middle age, he was ready to let go. He had already anointed Skilling as his successor. If he didn't join the Bush administration, maybe he would run for mayor of Houston. Whatever he did, it would be big. But on this particular morning Lay was focused solely on Enron. "Our future has never looked rosier," he told his many heirs. Enron was in businesses today it had not been in just five years earlier; he hoped that in ten years Enron would find more new business worlds to invent and dominate. At Enron it was always the future that mattered: inventing it, shaping it, ruling it.

The ashen, hung-over executives applauded politely. They'd heard this before.

And so it went for the next several hours. The editor of the hip *Red Herring* magazine extolled the glories of the Internet, followed by a pep talk from Gary Hamel, a stylishly shabby Harvard professor and the author of the best-selling *Leading the Revolution*, in which he championed the corporate innovators of the late nineties, especially Enron. "It pays to hire the best," Hamel said of the company. "You can't build a forever restless, opportunity-seeking company unless you're willing to hire forever restless, opportunity-seeking individuals." That Hamel was also a paid adviser to Enron didn't seem to bother anyone in the crowd. He was a Harvard professor, after all, and behavior that would once have been characterized as a conflict of interest was, by the late nineties, simply viewed as synergistic.

Finally, Skilling took the podium, and the enthusiasm in the room contracted noticeably. Skilling,

From Mimi Swartz, with Sherron Watkins, *Power Failure* (New York: Doubleday, 2003).

like Lay, was small in stature. (In fact, almost everyone who got ahead at Enron was short.) But where Lay was soft and self-assuredly self-deprecating—almost Sunday schoolish—Skilling was sharp and cool. He was dressed casually, almost carelessly, like his troops, and he wore his hair combed off his face in the style of Hollywood producers and Wall Street financiers. He was assiduously fit; his eyes were ice blue and his gaze was steady, and he spoke in clipped, flat, supremely confident tones. Everyone at Enron knew that Jeff was twice as smart as they were—twice as smart as they could ever hope to be—and they hung on every word. It was Skilling who had made the revenues grow from $4 billion to more than $60 billion, an increase of nearly 2,000 percent. It was Skilling who had made the stock price ascend to the heavens. So it was Skilling who made Enron's troops frantic to live in fast-forward mode, who made them anxious to prove that they could deliver any concept he could dream up, who made them desperate to tag along on his extreme adventures—rock climbing, bungee jumping—around the globe. Because if Jeff Skilling thought you "got it," you really did.

Skilling's appearance onstage signaled the arrival of an annual event: his stock-price prediction. In years past he had been on the money—Enron had gone from $40 to $60 a share in 1998, and soared to $80 in 1999. Now he stood before his faithful and bowed his head, as if he had to think about what he had to say. When he looked at the crowd again, he was beaming. Enron stock, he told them, would hit $126 a share in 2001. There was just a second of stunned silence before the crowd burst into applause. No one quite knew how the stock was going to increase another 30 percent, even with the success of Broadband, which was not exactly a sure thing. Neither was Enron Energy Services, the company's foray into the management of power needs for large corporations. And a few people in the crowd had heard of problems in Fastow's finance group. But no one was that worried. They reminded themselves that they worked for Enron and, no matter what, Jeff would find a way. Because he always did.

There was, in fact, only one cautionary note sounded that morning. Skilling introduced the crowd to Tom Peters, the author of the best-selling business bible *In Search of Excellence*. Before abandoning the stage to Peters, Skilling wanted to boost morale a little higher. Enron, he reminded the crowd, had found the one successful business model that could be applied to any market.

Peters strode to the stage, abandoned his prepared speech, and started pacing back and forth. He was even sweating slightly, which made some in the audience think he might be another loser. "That's the scariest thing I've ever heard," Peters said to Skilling, his former colleague at McKinsey. What, exactly, had Enron done that was so novel? he asked. What accounted for such self-congratulation? The company had taken a model and replicated it in other fields—Enron had created markets where none had existed before, in gas, in power, probably in telecom. But everyone knew that now. Other businesses were already copying Enron, and the novelty would soon wear off. And then where would Enron be? Where were the company's new new ideas? "An excess of self-confidence kills companies," Peters warned.

In the audience, Sherron Watkins scribbled notes furiously on a pad, listing Peters' signs of a company in trouble:

1. Denial of problems.
2. Nostalgia.
3. Arrogance.

Listening, Skilling and Lay sat frozen in their seats, smiles locked on their faces. When Peters stopped speaking, Skilling jumped up to the dais, thanked him, and repeated himself: *Remember*, he said, *Enron had found the one successful business model that could be applied to any market.*

## QUESTIONS

1. Should Watkins have spoken up earlier? How does a whistle-blower know when to whistle?
2. If you could go back in time and advise Enron, what would you tell them?

# CASE 10.2
## Would You Blow the Whistle on Yourself?
Pat L. Burr

In the course of teaching business classes through the semesters, I have been the butt of a great many accusations about the unethical behavior of American entrepreneurs, the deceptive advertising of Madison Avenue silver tongues, and even the rolling back of odometers by the local used-car dealers. I have not been personally involved in any of the activity, I hasten to add, I have simply been held accountable for it. All of it. By business students.

Enough, I said one day. I have done nothing wrong. I am not a crook. I vowed to bring the issue to the surface.

I set about my plan by inviting comments from my business students . . . about the structure of the system. The real question, as I saw it, was whether our business activity is inherently unethical or whether business persons are simply a product of our social system and therefore a reflection of our collective social values. Hogwash, they said. . . .

In pressing for more substance in their arguments, each semester I posed the same question to them at least once on written exams. I asked for detailed discussion. And on those very exams, I deliberately made grading mistakes on the numerous other questions, giving my students the advantage by two to five points. In short, I gave them grades which clearly were too high.

I turned back their papers, smugly awaiting the rush of feet to my desk to point out my error and to bring their unquestionably ethical behavior to a shining apex. I was confident of my students' motives. When none of them rushed forward, I pointed out the need for them to review my grading

lest I had made a mistake on their papers. Still no comment. . . . Not one student, in my seven years of teaching, has ever come forward to point out my error in their favor. . . .

My game usually ends each semester when I nonchalantly explain my own dirty trick on the last class day, thus giving them every opportunity to come clean before final exam day. . . . "Surely, it is a hoax," they say. "For shame," I mumble under my breath, enunciating clearly so they can hear me. I had caught them. Even set the trap. They were furious.

After years of refinement of my game of "values clarification," I have arrived at several conclusions:

1. It is . . . too late to reach business students with ethics courses.
2. One dirty trick in the hand is worth two fists of mud in the bush when the entire system is under attack.
3. Our economic system is closely tied to our social system.
4. Some of our business students, particularly those I have observed after they were exposed in my little test, would make terrific drama coaches.

## QUESTIONS

1. Would you have reported yourself? Why or why not? Should you have?

2. Do people ever blow the whistle on themselves? Is there something wrong with blowing the whistle on yourself? Is it irrational to do so? Explain.

*Business and Society Review*, 19, 1977–78.

## CASE 10.3

# Changing Jobs and Changing Loyalties

William H. Shaw and Vincent Barry

Cynthia Martinez was thrilled when she first received the job offer from David Newhoff at Crytex Systems. She had long admired Crytex, both as an industry leader and as an ideal employer, and the position the company was offering her was perfect. "It's just what I've always wanted," she told her husband, Tom, as they uncorked a bottle of champagne. But as she and Tom talked, he raised a few questions that began to trouble her.

"What about the big project you're working on at Altrue right now? It'll take three months to see that through," Tom had reminded her. "The company has a lot riding on it, and you've always said that you're the driving force behind the project. If you bolt, Altrue is going to be in a real jam."

Cynthia explained that she had mentioned the project to David Newhoff. "He said he could understand I'd like to see it through, but Crytex needs someone right now. He gave me a couple of days to think it over, but it's my big chance."

Tom looked at her thoughtfully and responded, "But Newhoff doesn't quite get it. It's not just that you'd like to see it through. It's that you'd be letting your whole project team down. They probably couldn't do it without you, at least not the way it needs to be done. Besides, Cyn, remember what you said about that guy who quit the Altrue branch in Baltimore."

"That was different," Cynthia responded. "He took an existing account with him when he went to another firm. It was like ripping Altrue off. I'm not going to rip them off, but I don't figure I owe them anything extra. It's just business. You know perfectly well that if Altrue could save some money by laying me off, the company wouldn't hesitate."

"I think you're rationalizing," Tom said. "You've done well at Altrue, and the company has always treated you fairly. Anyway, the issue is what's right for you to do, not what the company would or wouldn't do. Crytex is Altrue's big competitor. It's like you're switching sides. Besides, it's not just a matter of loyalty to the company, but to the people you work with. I know we could use the extra money, and it would be a great step for you, but still. . . ."

They continued to mull things over together, but the champagne no longer tasted quite as good. Fortunately, she and Tom never really argued about things they didn't see eye to eye on, and Tom wasn't the kind of guy who would try to tell her what she should or shouldn't do. But their conversation had started her wondering whether she really should accept that Crytex job she wanted so much.

## QUESTIONS

1. What should Cynthia do? What ideals, obligations, and effects should she take into account when making her decision?

2. Would it be unprofessional of Cynthia to drop everything and move to Crytex? Would it show a lack of integrity? Could moving abruptly to Crytex have negative career consequences for her?

3. What does loyalty to the company mean, and how important is it, morally? Under what circumstances, if any, do employees owe loyalty to their employers? When, if ever, do they owe loyalty to their coworkers?

William H. Shaw and Vincent Barry, *Moral Issues in Business*, 9th ed. (Belmont, CA: Wadsworth, 2004).

# CASE 10.4

## The Greenhouse Effect: Putting the Heat on Halliburton

Larry Margasak

The Army extended a Halliburton Co. troop support contract over the objections of a top contracting officer, even contending—and then withdrawing—a claim that U.S. forces faced an emergency if the company didn't get the extra work.

"I wrote directly on the document the weaknesses . . . so that all could clearly see," contracting official Bunnatine Greenhouse wrote a top general this month in questioning the extended troop support contract in the Balkans.

Halliburton was formerly headed by Vice President Dick Cheney.

Greenhouse has had problems with the $2 billion (€1.6 billion) contract at least since January 2002, when she wrote, "There is little or no incentive for the contractor to reduce or keep cost down."

The contracting officer has gone public with allegations of favoritism toward the company once headed by Vice President Dick Cheney. . . .

Greenhouse complained, in writing, Oct. 5 to Lt. Gen. Carl Strock, commander of the Army Corps of Engineers, that the Corps should not have halted plans to let companies compete for a successor Balkans contract. She is the Corps' top contracting officer.

Corps officials initially justified stopping the bidding by concluding that a "compelling emergency" would exist if Halliburton's work were to be interrupted.

When Greenhouse challenged the justification and sought an explanation of the emergency, however, Corps officials changed their reasoning. The new explanation was that Halliburton subsidiary KBR was the "one and only" company that could do the job.

Greenhouse wrote Strock that "the truth should be clearly explained" about the reason for halting competition.

She not only complained there was no explanation of what drove officials to cite an emergency, but, referring to the second justification, added: "It is not reasonable to believe that only one source responded to the solicitation."

Greenhouse, who has said she was frozen out of decisions on Halliburton, went public last weekend with allegations that Army officials showed favoritism to the company.

The FBI has asked Greenhouse's lawyers for an interview with her. The bureau has launched a criminal investigation of Halliburton's no-bid work.

The Associated Press has obtained dozens of documents that Greenhouse intends to provide to investigators.

The Balkans contract was to have ended May 27 but has been extended through next April.

The extension was so politically sensitive that Corps official, William Ryals, sent a memo to Corp headquarters in July seeking high-level approval.

"The reason for sending it to (headquarters) for approval is because this is so controversial in regard to this firm," the memo said. "If it had been any other firm, we would have done this and moved forward without any further consideration. Given that the firm is KBRS (the Halliburton subsidiary) and that we are in an election year and coming up to the peak in the election season soon, I sent to (headquarters) for concurrence."

Halliburton spokeswoman Wendy Hall said "This is very old information. The issue mentioned about the Balkans was fully dealt with and resolved several years ago, and since then KBR has received high marks from the Army on our Balkans Support Contract."

In a letter to Corps employees on Friday, Strock said the Army is investigating Greenhouse's allegations and therefore would not respond to the allegations "to ensure that a fair investigation can proceed."

The Army has cited severe problems with Halliburton's work in the Balkans, many documented in the Jan. 4, 2002, report by Greenhouse, who reviewed findings of investigators known as a "tiger" team.

"The general feeling in the theater is that the contractor is 'out of control,'" she wrote.

Greenhouse said it appeared the Halliburton subsidiary "makes the decisions of what is constructed, purchased or provided and it appears that oftentimes the products and services delivered reflect gold-plating since the contractor proudly touts that they provide the very, very best."

Greenhouse said Army contracting officials must work as a team because "divided—the contractor will 'eat our lunch.'"

## QUESTIONS

1. Should no-bid contracts ever be allowed? What might be a good argument in favor of no-bid contracts?

2. Do you think a problem arises when former members of company boards acquire a great deal of political power (such as becoming vice president or president)? What is presently done to control this? What more should be done?

# CASE 10.5

# Whistleblowing at the Phone Company

Joseph R. Desjardins and John J. McCall

Michael J., an employee of the phone company, recognizes that he has divided loyalties. The company has treated him well and, despite some minor disagreements, he gets along quite well with upper management and his own department. However, the phone company is a public utility, regulated for the public interest by the state's Public Utility Commission (PUC). As such, Michael J. recognizes that his firm owes a loyalty to citizens that goes beyond the simple responsibility that other firms owe to their consumers.

Once a year, as part of a major fund-raising drive for a local charity, the phone company encourages its employees to donate their personal time and money to this charity. This year, however, Michael J. discovers that a significant amount of company resources are being used to support the charity. The company is printing posters and sending out mail at its own expense and is using employees on company time to

promote the fund-raiser. When Michael J. brought this to the attention of his manager, the whole incident was dismissed as trivial. After all, the resources were going to charity.

After some consideration, Michael J. judged that these charitable efforts were betraying the public trust. The public, and not private individuals acting as their agents, ought to decide for themselves when to contribute to charity. As a result, he notified the PUC of this misallocation of funds. Knowing that records of calls from his desk could easily be traced, Michael J. made the calls from pay phones and from his house.

As required by law, the PUC investigated the charges. Although the facts were as Michael J. reported, the PUC judged that the misallocation was not substantial enough to constitute a violation of the public trust. However, executives of the phone company were less willing to dismiss the incident.

From Joseph R. Desjardins and John J. McCall, *Contemporary Issues in Business Ethics*, 2nd ed. (Belmont, CA: Wadsworth, 1990).

They were upset at what they judged to be serious disloyalty among their employees.

Although they suspected that Michael J. was the whistleblower, there was no proof that he was. A check of his office phone records showed no calls placed to the PUC. However, since this was the phone company, it was easy enough to trace calls made from Michael J.'s home and cross-check these against calls made to and from the PUC's offices. They did so, confirmed their suspicions, and disciplined Michael J.

## QUESTIONS

1. Do employees of public utilities have special responsibilities to protect the public interest? Why or why not? Should these responsibilities be extended to employees of some private firms, for example, large defense contractors?

2. Did the phone company do anything unethical in checking its own records to trace Michael J.'s phone calls? Should the PUC investigate further?

3. Would your opinion of this case change if large sums of money or something other than a charity was involved?

# CHAPTER QUESTIONS

1. When should you blow the whistle?

2. How is loyalty created? What ethical demands are created by loyalty? Does loyalty ever entirely outweigh other ethical concerns? Should it?

# 11

# Think Local, Act Global

## *International Business*

## Introduction

You have just been transferred to the international division of your company. Your new job requires you to work with company operations all over the world. Navigating various cultural customs can be tricky, but the most difficult problems you will face concern navigating different ethical norms of behavior. Sometimes it is not easy to distinguish between customs that you should follow to be polite and respectful and practices that are morally unacceptable, regardless of what appears to be common practice in the culture. As soon as you leave your home country, you find yourself grappling with variations on a major philosophical question: Are ethical principles universal, or does every culture have its own ethics? In a practical sense, when you are in Rome, should you do what the Romans do, even if it is morally repugnant? Or should you follow what you take to be the moral path, even if it makes you unpopular and is bad for your business? Sometimes, perhaps, we can be mistaken about what is really the moral path. You may not understand the situation because it is complex in ways that you have never had to deal with. In some cases, you may discover that your stereotype about the local culture and what is right in it is wrong. A Kenyan friend told me that paying small bribes is a part of everyday life in Kenya. This is not because Kenyans think bribery is acceptable, but because they cannot do anything about it. When you are in another culture, it is important to find out what people in that culture think life requires as they actually live it. It is not enough for you to imagine an idealized version of their life as it might be with a major change in their institutions. There is what is morally necessary. There is also what is morally preferable. But there is also what is morally possible, and confusing them when you are in a position of power or influence can do a lot of people a lot of harm.

At the same time, it is a good idea for you and your organization to have a clear picture of your own values and ethical standards of behavior *before* you go to do business in another country. While your company may have its rules and regulations, there is always an open question whether these rules and regulations will make sense elsewhere. (Indeed, it may be a matter of ongoing debate whether or not some of them make sense at home.) Furthermore, you also have to have your own sense of what you personally will and will not do, anywhere, as a person and as a professional. You may be able to justify paying "facilitating payments" to an official abroad, on the grounds that everyone in the culture expects it, but you should resolve ahead of time that you are unwilling to engage in the local customs of hiring children to do dangerous work, of denigrating women on the job, of physically abusing employees who fail to make their quotas, and of lying to the home office about how the work is going or to officials about the nature of the product or the services you provide. Making such decisions on the spot may be much more difficult if it is not backed up by prior understanding or, preferably, by company policy as well.

Navigating a business in a foreign culture can be confusing. How do you balance respect for other cultures with what you believe is morally right? For example, if companies in another country pay female employees less than men to do the same work, should you do the same? Businesses and individuals in some overseas countries are tempted to slip into the lax standards of health, safety, and human rights. In the name of "staying competitive," are you justified in doing the same? It isn't always easy to act on your own or to enforce your company's values in another place where the customs are going against you because an essential part of business is about gaining favor and building relationships. So the practical question is, how can you build a relationship by adhering to local expectations and preferences and, at the same time, stay true to your own and your company's values? More than anything, you will need the moral imagination to comprehend both the values of the local culture and your own in order to figure out how best to act both ethically and without seeming disrespectful, arrogant, unfriendly, or uncooperative.

Globalization intertwines the economic fates of nations and tends to promote shared values on the basis of shared business interests, but it also accentuates real differences in cultural values. People from other countries often think of Americans as ethical imperialists who try to impose their values on the world. Much worse, they tend to think of us as hypocrites who espouse values like justice, liberty, and equality but do not actually act in ways that promote these values in other countries. But global business is, ethically, a double-edged sword. On the one hand, multinational corporations can and do exploit people in poorer countries and market products and values that are undesirable, undermining whatever respect those people may have had for "our values" and our way of life. On the other hand, multinationals can be a positive force for improving the welfare and opportunities of people in other countries and prove by doing what those lofty values have promised.

The first article in this chapter, by Anthony Kwame Appiah, argues that the problem with the view that every culture has its own ethical values is that very few cultures are homogeneous. He says most cultures have been "contaminated" by other cultures. People choose what they want to adopt from other cultures and hold on to what they think is better in their own culture. The next article puts you on the street and doing business in a foreign culture. Thomas Donaldson's article, "Values in Tension: Ethics Away from Home," looks at some of the practical problems that you may encounter in a foreign environment. He offers some excellent advice on how to behave ethically in places that have different value systems.

Florian Wettstein addresses the question of whether companies have a duty to protect human rights in a foreign country. He argues that when a company simply goes about its business in countries where there are human rights violations, they become complicit in those violations. According to Wettstein, the nature of wrongdoing in international business is changing. It used to be that all a business had to do was behave ethically while doing business. Wettstein argues that in today's world, businesses can operate ethically but behave unethically by being silent about human rights violations in the culture around them.

In John T. Noonan's take on the history of bribes, we see that bribery is not a cultural quirk, because it has been considered wrong for a very long time in most parts of the world. People often think that because bribery is a ubiquitous practice, it is an ethically acceptable practice. This is rarely true. Often bribery seems to be acceptable because no one is able to, or no one wants to, do anything about it. The final article helps us better understand some of the Confucian values that underpin the way that some business people behave in China and other Asian cultures. The Confucian emphasis on relationships and family loyalty can be especially difficult for Westerners who believe that nepotism is wrong and that contracts and laws should govern business—not who you know. The conflict between these two ethical systems is not about which one is right or wrong. It is about how to do business ethically in countries where their ethical systems differ from your own.

The cases in this chapter are about how to treat people, how to make ethical decisions in international business, and the responsibilities of multinationals for what goes on the in the places in which they operate. The "Oil Rig" raises questions about respect for persons, equality, and employees' rights when working in developing countries. "Foreign Assignment" is a personal case about how you should act and what kind of treatment you should tolerate in another country. In the "PureDrug" case, you will think about a company's obligations when someone from another country wants to buy a product that is considered unsafe in your own country. "IBM's Business with Hitler" describes how IBM knowingly sold the Nazis machines that would help them keep the records that were used to carry out the holocaust. It is a historical case that raises a number of questions about doing business today with countries that kill or harm their citizens, support terrorism, or are a threat to the rest of the world. In other words, to what extent does the morality of your customer and your customer's country matter when doing business? These are serious questions in a world where doing business in another country may require companies to be responsible for more than just their business.

Supply chains raise another set of ethical problems for international business. Much has already been written about sweatshops. In the Foxconn case, employees at the factory are committing suicide at an alarming rate. Foxconn produces, among other things, iPhones for Apple. To what extent is Apple responsible for the conditions that led to these suicides? How responsible are companies for the way that firms in their supply chain operate? The last case is another personal one. A foreign employee of a multinational company is assigned to his home country. Instead of living in safe comfortable housing, the employee lives in a ghetto and spends his housing allowance on his poor family members who live there. This case illustrates the problems that can come from the strong pull of family loyalty in some cultures.

Ultimately these readings intend to help you ponder how you would navigate value conflicts in other cultures and where you would draw the line when the norms of a foreign culture violate the norms of your value system. In the end, all the readings and cases in this chapter intend to help you reflect on what values and standards you want to live and work by, no matter where you are in the world. It helps to be clear on this point before you take a foreign assignment or a job with a multinational firm because you will be miserable working with an organization that does not allow you to behave ethically, especially in regard to respecting and protecting human rights. Furthermore, working for such an employer may be harmful to your moral and physical health.

| Anthony Kwame Appiah | Global Villages |

Anthony Kwame Appiah is Lawrence J. Rockefeller University Professor of Philosophy at Princeton University.

People who complain about the homogeneity produced by globalization often fail to notice that globalization is, equally, a threat to homogeneity. You can see this as clearly in Kumasi as anywhere. The capital of Asante is accessible to you, whoever you are—emotionally, intellectually, and, of course, physically. It is integrated into the global markets. None of this makes it Western, or American, or British. It is still Kumasi. What it isn't, just because it's a city, is homogeneous. English, German, Chinese, Syrian, Lebanese, Burkinabe, Ivorian, Nigerian, Indian: I can find you families of each description. I can find you Asante people, whose ancestors have lived in this town for centuries, but also Hausa households that have been around for centuries, too. There are people there from all the regions, speaking all the scores of languages of Ghana as well. And while people in Kumasi come from a wider variety of places than they did a hundred or two hundred years ago, even then there were already people from all over the place coming and going. I don't know who was the first Asante to make the pilgrimage to Mecca, but his trip would have followed trade routes that are far older than the kingdom. Gold, salt, kola nuts, and, alas, slaves have connected my hometown to the world for a very long time. And trade

means travelers. If by globalization you have in mind something new and recent, the ethnic eclecticism of Kumasi is not the result of it.

But if you go outside Kumasi, only a little way—twenty miles, say, in the right direction—and if you drive off the main road down one of the many potholed side roads of red laterite, you can arrive pretty soon in villages that are fairly homogeneous. The people have mostly been to Kumasi and seen the big, polyglot, diverse world of the city. Here, though, where they live, there is one everyday language (aside from the English in the government schools), a few Asante families, and an agrarian way of life that is based on some old crops, like yam, and some new ones, like cocoa, which arrived in the late nineteenth century as a commercial product for export. They may or may not have electricity (this close to Kumasi, they probably do). When people talk of the homogeneity produced by globalization, what they are talking about is this: the villagers will have radios; you will be able to get a discussion going about the World Cup in soccer, Muhammad Ali, Mike Tyson, and hip-hop; and you will probably be able to find a bottle of Guinness or Coca-Cola (as well as Star or Club, Ghana's own delicious lagers). Then again, the language on the radio won't be a world language, the soccer teams they know best will be Ghanaian, and what can you tell about someone's soul from the fact that she drinks Coca-Cola? These villages are connected with more places than they were a couple of centuries ago. Their homogeneity, though, is still the local kind.

In the era of globalization—in Asante as in New Jersey—people make pockets of homogeneity. Are all these pockets of homogeneity less distinctive than they were a century ago? Well, yes, but mostly in good ways. More of them have access to medicines that work. More of them have access to clean drinking water. More of them have schools. Where, as is still too common, they don't have these things, this is not something to celebrate but to deplore. And whatever loss of difference there has been, they are constantly inventing new forms of difference: new hairstyles, new slang, even, from time to time, new religions. No one could say that the world's villages are—or are about to become—anything like the same.

So why do people in these places sometimes feel that their identity is threatened? Because the world, their world, is changing, and some of them don't like it. The pull of the global economy—witness those cocoa trees whose chocolate is eaten all around the world—created some of the life they now live. If the economy changes—if cocoa prices collapse again as they did in the early 1990s—they may have to find new crops or new forms of livelihood. That is unsettling for some people (just as it is exciting for others). Missionaries came a while ago, so many of these villagers will be Christian, even if they also have kept some of the rites from earlier days. But new Pentecostal messengers are challenging the churches they know and condemning the old rites as idolatrous. Again, some like it; some don't.

Above all, relationships are changing. When my father was young, a man in a village would farm some land that a chief had granted him, and his *abusua*, his matriclan, (including his younger brothers) would work it with him. If extra hands were needed in the harvest season, he would pay the migrant workers who came from the north. When a new house needed building, he would organize it. He would also make sure his dependents were fed and clothed, the children educated, marriages and funerals arranged and paid for. He could expect to pass the farm and the responsibilities eventually to one of his nephews.

Nowadays, everything has changed. Cocoa prices have not kept pace with the cost of living. Gas prices have made the transportation of the crop more expensive. And there are new possibilities for the young in the towns, in other parts of the country, and in other parts of the world. Once, perhaps, you could have commanded your nephews and nieces to stay. Now they have the right to leave; in any case, you may not make enough to feed and clothe and educate them all. So the time of the successful farming family has gone; and those who were settled in that way of life are as sad to see it go as some of the American family farmers whose lands are being accumulated by giant agribusinesses. We can sympathize with them. But we cannot force their children to stay in the name of protecting their authentic culture; and we cannot afford to subsidize indefinitely thousands of distinct islands of homogeneity that no longer make economic sense.

Nor should we want to. Cosmopolitans think human variety matters because people are entitled to the options they need to shape their lives in partnership with others. What John Stuart Mill said more than a century ago in *On Liberty* about diversity within a society serves just as well as an argument for variety across the globe:

> If it were only that people have diversities of taste, that is reason enough for not attempting to shape them all after one model. But different persons also require different conditions for their spiritual development; and can no more exist healthily in the same moral, than all the variety of plants can exist in the same physical, atmosphere and climate. The same things which are helps to one person towards the cultivation of his higher nature, are hindrances to another. . . . Unless there is a corresponding diversity in their modes of life, they neither obtain their fair share of happiness, nor grow up to the mental, moral, and aesthetic stature of which their nature is capable.

If we want to preserve a wide range of human conditions because it allows free people the best chance to make their own lives, there is no place for the enforcement of diversity by trapping people within a kind of difference they long to escape. There simply is no decent way to sustain those communities of difference that will not survive without the free allegiance of their members.

## DON'T EVER CHANGE

Even if you grant that people shouldn't be forced into sustaining authentic cultural practices, you might suppose that a cosmopolitan should side with those who are busy around the world "preserving culture" and resisting "cultural imperialism." But behind these slogans you often find some curious assumptions. Take "preserving culture." It's one thing to provide people with help to sustain arts they want to sustain. I am all for festivals of Welsh bards in Llandudno funded by the Welsh Arts Council, if there are people who want to recite and people who care to listen. I am delighted with the Ghana National Cultural Center in Kumasi, where you can go and learn traditional Akan dancing and drumming, especially since its classes are spirited and overflowing. Restore the deteriorating film stock of early Hollywood movies; continue the preservation of Old Norse and early Chinese and Ethiopian manuscripts; record, transcribe, and analyze the oral narratives of Malay and Maasai and Maori: all these are a valuable part of our human heritage. But preserving *culture*—in the sense of cultural artifacts, broadly conceived—is different from preserving *cultures*. And the preservers of cultures are busy trying to ensure that the Huli of Papua New Guinea or, for that matter, Sikhs in Toronto or Hmong in New Orleans keep their "authentic" ways. What makes a cultural expression authentic, though? Are we to stop the importation of baseball caps into Vietnam, so that the Zao will continue with their colorful red headdresses? Why not ask the Zao? Shouldn't the choice be theirs?

"They *have* no real choice," the cultural preservationists may say. "We have dumped cheap Western clothes into their markets; and they can no longer afford the silk they used to wear. If they had what they really wanted, they'd still be dressed

traditionally." Notice that this is no longer an argument about authenticity. The claim is that they can't afford to do something that they'd really like to do, something that is expressive of an identity they care about and want to sustain. This is a genuine problem, one that afflicts people in many communities: they're too poor to live the life they want to lead. If that's true, it's an argument for trying to see whether we can help them get richer. But if they do get richer and they still run around in T-shirts, so much the worse, I say, for authenticity.

Not that this is likely to be a problem in the real world. People who can afford it mostly *like* to put on traditional garb from time to time. American boys wear tuxedos to proms. I was best man once at a Scottish wedding. The bridegroom wore a kilt, of course. (I wore a *kɛnte* cloth. Andrew Oransay, who piped us up the aisle, whispered in my ear at one point, "Here we all are then, in our tribal gear.") In Kumasi, people who can afford them, love to put on their *kɛnte* cloths, especially the most "traditional" ones, woven in colorful silk strips in the town of Bonwire, as they have been for a couple of centuries. (The prices have risen in part because demand outside Asante has risen. A fine *kɛnte* for a man now costs more than the average Ghanaian earns in a year. Is that bad? Not for the people of Bonwire.) But trying to find some primordially authentic culture can be like peeling an onion. The textiles most people think of as traditional West African cloths are known as java prints, and arrived with the Javanese batiks sold, and often milled by, the Dutch. The traditional garb of Herero women derives from the attire of nineteenth-century German missionaries, though it's still unmistakably Herero, not least because the fabrics they use have a distinctly un-Lutheran range of colors. And so with our *kɛnte* cloth: the silk was always imported, traded by Europeans, produced in Asia. This tradition was once an innovation. Should we reject *it* for that reason as untraditional? How far back must one go? Should we condemn the young men and women of the University of Science and Technology, a few miles outside Kumasi, who wear European-style gowns for graduation, lined with *kɛnte* strips (as they do, now, at Howard and Morehouse, too). Cultures are made of continuities *and* changes, and the identity of a society can survive through these changes, just as each individual survives the alterations of Jacques's "seven ages of man."

## THE TROUBLE WITH "CULTURAL IMPERALISM"

Cultural preservationists often make their case by invoking the evil of "cultural imperialism." And its victims aren't necessarily the formerly colonized "natives." In fact, the French have a penchant for talking of "cultural imperialism" to make the point that French people like to watch American movies and visit English-language sites on the Internet. (*Évidemment*, the American taste for French movies is something to be encouraged.) This is surely very odd. No army, no threat of sanctions, no political saber rattling, imposes Hollywood on the French.

There is a genuine issue here, I think, but it is not imperialism. France's movie industry requires government subsidy. Part of the reason, no doubt, is just that Americans have the advantage of speaking a language with many more speakers than France (though this can't be the whole explanation, since the British film industry seems to require subsidy, too). Still, whatever the reason, the French would like to have a significant number of films rooted deeply in French life, which they watch alongside all those American movies. Since the resulting films are often wonderful, in subsidizing them for themselves, they have also enriched the treasury of cosmopolitan cultural experience. So far, I think, so good.

What would justify genuine concern would be an attempt by the United States through the World Trade Organization, say, to have these culturally motivated subsidies banned. Even in the United States, most of us believe it is perfectly proper to subsidize programs on public television. We grant tax-exempt status to our opera and ballet companies; cities and states subsidize sports stadiums. It is an empirical question, not one to be settled by appeal to a free-market ideology, how much of the public culture the citizens of a democratic nation want can be produced solely by the market.

But to concede this much is not to accept what the theorists of cultural imperialism want. In broad

strokes, their underlying picture is this. There is a world system of capitalism. It has a center and a periphery. At the center—in Europe and the United States—is a set of multinational corporations. Some of these are in the media business. The products they sell around the world promote the interests of capitalism in general. They encourage consumption not just of films, television, and magazines but of the other non-media products of multinational capitalism. Herbert Schiller, a leading critic of "media/cultural imperialism" has claimed that it is "the imagery and cultural perspectives of the ruling sector in the center that shape and structure consciousness throughout the system at large."

People who believe this story have been taking the pitches of magazine and television company executives selling advertising space for a description of reality. The evidence doesn't bear it out. As it happens, researchers actually went out into the world and explored the responses to the hit television series *Dallas* in Holland and among Israeli Arabs, Moroccan Jewish immigrants, kibbutzniks, and new Russian immigrants to Israel. They have examined the actual content of the television media—whose penetration of everyday life far exceeds that of film—in Australia, Brazil, Canada, India, and Mexico. They have looked at how American popular culture was taken up by the artists of Sophiatown, in South Africa. They have discussed *Days of Our Lives* and the *The Bold and the Beautiful* with Zulu college students from traditional backgrounds.

And they have found two things, which you might already have guessed. The first is that, if there is a local product—as there is in France, but also in Australia, Brazil, Canada, India, Mexico, and South Africa—many people prefer it, especially when it comes to television. For more than a decade in Ghana, the one program you could discuss with almost anyone was a local soap opera in Twi called *Osofo Dadzie*, a lighthearted program with a serious message, each episode, about the problems of contemporary everyday life. We know, do we not, how the Mexicans love their *telenovelas?* (Indeed, people know it even in Ghana, where they are shown in crudely dubbed English versions, too.) The academic research confirms that people

131

tend to prefer television programming that's close to their own culture. (The Hollywood blockbuster has a special status around the world; but here, as American movie critics regularly complain, the nature of the product—heavy on the action sequences, light on clever badinage—is partly determined by what works in Bangkok and Berlin. From the point of view of the cultural-imperialism theorists, this is a case in which the empire has struck back.)

The second observation that the research supports is that how people respond to these American products depends on their existing cultural context. When the media scholar Larry Strelitz spoke to those students from KwaZulu-Natal, he found that they were anything but passive vessels. One of them, Sipho, reported both that he was a "very, very strong Zulu man" and that he had drawn lessons from watching the American soap opera *Days of Our Lives*—"especially relationship-wise." It fortified his view that "if a guy can tell a woman that he loves her she should be able to do the same." What's more, after watching the show, Sipho "realized that I should be allowed to speak to my father. He should be my friend rather than just my father. . . ." One doubts that that was the intended message of multinational capitalism's ruling sector.

But Sipho's response also confirmed what has been discovered over and over again. Cultural consumers are not dupes. They can resist. So he also said,

> In terms of our culture, a girl is expected to enter into relationships when she is about 20. In the Western culture, the girl can be exposed to a relationship as early as 15 or 16. That one we shouldn't adopt in our culture. Another thing we shouldn't adopt from the Western culture has to do with the way they treat elderly people. I wouldn't like my family to be sent into an old-age home.

The "old-age homes" in American soap operas may be safe places, full of kindly people. That doesn't sell the idea to Sipho. Dutch viewers of *Dallas* saw not the pleasures of conspicuous consumption among the super-rich—the message that theorists of "cultural imperialism" find in every episode— but a reminder that money and power don't protect you from tragedy. Israeli Arabs saw a program that confirmed that women abused by their husbands should return to their fathers. Mexican *telenovelas* remind Ghanaian women that, where sex is at issue, men are not to be trusted. If the *telenovelas* tried to tell them otherwise, they wouldn't believe it.

Talk of cultural imperialism structuring the consciousnesses of those in the periphery treats Sipho and people like him as tabulae rasae on which global capitalism's moving finger writes its message, leaving behind another homogenized consumer as it moves on. It is deeply condescending. And it isn't true.

## IN PRAISE OF CONTAMINATION

Behind much of the grumbling about the cultural effects of globalization is an image of how the world used to be—an image that is both unrealistic and unappealing. Our guide to what is wrong here might as well be another African. Publius Terentius Afer, whom we know as Terence, was born a slave in Carthage in North Africa, and taken to Rome in the late second century AD. Before long, his plays were widely admired among the city's literary elite; witty, elegant works that are, with Plautus's earlier, less cultivated works, essentially all we have of Roman comedy. Terence's own mode of writing—his free incorporation of earlier Greek plays into a single Latin drama—was known to Roman littérateurs as "*contamination*." It's a suggestive term. When people speak for an ideal of cultural purity, sustaining the authentic culture of the Asante or the American family farm, I find myself drawn to contamination as the name for a counter-ideal. Terence had a notably firm grasp on the range of human variety: "So many men, so many opinions" was an observation of his. And it's in his comedy *The Self-Tormentor* that you'll find what has proved something like the golden rule of cosmopolitanism: *Homo sum: humani nil a me alienum puto.* "I am human: nothing human is alien to me." The context is illuminating. The play's main character, a busybody farmer named Chremes, is told by his overworked neighbor to mind his own affairs; the *homo sum* credo is his breezy rejoinder. It isn't meant to be an ordinance from on high; it's just the case for gossip.

Then again, gossip—the fascination people have for the small doings of *other* people—shares a taproot with literature. Certainly the ideal of contamination has no more eloquent exponent than Salman Rushdie, who has insisted that the novel that occasioned his fatwa "celebrates hybridity, impurity, intermingling, the transformation that comes of new and unexpected combinations of human beings, cultures, ideas, politics, movies, songs. It rejoices in mongrelization and fears the absolutism of the Pure. Mélange, hotchpotch, a bit of this and a bit of that is how newness enters the world. It is the great possibility that mass migration gives the world, and I have tried to embrace it."[6] But it didn't take modern mass migration to create this great possibility. The early Cynics and Stoics took their contamination from the places they were born to the Greek cities where they taught. Many were strangers in those places; cosmopolitanism was invented by contaminators whose migrations were solitary. And the migrations that have contaminated the larger world were not all modern. Alexander's empire molded both the states and the sculpture of Egypt and North India; first the Mongols then the Mughals shaped great swaths of Asia; the Bantu migrations populated half the African continent. Islamic states stretch from Morocco to Indonesia; Christianity reached Africa, Europe, and Asia within a few centuries of the death of Jesus of Nazareth; Buddhism long ago migrated from India into much of East and Southeast Asia. Jews and people whose ancestors came from many parts of China have long lived in vast diasporas. The traders of the Silk Road changed the style of elite dress in Italy; someone brought Chinese pottery for burial in fifteenth-century Swahili graves. I have heard it said that the bagpipes started out in Egypt and came to Scotland with the Roman infantry. None of this is modern.

No doubt, there can be an easy and spurious utopianism of "mixture," as there is of "purity." And yet the larger human truth is on the side of Terence's contamination. We do not need, have never needed, settled community, a homogeneous system of values, in order to have a home. Cultural purity is an oxymoron. The odds are that, culturally speaking, you already live a cosmopolitan life, enriched by literature, art, and film that come from many places, and that contains influences from many more. And the marks of cosmopolitanism in that Asante village—soccer, Muhammad Ali, hip-hop—entered their lives, as they entered yours, not as work but as pleasure. There are some Western products and vendors that appeal to people in the rest of the world *because* they're seen as Western, as modern: McDonald's, Levis. But even here, cultural significance isn't just something that corporate headquarters gets to decree. People wear Levis on every continent. In some places they are informal wear; in others they're dressy. You can get Coca-Cola on every continent, too. In Kumasi you will get it at funerals. Not, in my experience, in the West of England, where hot milky Indian tea is favored. The point is that people in each place make their own uses even of the most famous global commodities.

A tenable cosmopolitanism tempers a respect for difference with a respect for actual human beings—and with a sentiment best captured in the credo, once comic, now commonplace, penned by that former slave from North Africa. Few remember what Chremes says next, but it's as important as the sentence everyone quotes: "Either I want to find out for myself or I want to advise you: think what you like. If you're right, I'll do what you do. If you're wrong, I'll set you straight."

## QUESTIONS

1. What assumptions should a business make about the ethical values of people in a particular culture? What is the problem with the idea "When in Rome, do as the Romans do"?

2. What is cultural imperialism? What does Appaiah say is the problem with cultural imperialism? Why does he like about cultural contamination?

3. Should public culture (e.g., movies, art, etc.) be subsidized by the government or left in the hands of private enterprise?

To: You
From: The Philosopher
Subject: "Isaiah Berlin on Values"

I hear that you will be traveling all over the world in your new job. The thing I like best about traveling is comparing home to what is better and worse in other countries. Americans often think that they have the best values and people in other places have got it all wrong, but as the philosopher Isaiah Berlin argues, disagreements about values are not always about who is right and who is wrong. Berlin doesn't think it is possible or desirable for everyone to agree on the same values. He says, "These collisions of values are of the essence of what they are and what we are." But, "We are doomed to choose, and every choice may entail an irreparable loss." Berlin writes:

> What is clear is that values can clash—that is why civilizations are incompatible. They can be incompatible between cultures, or groups in the same culture, or between you and me. You believe in always telling the truth, not matter what; I do not, because I believe that it can some-times be too painful and too destructive. We can discuss each other's point of view, we can try to reach common ground, but in the end what you pursue may not be reconcilable with the ends to which I find that I have dedicated my life. Values may easily clash within the breast of an individual; and it does not follow that, if they do, some must be true and others false. Justice, rigorous justice, is for some people an absolute value, but it is not compatible with what may be no less ultimate values for them—mercy, compassion—as arises in concrete cases.*

*Isaiah Berlin, "The Pursuit of the Ideal," *The Crooked Timber of Humanity* (Alfred A. Knopf), 1991, pp. 7–8.

Thomas Donaldson

# Values in Tension: Ethics Away from Home

Thomas Donaldson is Mark O. Winkelman Professor of Legal Studies at the Wharton School of Business, University of Pennsylvania.

When we leave home and cross our nation's boundaries, moral clarity often blurs. Without a backdrop of shared attitudes, and without familiar laws and judicial procedures that define standards of ethical conduct, certainty is elusive. Should a company invest in a foreign country where civil and political rights are violated? Should a company go along with a host country's discriminatory employment practices? If companies in developed countries shift facilities to developing nations that lack strict environmental and health regulations, or if those companies choose to fill management and other top-level positions in a host nation with people from the home country, whose standards should prevail?

Even the best-informed, best-intentioned executives must re-think their assumptions about business practice in foreign settings. What works in a company's home country can fail in a country with different standards of ethical conduct. Such difficulties are unavoidable for businesspeople who live and work abroad.

But how can managers resolve the problems? What are the principles that can help them work through the maze of cultural differences and establish codes of conduct for globally ethical business practice? How can companies answer the toughest question in global business ethics: What happens when a host country's ethical standards seem lower than the home country's?

## COMPETING ANSWERS

One answer is as old as philosophical discourse. According to cultural relativism, no culture's ethics are better than any other's; therefore there are no international rights and wrongs. If the people of Indonesia tolerate the bribery of their public officials, so what? Their attitude is no better or worse than that of people in Denmark or Singapore who refuse to offer or accept bribes. Likewise, if Belgians fail to find insider trading morally repugnant, who cares? Not enforcing insider-trading laws is no more or less ethical than enforcing such laws.

The cultural relativist's creed—When in Rome, do as the Romans do—is tempting, especially when failing to do as the locals do means forfeiting business opportunities. The inadequacy of cultural relativism, however, becomes apparent when the practices in question are more damaging than petty bribery or insider trading.

In the late 1980s, some European tanneries and pharmaceutical companies were looking for cheap waste-dumping sites. They approached virtually every country on Africa's west coast from Morocco to the Congo. Nigeria agreed to take highly toxic polychlorinated biphenyls. Unprotected local workers, wearing thongs and shorts, unloaded barrels of PCBs and placed them near a residential area. Neither the residents nor the workers knew that the barrels contained toxic waste.

We may denounce governments that permit such abuses, but many countries are unable to police transnational corporations adequately even if they want to. And in many countries, the combination of ineffective enforcement and inadequate regulations leads to behavior by unscrupulous companies that is clearly wrong. A few years ago, for example, a group of investors became interested in restoring the SS *United States*, once a luxurious ocean liner. Before the actual restoration could begin, the ship had to be stripped of its asbestos lining. A bid from a U.S. company, based on U.S. standards for asbestos removal, priced the job at more than $100 million. A company in the Ukranian city of Sevastopol offered to do the work for less than $2 million. In October 1993, the ship was towed to Sevastopol.

A cultural relativist would have no problem with that outcome, but I do. A country has the right to establish its own health and safety regulations, but in the case just described, the standards and the terms of the contract could not possibly have protected workers in Sevastopol from known health risks. Even if the contract met Ukranian standards, ethical businesspeople must object. Cultural relativism is morally blind. There are fundamental values that cross cultures, and companies must uphold them.

At the other end of the spectrum from cultural relativism is ethical imperialism, which directs people to do everywhere exactly as they do at home. Again, an understandably appealing approach but one that is clearly inadequate. Consider the large U.S. computer-products company that in 1993 introduced a course on sexual harassment in its Saudi Arabian facility. Under the banner of global consistency, instructors used the same approach to train Saudi Arabian managers that they had used with U.S. managers: the participants were asked to discuss a case in which a manager makes sexually explicit remarks to a new female employee over drinks in a bar. The instructors failed to consider how the exercise would work in a culture with strict conventions governing relationships between men and women. As a result, the training sessions were ludicrous. They baffled and offended the Saudi participants, and the message to avoid coercion and sexual discrimination was lost.

The theory behind ethical imperialism is absolutism, which is based on three problematic principles. Absolutists believe that there is a single list of truths, that they can be expressed only with one set of concepts, and that they call for exactly the same behavior around the world.

The first claim clashes with many people's belief that different cultural traditions must be respected. In some cultures, loyalty to a community—family, organization, or society—is the foundation of all ethical behavior. The Japanese, for example, define business ethics in terms of loyalty to their companies, their business networks, and their nation. Americans place a higher value on liberty than on loyalty; the U.S. tradition of rights emphasizes equality, fairness, and individual freedom. It is hard to conclude that truth lies on one side or the other, but an absolutist would have us select just one.

The second problem with absolutism is the presumption that people must express moral truth using only one set of concepts. For instance, some absolutists insist that the language of basic rights provide the framework for any discussion of ethics. That means, though, that entire cultural traditions must be ignored. The notion of a right evolved with the rise of democracy in post-Renaissance Europe and the United States, but the term is not found in either Confucian or Buddhist traditions. We all learn ethics in the context of our particular cultures, and the power in the principles is deeply tied to the way in which they are expressed. Internationally accepted lists of moral principles, such as the United Nations' Universal Declaration of Human Rights, draw on many cultural and religious traditions. As philosopher Michael Walzer has noted, "There is no Esperanto of global ethics."

The third problem with absolutism is the belief in a global standard of ethical behavior. Context must shape ethical practice. Very low wages, for example,

may be considered unethical in rich, advanced countries, but developing nations may be acting ethically if they encourage investment and improve living standards by accepting low wages. Likewise, when people are malnourished or starving, a government may be wise to use more fertilizer in order to improve crop yields, even though that means settling for relatively high levels of thermal water pollution.

When cultures have different standards of ethical behavior—and different ways of handling unethical behavior—a company that takes an absolutist approach may find itself making a disastrous mistake. When a manager at a large U.S. specialty-products company in China caught an employee stealing, she followed the company's practice and turned the employee over to the provincial authorities, who executed him. Managers cannot operate in another culture without being aware of that culture's attitudes toward ethics.

If companies can neither adopt a host country's ethics nor extend the home country's standards, what is the answer? Even the traditional litmus test—What would people think of your actions if they were written up on the front page of the newspaper?—is an unreliable guide, for there is no international consensus on standards of business conduct.

## BALANCING THE EXTREMES: THREE GUIDING PRINCIPLES

Companies must help managers distinguish between practices that are merely different and those that are wrong. For relativists, nothing is sacred and nothing is wrong. For absolutists, many things that are different are wrong. Neither extreme illuminates the real world of business decision making. The answer lies somewhere in between.

When it comes to shaping ethical behavior, companies must be guided by three principles.

• Respect for core human values, which determine the absolute moral threshold for all business activities.

- Respect for local traditions.
- The belief that context matters when deciding what is right and what is wrong.

Consider those principles in action. In Japan, people doing business together often exchange gifts—sometimes expensive ones—in keeping with longstanding Japanese tradition: When U.S. and European companies started doing a lot of business in Japan, many Western business-people thought that the practice of gift giving might be wrong rather than simply different. To them, accepting a gift felt like accepting a bribe. As Western companies have become more familiar with Japanese traditions, however, most have come to tolerate the practice and to set different limits on gift giving in Japan than they do elsewhere.

Respecting differences is a crucial ethical practice. Research shows that management ethics differ among cultures; respecting those differences means recognizing that some cultures have obvious weaknesses—as well as hidden strengths. Managers in Hong Kong, for example, have a higher tolerance for some forms of bribery than their Western counterparts, but they have a much lower tolerance for the failure to acknowledge a subordinate's work. In some parts of the Far East, stealing credit from a subordinate is nearly an unpardonable sin.

People often equate respect for local traditions with cultural relativism. That is incorrect. Some practices are clearly wrong. Union Carbide's tragic experience in Bhopal, India, provides one example. The company's executives seriously underestimated how much on-site management involvement was needed at the Bhopal plant to compensate for the country's poor infrastructure and regulatory capabilities. In the aftermath of the disastrous gas leak, the lesson is clear companies using sophisticated technology in a developing country must evaluate that country's ability to oversee its safe use. Since the incident at Bhopal, Union Carbide has become a leader in advising companies on using hazardous technologies safely in developing countries.

Some activities are wrong no matter where they take place. But some practices that are unethical in one setting may be acceptable in another. For instance, the chemical EDB, a soil fungicide, is banned for use in the United States. In hot climates, however, it quickly becomes harmless through exposure to intense solar radiation and high soil temperatures. As long as the chemical is monitored, companies may be able to use EDB ethically in certain parts of the world.

## DEFINING THE ETHICAL THRESHOLD: CORE VALUES

Few ethical questions are easy for managers to answer. But there are some hard truths that must guide managers' actions, a set of what I call *core human values*, which define minimum ethical standards for all companies.[1] The right to good health and the right to economic advancement and an improved standard of living are two core human values. Another is what Westerners call the Golden Rule, which is recognizable in every major religious and ethical tradition around the world. In Book 15 of his *Analects*, for instance, Confucius counsels people to maintain reciprocity, or not to do to others what they do not want done to themselves.

Although no single list would satisfy every scholar, I believe it is possible to articulate three core values that incorporate the work of scores of theologians and philosophers around the world. To be broadly relevant, these values must include elements found in both Western and non-Western cultural and religious traditions. Consider the examples of values in the [box] "What Do These Values Have in Common?"

At first glance, the values expressed in the two lists seem quite different. Nonetheless, in the spirit of what philosopher John Rawls calls *overlapping consensus*, one can see that the seemingly divergent values converge at key points. Despite important differences between Western and non-Western cultural and religious traditions, both express shared attitudes about what it means to be human. First, individuals must not treat others simply as tools; in other words, they must recognize a person's value as a human being. Next, individuals and communities must treat people in ways that respect people's basic

# What Do These Values Have in Common?

**Non-Western**

Kyosei (Japanese): Living and working together for a
   Common good
Dharma (Hindu): The fulfillment of inherited duty
Santutthi (Buddhist): The importance of limited desires
Zakat (Muslim): The Muslin duty to give alms to the poor.

**Western**

Individual liberty

Egalitarianism
Political Participation
Human rights

rights. Finally, members of a community must work together to support and improve the institutions on which the community depends. I call those three values *respect for human dignity, respect for basic rights*, and *good citizenship*.

Those values must be the starting point for all companies as they formulate and evaluate standards of ethical conduct at home and abroad. But they are only a starting point. Companies need much more specific guidelines, and the first step to developing those is to translate the core human values into core values for business. What does it mean, for example, for a company to respect human dignity? How can a company be a good citizen?

I believe that companies can respect human dignity by creating and sustaining a corporate culture in which employees, customers, and suppliers are treated not as means to an end but as people whose intrinsic value must be acknowledged, and by producing safe products and services in a safe workplace. Companies can respect basic rights by acting in ways that support and protect the individual rights of employees, customers, and surrounding communities, and by avoiding relationships that violate human beings' rights to health, education, safety, and an adequate standard of living. And companies can be good citizens by supporting essential social institutions, such as the economic system and the education system, and by working with host governments and other organizations to protect the environment.

The core values establish a moral compass for business practice. They can help companies identify practices that are acceptable and those that are intolerable—even if the practices are compatible with a host country's norms and laws. Dumping pollutants near people's homes and accepting inadequate standards for handling hazardous materials are two examples of actions that violate core values.

Similarly, if employing children prevents them from receiving a basic education, the practice is intolerable. Lying about product specifications in the act of selling may not affect human lives directly, but it too is intolerable because it violates the trust that is needed to sustain a corporate culture in which customers are respected.

Sometimes it is not a company's actions but those of a supplier or customer that pose problems. Take the case of the Tan family, a large supplier for Levi Strauss. The Tans were allegedly forcing 1,200 Chinese and Filipino women to work 74 hours per week in guarded compounds on the Mariana Islands. In 1992, after repeated warnings to the Tans, Levi Strauss broke off business relations with them.

## CREATING AN ETHICAL CORPORATE CULTURE

The core values for business that I have enumerated can help companies begin to exercise ethical judgment and think about how to operate ethically in foreign cultures, but they are not specific enough to guide managers through actual ethical dilemmas. Levi Strauss relied on a written code of conduct when figuring out how to deal with the Tan family. The company's Global Sourcing and Operating Guidelines, formerly called the Business Partner Terms of Engagement, state that Levi Strauss will "seek to identify and utilize business partners who aspire as individuals and in the conduct of all their businesses to a set of ethical standards not incompatible with our own." Whenever intolerable business situations arise, managers should be guided by precise statements that spell out the behavior and operating practices that the company demands.

Ninety percent of all *Fortune* 500 companies have codes of conduct, and 70% have statements of vision and values. In Europe and the Far East, the percentages are lower but are increasing rapidly. Does that mean that most companies have what they need? Hardly. Even though most large U.S. companies have both statements of values and codes of conduct, many might be better off if they didn't. Too many companies don't do anything with the documents; they simply paste them on the wall to impress employees, customers, suppliers, and the public. As a result, the senior managers who drafted the statements lose credibility by proclaiming values and not living up to them. Companies such as Johnson & Johnson, Levi Strauss, Motorola, Texas Instruments, and Lockheed Martin, however, do a great deal to make the words meaningful. Johnson & Johnson, for example, has become well known for its Credo Challenge sessions, in which managers discuss ethics in the context of their current business problems and are invited to criticize the company's credo and make suggestions for changes. The participants' ideas are passed on to the company's senior managers. Lockheed Martin has created an innovative site on the World Wide Web and on its local network that gives employees, customers, and suppliers access to the company's ethical code and the chance to voice complaints.

Codes of conduct must provide clear direction about ethical behavior when the temptation to behave unethically is strongest. The pronouncement in a code of conduct that bribery is unacceptable is useless unless accompanied by guidelines for gift giving, payments to get goods through customs, and "requests" from intermediaries who are hired to ask for bribes.

Motorola's values are stated very simply as "How we will always act: [with] constant respect for people [and] uncompromising integrity." The company's code of conduct, however, is explicit about actual business practice. With respect to bribery, for example; the code states that the "funds and assets of Motorola shall not be used, directly or indirectly, for illegal payments of any kind." It is unambiguous about what sort of payment is illegal: "the payment of a bribe to a public official or the kickback of funds to an employee of a customer. . . ." The code goes on to prescribe specific procedures for handling commissions to intermediaries, issuing sales invoices, and disclosing confidential information in a sales transaction—all situations in which employees might have an opportunity to accept or offer bribes.

Codes of conduct must be explicit to be useful, but they must also leave room for a manager to use his or her judgment in situations requiring cultural sensitivity. Host-country employees shouldn't be forced to adopt all home-country values and renounce their own. Again, Motorola's code is exemplary. First, it gives clear direction: "Employees of Motorola will respect the laws, customs, and traditions of each country in which they operate, but will, at the same time, engage in no course of conduct which, even if legal, customary, and accepted in any such country, could be deemed to be in violation of the accepted business ethics of Motorola or the laws of the United States relating to business ethics." After laying down such absolutes, Motorola's code then makes clear when individual judgment will be necessary. For example, employees may sometimes accept certain kinds of small gifts "in rare circumstances, where the refusal to accept a gift" would injure Motorola's "legitimate business interests." Under certain circumstances, such gifts "may be accepted so long as the gift inures to the benefit of Motorola" and not "to the benefit of the Motorola employee."

Striking the appropriate balance between providing clear direction and leaving room for individual judgment makes crafting corporate values statements and ethics codes one of the hardest tasks that executives confront. The words are only a start. A company's leaders need to refer often to their organization's credo and code and must themselves be credible, committed, and consistent. If senior managers act as though ethics don't matter, the rest of the company's employees won't think they do, either.

## CONFLICTS OF DEVELOPMENT AND CONFLICTS OF TRADITION

Managers living and working abroad who are not prepared to grapple with moral ambiguity and tension should pack their bags and come home. The view that all business practices can be categorized as either ethical or unethical is too simple. As Einstein is reported to have said, "Things should be as simple as possible—but no simpler." Many business practices that are considered unethical in one setting may be ethical in another. Such activities are neither black nor white but exist in what Thomas Dunfee and I have called *moral free space*.[2] In this gray zone, there are no tight prescriptions for a company's behavior. Managers must chart their own courses—as long as they do not violate core human values.

## GUIDELINES FOR ETHICAL LEADERSHIP

Learning to spot intolerable practices and to exercise good judgment when ethical conflicts arise requires practice. Creating a company culture that rewards ethical behavior is essential. The following guidelines for developing a global ethical perspective among managers can help.

**Treat corporate values and formal standards of conduct as absolutes.** Whatever ethical standards a company chooses, it cannot waver on its principles

either at home or abroad. Consider what has become part of company lore at Motorola. Around 1950, a senior executive was negotiating with officials of a South American government on a $10 million sale that would have increased the company's annual net profits by nearly 25%. As the negotiations neared completion, however, the executive walked away from the deal because the officials were asking for $1 million for "fees." CEO Robert Galvin not only supported the executive's decision but also made it clear that Motorola would neither accept the sale on any terms nor do business with those government officials again. Retold over the decades, this story demonstrating Galvin's resolve has helped cement a culture of ethics for thousands of employees at Motorola.

**Design and implement conditions of engagement for suppliers and customers.** Will your company do business with any customer or supplier? What if a customer or supplier uses child labor? What if it has strong links with organized crime? What if it pressures your company to break a host country's laws? Such issues are best not left for spur-of-the-moment decisions. Some companies have realized that. Sears, for instance, has developed a policy of not contracting production to companies that use prison labor or infringe on workers' rights to health and safety. And BankAmerica has specified as a condition for many of its loans to developing countries that environmental standards and human rights must be observed.

**Allow foreign business units to help formulate ethical standards and interpret ethical issues.** The French pharmaceutical company Rhône-Poulenc Rorer has allowed foreign subsidiaries to augment lists of corporate ethical principles with their own suggestions. Texas Instruments has paid special attention to issues of international business ethics by creating the Global Business Practices Council, which is made up of managers from countries in which the company operates. With the overarching intent to create a "global ethics strategy, locally deployed," the council's mandate is to provide ethics education and create local processes that will help managers in the company's foreign business units resolve ethical conflicts.

140

**In host countries, support efforts to decrease institutional corruption.** Individual managers will not be able to wipe out corruption in a host country, no matter how many bribes they turn down. When a host country's tax system, import and export procedures, and procurement practices favor unethical players, companies must take action.

Many companies have begun to participate in reforming host-country institutions. General Electric, for example, has taken a strong stand in India, using the media to make repeated condemnations of bribery in business and government. General Electric and others have found, however, that a single company usually cannot drive out entrenched corruption. Transparency International, an organization based in Germany, has been effective in helping coalitions of companies, government officials, and others work to reform bribery-ridden bureaucracies in Russia, Bangladesh, and elsewhere.

**Exercise moral imagination.** Using moral imagination means resolving tensions responsibly and creatively. Coca-Cola, for instance, has consistently turned down requests for bribes from Egyptian officials but has managed to gain political support and public trust by sponsoring a project to plant fruit trees. And take the example of Levi Strauss, which discovered in the early 1990s that two of its suppliers in Bangladesh were employing children under the age of 14—a practice that violated the company's principles but was tolerated in Bangladesh. Forcing the suppliers to fire the children would not have ensured that the children received an education, and it would have caused serious hardship for the families depending on the children's wages. In a creative arrangement, the suppliers agreed to pay the children's regular wages while they attended school and to offer each child a job at age 14. Levi Strauss, in turn, agreed to pay the children's tuition and provide books and uniforms. That arrangement allowed Levi Strauss to uphold its principles and provide longterm benefits to its host country.

Many people think of values as soft; to some they are usually unspoken. A South Seas island society uses the word *Mokita*, which means, "the truth that everybody knows but nobody speaks." However difficult they are to articulate, values affect how we all behave. In a global business environment, values in tension are the rule rather than the exception. Without a company's commitment, statements of values and codes of ethics end up as empty platitudes that provide managers with no foundation for behaving ethically. Employees need and deserve more, and responsible members of the global business community can set examples for others to follow. The dark consequences of incidents such as Union Carbide's disaster in Bhopal remind us how high the stakes can be.

## NOTES

1. In other writings, Thomas W. Dunfee and I have used the term *hypernorm* instead of *core human value*.

2. Thomas Donaldson and Thomas W. Dunfee, "Toward a Unified Conception of Business Ethics: Integrative Social Contracts Theory," *Academy of Management Review*, April 1994; and "Integrative Social Contracts Theory: A Communitarian Conception of Economic Ethics," *Economics and Philosophy*, spring 1995.

## QUESTIONS

1. When should companies and/or the people who work in them attempt to assert their own moral values over the values of another culture?

2. When you have traveled to other countries, which cultural values and practices did you find more ethical than your home culture, and which ones did you find less ethical? Why?

3. Under what conditions do you think it is right for a business to try and change the values of employees and others in a foreign culture? What sorts of initiatives do you think are appropriate changes and what sorts of initiative are not appropriate?

# Silence as Complicity: Elements of a Corporate Duty to Speak Out Against the Violation of Human Rights

Florian Wettstein

Florian Wettstein is an Assistant Professor in the Ethics and Business Law Department of the University of St. Thomas.

The vast majority of corporate rights violations," as Stephen Kobrin observes, "involve complicity, aiding and abetting violations by another actor, most often the host government." Kobrin's claim certainly seems plausible. In an increasingly interconnected world our actions affect the lives of others in ever more profound ways. Thus, increasingly we may contribute to harm without being aware of it, or at least without intending to do so. It is in the very nature of complicity that it falls "outside the paradigm of individual, intentional wrongdoing." The problem deepens if we are not merely looking at the actions of individuals, but at those of organizations that operate globally and on a large scale, such as multinational corporations. Corporations may become complicit in human rights violations although they are not doing anything wrong in a conventional sense or engaging in any unlawful conduct; they may simply be going about their business. This contributes to the pervasiveness of corporate complicity and renders it notoriously hard to grasp and, not least, to condemn. The very nature of wrongdoing is changing in the process of today's globalization.

The changing nature of wrongdoing in the global age must be followed by our rethinking of the parameters of moral responsibility. The fact that corporations often contribute to wrongdoings in the course of their "regular" business conduct rather than by engaging in some specific, overt and deliberate harmful activity, poses new challenges to our moral intuition and our natural sense of justice. This is why cases of corporate complicity are in a sense symptomatic for our time; they require us to rethink some of the certainties of the Westphalian age and to come up with new normative visions and concepts to deal with the new problems with which we are faced in a transnational world.

The aim of this paper then is to assess under what conditions it is plausible to speak of corporations as silently complicit in human rights abuses and thus under what circumstances such a positive duty to speak out can be assumed.

## SILENT COMPLICITY AND THE MORAL DUTY TO HELP PROTECT

Corporate complicity is commonly defined as "aiding and abetting" in the violation of human rights committed by a third party. Aiding and abetting is to be interpreted broadly; it includes not merely direct involvement of corporations, but also various forms of indirect facilitation.

Thus, corporate complicity can be categorized by the nature of its contribution to the wrongdoing in play. The literature on the topic commonly refers to four different forms of complicity: direct complicity, indirect complicity, beneficial complicity and silent complicity. While direct complicity implies direct involvement of the corporation in a human rights abuse, indirect complicity involves mere facilitation, that is, an indirect contribution to the general ability of a perpetrator to commit human rights violations. There is increasing agreement that the scope of complicity may extend beyond *active* assistance given to a primary perpetrator. Cases of beneficial complicity, for example, do not require an active contribution by the corporation, but merely that the corporation directly or indirectly benefits from the violation of human rights. In the case of silent complicity, even "merely" standing by while human rights are violated is increasingly perceived as a form of complicity.

In contrast to other, more "conventional" forms of complicity, silent and in most cases also beneficial complicity are not established by a corporation's active contribution, but by its passive stance toward the violation of human rights. Knowingly looking the other way while the most basic rights of human beings are trampled underfoot by a host government can constitute not merely indifference, but actual support. In such cases, silence can have a potentially *legitimizing or encouraging effect* on a perpetrator, which in turn grounds the accusation of silent complicity. For John M. Kline, silent complicity "suggests that a non-participant is aware of abusive action and, although possessing some degree of ability to act, chooses neither to help protect nor to assist victims of the abuse, remaining content to meet the minimal ethical requirement to do no (direct) harm." Hence, moral blame in cases of silent complicity is not attached to certain harmful actions conducted by the corporation, but to its failure to give assistance to those in need when it is in a position to do so. In short, the main difference between silent complicity and most other forms of complicity is that its moral basis is not commission, but omission.

The normative implications of this insight are far-reaching. Omission denotes a failure to act in response to wrongdoing. Thus, rather than to merely passively refrain from specific harmful actions, the agent in danger of becoming silently complicit is under a moral obligation to confront and possibly counteract the wrongdoing. If silence renders companies complicit, speaking out to help protect the victims is what is required to diffuse such allegations. The claim that a corporation is silently complicit in human rights violations, as

Wiggen and Bomann-Larsen conclude, implies that it is guilty of omitting to fulfill an actual *positive duty*.

In sum, there are two constitutive requirements that need to be fulfilled in order for an agent to be guilty of silent complicity: first, the agent must have failed to speak out and help protect the victims. I will call this the "omission requirement." Second, the omission of this positive duty must have a legitimizing or encouraging effect on the human rights violation and the perpetrator who is committing it. I will call this the "legitimization requirement." This, in turn, raises the question: under what conditions can corporations indeed be said to be silently complicit in a host government's human rights abuse? That is, under what circumstances or conditions can these two requirements plausibly be said to be fulfilled? In what follows I will assess both requirements separately. The "omission requirement," I will argue, hinges on one general and two qualified conditions, while the "legitimization requirement" depends on a fourth condition.

## ASSESSING THE "OMISSION REQUIREMENT": ELEMENTS OF A POSITIVE DUTY TO SPEAK OUT AGAINST THE VIOLATION OF HUMAN RIGHTS

A first important distinction that needs to be drawn in order to assess the "omission requirement" is the one between negative and positive duties. A *negative duty* is a duty to do no harm, while a *positive duty* is a duty to assist or "help persons in [acute] distress." Thus, a negative duty is a duty not to make a situation worse, while a positive duty is a duty to improve a given state of affairs. Negative duties are commonly seen as stricter than positive ones, which is at the root of the controversy surrounding any argument that assigns positive duties to corporations.

The distinction between negative and positive duties is not to be confused with the one between passive and active duties. *Passive duties* command us to merely abstain from certain (harmful) activities while *active duties* require us to actively perform specific actions. Negative duties can be active or passive. Doing no harm may be as simple as abstaining from actively hurting someone (passive), but, depending on the situation, it may also require to *actively* eliminate risks or dangers to others, such as cutting the tree in one's yard that threatens to fall onto the sidewalk. Passive duties are always negative, since passively abstaining from specific actions is obligatory only if those actions are harmful to others (or, in some cases, to oneself). As a consequence, positive duties are always active.

The duty to speak out against human rights violations is a positive duty. That is to say, it is a duty to speak out to *help protect* the victims. It is from this perspective that commonly the duty to speak out is not perceived merely as a duty to make a statement, but as a broader duty to *address* the issue with the appropriate authorities.

Generally, for there to be a passive negative duty to do no harm, only one condition needs to be fulfilled, which is that an agent has some level of autonomy to act. It is against this background that the passive negative duty to do no harm is of general nature and of universal reach; it applies to everyone at the same time and to the same extent. I will refer to this as the criterion of voluntariness. Second, for a negative duty to become active there must be a morally significant connection between the respective agent and the human rights violation. In contrast to passive duties, active duties (negative or positive) are specific and dependent on the context and situation; they apply to particular agents to varying degrees and extent. However, for active duties to apply to some agents but not to others, there must be something that specifically links those agents to the human rights violations at stake. I will call this the connection criterion. For there to be a positive duty to help protect, these two conditions must be complemented with a third one; a positive duty to improve a given state of affairs presupposes that a duty-bearer has the power to exert influence on the situation in a positive way. Thus, I will refer to this as the criterion of influence/power. The first two conditions aim at the non-violation of human rights, which means that they can be justified on a deontological basis. The third condition, however, aims at the improvement of a given situation. Thus, its justification or plausibility requires at least some sensitivity to consequences (not, however, consequentialism). Let us analyze all three conditions in some more detail.

*Voluntariness*: Passive negative duties apply to all responsible individuals at all times and to the same extent; we all have the same duty to abstain from harming others. For any rational, adult human being this responsibility can only be mitigated or eliminated if the action causing harm is not freely chosen or if the harmful consequences are not foreseeable. Thus, moral responsibility, as opposed to mere causal responsibility, depends on autonomous and thus voluntary or intentional action. We can only be held morally responsible for actions we freely and willingly choose, but not for those over which we have no control or which we are forced to commit.

*Connection:* For there to be an active negative duty, voluntariness must be combined with connection. As pointed out earlier, silence turns into complicity only if, based on the perception of implicit endorsement or approval, it has a legitimizing or encouraging effect on the wrongdoing. This, it seems, presupposes a significant connection between the agent and the human rights violation. After all, the very claim that agents have an active duty to *disassociate* themselves from a particular human rights violation or its perpetrator already implies that there is an actual connection that links them to the violation in a morally relevant way. The crucial question is what qualifies connections as morally significant in this context of silent complicity. Generally, we can distinguish between two categories of connections: an agent can either be *actively* connected or *passively* connected to the violation. Active connection essentially means actual involvement, that is, the agent actively contributes to the violation of human rights committed by the primary perpetrator. However, such cases of active involvement belong to the category of direct complicity, which establishes a passive negative obligation to do no harm. In such cases, active involvement or contribution to the human rights violation is the problem, rather than the agent's silence. Hence, the connections that are relevant for silent complicity are of the passive kind.

*Influence/Power:* While voluntariness and connection are necessary conditions for there to be a moral obligation for a company to speak out against human rights abuse, they merely establish a negative obligation for the company, that is, an obligation to disassociate itself from the perpetrator and its harmful actions. However, on their own, these two conditions are insufficient to establish a positive duty to speak out to help protect the victims. For the company to have a positive obligation to speak out, it must be in a position to exert pressure or influence for the purpose of improving the situation of the victims.

*Legitimization Requirement:* The legitimization requirement consists of two elements. First, an agent's silence must imply implicit endorsement of the human rights violation. Second, this implied endorsement must serve to legitimize or encourage the violation. The implied endorsement derives from the combination of voluntariness, connection, and power as discussed above. Hence, an agent who is connected to the human rights violation and would be in a sufficiently powerful position to speak out against it can be perceived as endorsing it, if she *chooses* not to speak out. In order for an agent's implied endorsement to add legitimacy to the incident, her stance on the issue must carry some weight in the public perception. For this to be the case, the agent must be of a certain status or standing. This may involve high social regard and prestige. It may imply that the agent is epresentative of society or a relevant subset thereof.

## INNOCENT BYSTANDER OR SILENTLY COMPLICIT?: THE EXECUTION OF KEN SARO-WIWA AND SHELL'S "ECOLOGICAL WAR" IN THE NIGER DELTA

On Tuesday, 31 October 1995, Nigerian playwright and minority-rights activist Ken Saro-Wiwa, along with eight of his followers, were sentenced to death by a specially convened, "hand-picked" tribunal of the Abacha regime in Nigeria for inciting the murder of four conservative, pro-government Ogoni chiefs. The four Ogoni chiefs were rounded up and killed by a rioting mob on 21 May 1994. On 10 November 1995, just ten days after the sentence was passed, Saro-Wiwa and his friends were executed while the world watched in outrage.

At the time of his arrest, Ken Saro-Wiwa and his activist group "Movement for the Survival of the Ogoni People" (MOSOP) were spearheading widespread protests against exploitation and environmental degradation by oil companies in the Ogoni land. Protests against the environmental destruction caused by oil companies had been growing throughout the Niger Delta since the 1970s. When the protests grew bigger and more numerous in the early 1990s, the government started to repress them violently—often at the specific request of Shell. Growing tension between Shell and the indigenous people in the Niger Delta led to increasing numbers of increasingly violent protests. The most devastating of these protests occurred in January 1993, when, at the dawn of the UN Year of Indigenous Peoples, the largest peaceful rally against oil companies to that point in time was silenced violently by government forces, resulting in the destruction of 27 villages, displacing 80,000 Ogoni villagers, and leaving some 2000 people dead. As the struggle evolved, the Ogoni people became the "vanguard movement for adequate compensation and ecological self-determination" in the Niger Delta and Shell became the symbol of their oppression. Saro-Wiwa was the driving force behind the Ogoni movement; "No other person in Nigeria," as one member of the Nigerian Civil Liberties Organisation put it, "can get 100,000 people on the streets."

The murder of the four chiefs provided the Nigerian government with an opportunity to arrest Saro-Wiwa and eight other leaders of his organization. The charges against Saro-Wiwa and his colleagues were anything but uncontroversial. It was even suggested that the Nigerian government itself was involved in provoking the murders as a justification for stronger military presence in the region. Not only was Saro-Wiwa "miles away" when the murders took place, but he was, in fact, under military escort. Key witnesses admitted that they had been bribed to provide false evidence and the tribunal, which was controlled by the military, was denounced as illegitimate by the international community due to blatant violations of international fair trial standards and a lack of respect for due process. The British government condemned the trial as "judicial murder."

The international protests did not remain limited to the Nigerian government. Shell too came under attack for idly standing by while the tragedy unfolded. Shell was accused of not using its influence in Nigeria to stop the execution, the torturing of protesters, and the violent crack-down of demonstrations. In other words, Shell was seen as being silently complicit by violating a positive duty to help protect them against the human rights violations of the Abacha junta. Our analysis now provides a tool with which to assess the validity of this claim. For Shell to be silently complicit, the two qualified conditions underlying the omission requirement (i.e., connection and influence/power) as well as the status condition underlying the legitimization requirement all need to have been met.

*Connection:* The connection between Shell and Ken Saro-Wiwa's and the roughly 2000 other Ogoni deaths is undisputed. The uprising of the Ogoni people was a direct response to Shell's operations in the Niger Delta; their protests were directly aimed at Shell. In some instances the police forces that put the demonstrations down were requested by Shell. Even when they were not requested, the suppression of large scale protests benefitted Shell and secured the continuation of its operations. In his closing statement to the tribunal, Ken Saro-Wiwa explicitly addressed Shell's role and connection to the incidence:

> I repeat that we all stand before history. I and my colleagues are not the only ones on trial. Shell is on trial here, and it is as well that it is represented by counsel said to be holding a watching brief. The company has, indeed, ducked this particular trial, but its day will surely come and the lessons learned here may prove useful to it, for there is no doubt in my mind that the ecological war the company has waged in the delta will be called to question sooner than later and the crimes of that war be duly punished. The crime of the company's dirty wars against the Ogoni people will also be punished.

Shell was the main cause for the formation of the Ogoni protests and was also the main reason for the violent crack down. Shell was, by every definition of the word, linked to the execution of Ken Saro-Wiwa and his friends in a morally significant way.

*Influence/Power:* For Shell to have a positive duty to help protect and thus to speak out against the trial and to put pressure on the Nigerian government, their connection to the incidence must come with a position of influence or power. While the degree of Shell's real influence at the time ultimately is subject to speculation, most of the evidence and, as we will see shortly, also Shell's own assessment of its influence in Nigeria suggest that this condition too was met. Shell's position in Nigeria was and still is exceptionally powerful. The military government's power was dependent on the foreign earnings generated by oil and Shell was by far the major oil producer not only in the area but in the whole country. At the time of Saro-Wiwa's execution, Shell produced roughly half of Nigeria's crude oil output. As a result, Shell's power and influence was by any measure considerable.[22] Thus, Andrew Rowell observes that Shell's position in Nigeria was "both powerful and unique." Quoting an anonymous Ogoni activist, he says: "With such an illegitimate political system, each bunch of unelected military rulers that comes into power, simply dances to the tune of this company. . . . Shell is in the position to dictate, because Nigeria is economically and politically weak."

*Status:* At the time of the execution Shell enjoyed the prestige of a company with global brand recognition. In the mid-1990s, Shell was the world's biggest oil company not owned by a government, it was producing 3 percent of the world's crude oil and 4 percent of its natural gas. It was the world's only private company to rank among the top ten biggest holders of oil and gas reserves. Its influence both in Nigeria and globally was substantial. It was without doubt a company that led, molded, and directed, a company that disrupted old social orders and dictated the pace of daily life in Nigeria and the Niger Delta. The very protests that erupted first in Nigeria against Shell's environmental record and later on an international scale against Shell's way of handling the turmoil in Nigeria underscore Shell's standing relative to society at large. Furthermore, they are a case in point regarding the politicization of corporations and the subsequent call for deliberative public engagement. In light of the worldwide attention that the Shell case received, it seems that it would at least be difficult to argue that the company lacked the status necessary to be implicated with silent complicity.

Based on such assessments there certainly is a case to be made for Shell's silent complicity in Saro-Wiwa's execution. Many commentators believed and continue to believe that Shell was in a position to speak out against the trial. Saro-Wiwa's brother, Owens Wiwa goes so far as to claim that if Shell "had threatened to withdraw from Nigeria unless Ken was released, he would have been alive today. There is no question of that." Andrew Rowell's conclusions even reach beyond the specific incident around Saro-Wiwa: "[S]uch is the economic strength of the company that few people in Nigeria or Britain doubt that it could have stopped the conflict outright—or at least stopped the use of excessive force against demonstration." Shell was well aware of its powerful position in the country and its potential to turn the events around. In fact, as *The Observer* reported nine days after Saro-Wiwa's execution, Brian Anderson, who was head of Shell Nigeria at the time, had in fact offered to Owens Wiwa to use Shell's influence with Nigeria's military regime to try to free his brother; however, his offer was conditional on the Ogoni leaders calling off any global protests against Shell. This bargain, irrespective of its questionable ethical quality, was unattainable for Wiwa: "Even if I had wanted to, I didn't have the power to control the international environmental protests."

Shell defended its position of inactivity against the growing public outrage. The company's official position was that it would be "dangerous and wrong" for Shell to "intervene and use its perceived 'influence' to have the judgment overturned." "A commercial organization like Shell," as they claimed further, "cannot and must never interfere with the legal processes of any sovereign state." A Shell manager reportedly stated in 1996:

> I am afraid I cannot comment on the issue of the Ogoni 9, the tribunal and the hanging. This country has certain rules and regulations on how trials can take place. Those are the rules of Nigeria. Nigeria makes its rules and it is not for private companies like us to comment on such processes in the country.

## QUESTIONS

1. What does it mean for a corporation to be complicit in human rights violations? Can you give some cases outside of this article where corporations could have prevented the abuse of human rights?

2. To what extent do you think that Shell was responsible for the 2000 Ogoni deaths? What could they have done to prevent them?

3. How can companies leverage their status in another country to bring about change without affecting their competitive position?

---

To: You
From: The Philosopher
RE: The Global Compact

Have you heard about this Global Compact that the United Nations launched in 2000? It's a set of 10 ethical principles for businesses. Companies voluntarily sign it and pledge to align their business practices and strategies with its principles. It is the largest voluntary corporate responsibility initiative in the world, with over 8700 signatories from 130 countries. I am skeptical about these things. Some companies may only do this for public relations purposes. What do you think? Do these sorts of initiatives really make a difference in how the companies that sign it do business? What do you think of the principles in the compact?

Principle 1: Businesses should support and respect the protection of internationally proclaimed human rights.

Principle 2: Make sure that they are not complicit in human rights abuses.

Principle 3: Businesses should uphold the freedom of association and the effective recognition of the right to collective bargaining.

Principle 4: The elimination of all forms of forced and compulsory labor.

Principle 5: The effective abolition of child labor.

Principle 6: The elimination of discrimination in respect of employment and occupation.

Principle 7: Businesses should support a precautionary approach to environmental challenges.

Principle 8: Undertake initiatives to promote greater environmental responsibility.

Principle 9: Encourage the development and diffusion of environmentally friendly technologies.

Principle 10: Businesses should work against corruption in all its forms, including extortion and bribery.

John T. Noonan, Jr. | # A Quick Look at the History of Bribes

John T. Noonan, Jr., is a judge in the United States Ninth Circuit Court of Appeals.

*First.* Bribes—socially disapproved inducements of official action meant to be gratuitously exercised—are ancient, almost as ancient as the invention in Egypt of scales which symbolized and showed social acceptance of the idea of objective judgment.

*Second.* The bribe has a history, divisible into discernible epochs. From approximately 3000 B.C. to 1000 A.D. the idea of nonreciprocity struggles against the norms of reciprocation which cement societies whose rulers are both judges and the recipients of

offerings. In the second period from, say, 1000 A.D. to 1550 A.D., the antibribery ideal is dominant in religious, legal, and literary expressions; its active enforcement is attempted in successive waves of reformation. The third period of the idea, as far as English-speaking people are concerned, begins in the sixteenth century with its domestication in English bibles and English plays and English law and ends in the eighteenth century with its proclamation as a norm for the English empire. The fourth stage is the American, when the heirs of the successive reformations and of English politics begin to apply it and then to expand its sway until it is asserted as an

John T. Noonan, Jr. "A Quick Look at the History of Bribes" in *Bribes* (New York: Macmillan Publishers, 1984), pp. xx–xxiii.

American norm around the earth; and the rest of the world—not merely as a result of American influence but because of the general expansion of the Western moral tradition—makes at least verbal acknowledgment of the norm.

*Third*. Bribes are today universal; that is, every culture, with insignificant exceptions, treats certain reciprocities with officials as disapproved.

*Fourth*. The bribe is a concept running counter to normal expectations in approaching a powerful stranger. Linguistic ambiguity in the term for bribe in Hebrew, Greek, and Latin marks the cultural resistance encountered by the concept. Historically, the limitation of the concept to one class of officials— judges—is a second sign of the resistance. Reluctance to apply the concept against the bribegiver is a third. Lack of specific sanctions against the bribetaker is a fourth indication of the precarious hold the concept, historically, has enjoyed.

*Fifth*. The bribe in its origins depends on religious teaching. Reciprocity is so regularly the norm of human relations that the conception of a transcendental figure, a Judge beyond the reach of ordinary reciprocities, was of enormous importance for the idea that certain reciprocities with earthly officials were intolerable. That conception of a transcendental Judge was shaped in the ancient Near East. Communication of this image to the West was largely dependent on religion. Accepted as divine revelation, Scripture by commandment and paradigm inculcated a teaching on impartial judgment. The concept of the bribe was cast in a biblical mold.

*Sixth*. Religion—Jewish, Christian, pagan—has been, however, profoundly ambivalent in its teaching on reciprocity. The Judge beyond influence has been placated by pagans, offered prayers and slaughtered animals by Jews, and seen by Christians as accepting a special redeeming sacrifice. Religion can be viewed as bribery on a grand scale, organized for the highest end, man's salvation, and practiced to persuade the Supreme Authority. Indulgences, systematized to support enterprises from basilicas to bridges, constitute an especially striking example of this kind of religion. Even in its most primitive form, Christianity rests on a transaction carried out between God and the Son of God which theology labeled the Buy Back, a term in Roman civilization often used to mean payoff to a judge to escape punishment. Job and Jesus himself to the contrary, religion can be read as reinforcement of the iron law, "I give that you may give," a law requiring reciprocity with every power-holder including God.

*Seventh*. The double message conveyed by the several religious traditions is paralleled in Western cultures by the elimination of certain reciprocities as bribes and the retention of others as acceptable quid pro quos. Words alone seem to mark the distinction between certain acceptable and condemned offerings. In sixteenth-century Europe payment to obtain a spiritual favor was the sin of simony; a *contributio* to obtain an indulgence was legitimate. In twentieth-century America, payment to a candidate for his vote is a penal offense; a licensed contribution to a campaign committee is lawful. In some instances, there is only verbal camouflage; in some instances, the verbal distinction points to a real difference.

*Eighth*. Although the definition of a bribe depends on the conventions of the culture, so that ceremony and context, form and intention, determine whether an exchange counts as a crime or a virtuous act, ultimately the distinction between bribe and gift has become fundamental. Without this distinction the condemnation of bribes appears arbitrary, and intermediate offerings such as a tip or a campaign contribution are indiscriminately lumped into a single category which includes all reciprocities. With bribe and gift set at polar opposites, a spectrum with shades of discrimination exists. For our culture— Western culture, now the dominant world culture— the difference between bribe and gift has been most powerfully developed by reflection, theological and literary, on the Redemption.

*Ninth*. Bribes come openly or covertly, disguised as an interest in a business, as a lawyer's fee, or, very often, as a loan. Bribes come directly, paid into the waiting hands of the bribee or, more commonly, indirectly to the subordinate or friend performing the nearly indispensable office of bagman. Bribes come in all shapes as sex, commodities, appointments, and, most often, cash. In the shape of sex, bribes have been both male and female: a slave, a wife, a noble boy. As commodities, they have included bedspreads, cups, dogs, fruits, furniture, furs, golf balls, jewels, livestock, peacocks, pork, sturgeon, travel, wine—the gamut of enjoyable goods. As appointments, they have often been rationalized or justified by the merits of the appointee—a double effect, one good, one bad, being achieved by the bribe. As cash they have come as contingent payments and down payments, as payments for the life of the contract and payments for the life of the recipient and as cash on the spot. They have come at the rate of so much a car towed, so much a prostitute undisturbed, so much a plane purchased, so much a guinea spent, at such a percentage, and at a flat rate. They have been as little as 1 percent of a contract and as high as 20 percent or more. They have been as small as $2.50 for a Connecticut voter and as much as $12,000,000 for the prime minister of Japan and his associates. . . .

*Tenth*. Bribers have included every variety of business, from very small to multinational; all the professions; every manner of criminal defendant; and the ordinary citizen in line for an inheritance or in need of a traffic ticket being fixed. Bribees have ranged from constables and sheriffs to the Speaker of the House (U.S., nineteenth century), the Speaker of the House of Commons (U.K., seventeenth century), the president of Honduras, the president of Italy, the prime minister of Japan, the prince-consort of the Netherlands, the Lord Chancellor of England (seventeenth century). Bribe-takers and bribe-givers are not distinguished by any of the characteristics commonly associated with criminality. Sometimes they are oppressed and bribe to escape harassment. Sometimes they are oppressed and therefore accept bribes. Often they are possessed of high office and comfortable income, bribe to maintain or expand their power or wealth, and accept bribes given as tributes to their power or wealth. Their crimes have not been shown to depend on any oedipal fixation, sexual need or malfunction, or uncontrollable instinct. They are not vicious in all respects; they are often otherwise decent individuals. They are of all nationalities and sects and have been in the past more often men than women.

*Eleventh*. The bribe is ideologically neutral—that is, charges of bribery can be made by an established class attacking a new class (John Randolph pursuing the Yazoo speculators; George Templeton Strong

scorning the Tweed Ring); by a new class attacking an old class (the Protestants assailing the papacy; Andrew Jackson censuring Adams and Clay); and in intraclass warfare (Coke against Bacon; the Carter administration against the Abscam defendants). The bribe is a concept which can be effectively evoked by "the center" or existing hierarchy, as fourth-century Roman emperors and popes like Gregory I, Gregory VII, and Innocent III illustrate. It is a concept which is useful to "the border" or sectarian groupings within a society, as is shown by the writings of John Wyclif and Jan Hus.

*Twelfth*. Enforcement of law against bribes has nearly always been a function of prosecutorial discretion. Prosecutions for bribery have often depended on motivations distinct from the desire to punish the bribe. The watershed for widespread federal prosecution of bribery occurred in the 1960s. Whatever social causes account for it, at this time the pursuit of bribery became a national enterprise in the United States. Watergate is the consequence not the cause of this phenomenon. In the Orwellian prophecy for the year 1984, sexual Puritanism is the rule, enforced by electronics. In the actual America of 1984, it is the purity of political reciprocities that is enforced by wire taps, tape recordings, and television cameras.

*Thirteenth*. The commonest sanctions against bribes are moral—the invocation of guilt before God and shame before society, guilt and shame being equally relied on. Political sanctions—repudiation at the polls, forced resignation from office, loss of promotion—are frequently invoked. Sanctions prescribed by law are more often indirect than direct—not the crime of bribery itself but a related offense is usually punished. Until very recent times application of direct criminal sanctions to highly placed bribe-takers was rare.

*Fourteenth*. Prosecutors, politicians, and journalists are those most attentive to contemporary corruption. Academic lawyers, anthropologists, psychoanalysts, and theologians have had little to say. Political scientists and sociologists, intent on understanding the function of social practices, sometimes give little weight to the moral impact of corruption. Biographers and historians, despite a tendency at times to act as advocates or apologists, give a kind of secular last judgment on the corrupt. Those who have most powerfully articulated the antibribery ethic are the masters of Western literature—above, all, Chaucer, Dante, and Shakespeare.

*Fifteenth.* The material injury bribers and bribees inflict is often undemonstrable. Their actions always subvert the trust that accompanies public office and distinguishes office from power. For Jews, for Christians, for those who share their moral heritage, the bribe is not a morally neutral concept.

Writing at this interesting time in the history of the bribe, I venture a prediction that is a projection of my values. That will come at the end. History itself is not prediction but the selection of significant actions, words, and characters to be remembered—drama more than process. "Remember! Remember! Remember!"—Burke's incantation after his prosecution of Warren Hastings had ended in defeat. If all that is collected here survives in memory, this account has been worth making.

## QUESTIONS

1. How would you delineate the difference between a bribe and a gift?

2. What is it about a bribe that makes it such a prevalent ethical problem in history? Why has bribery been discredited for so long in so many places?

3. Are anti-bribery rules the luxury of wealthy countries and a hindrance to people in developing countries? Are countries corrupt because they are poor or poor because they are corrupt?

---

To: You
From: The Philosopher
Subject: The Foreign Corrupt Practices Act

I always thought that the Foreign Corrupt Practices Act (FCPA) put American Companies at a disadvantage. After all, how can they compete in some markets when other companies can pay bribes to get business? Then I read that in 2008 Siemens paid $800 million to the U.S. and Germany to settle a bribery case. The company was later charged for paying $100 million in bribes to the Carlos Menem, the then President of Argentina, and other Argentine officials to secure a $1 billion project.* The bribery took place in Argentina and the people who paid, demanded, and received the bribes were Argentine, and Siemans is a German company. Yet, Siemans was prosecuted and fined for violating a US law! I did not know that in 1998, the U.S. extended the FPCA to foreign companies, like Siemans, that traded their securities in the United States.

While this amendment sounds good for U.S. companies, it also makes me wonder: Is it fair to force companies from other countries to play by laws based on the U.S. values? Here is what the law says:

The Foreign Corrupt Practices Act of 1977 was enacted for the purpose of making it unlawful for certain classes of persons and entities to make payments to foreign government officials to assist in obtaining or retaining business. Specifically, the anti-bribery provisions of the FCPA prohibit the willful use of the mails or any means of instrumentality of interstate commerce corruptly in furtherance of any offer, payment, promise to pay, or authorization of the payment of money or anything of value to any person, while knowing that all or a portion of such money or thing of value will be offered, given or promised, directly or indirectly, to a foreign official to influence the foreign official in his or her official capacity, induce the foreign official to do or omit to do an act in violation of his or her lawful duty, or to secure any improper advantage in order to assist in obtaining or retaining business for or with, or directing business to, any person.

Since 1977, the anti-bribery provisions of the FCPA have applied to all U.S. persons and certain foreign issuers of securities. With the enactment of certain amendments in 1998, the anti-bribery provisions of the FCPA now also apply to foreign firms and persons who cause, directly or through agents, an act in furtherance of such a corrupt payment to take place within the territory of the United States.

The FCPA also requires companies whose securities are listed in the United States to meet its accounting provisions. See 15 U.S.C. § 78m. These accounting provisions, which were designed to operate in tandem with the anti-bribery provisions of the FCPA, require corporations covered by the provisions to (a) make and keep books and records that accurately and fairly reflect the transactions of the corporation and (b) devise and maintain an adequate system of internal accounting controls.**

*Leslie Wayne, "Foreign Firms Most Affected by a U.S. Law Baring Bribes," *The New York Times*, September 3, 2012.
**Quoted from: http://www.justice.gov/criminal/fraud/fcpa/

---

Daryl Koehn                    | # Confucian Trustworthiness

Daryl Koehn is a Professor in the Ethics and Business Law Department of the University of St. Thomas.

*It is not the failure of others to appreciate your abilities that should trouble you, but rather your own lack of them.*[1]

—*Confucius*

Confucius contends that individuals are ethically obligated to refine themselves and to become exemplary human beings. Such refinement (jen*) requires education. Becoming an educated and influential individual depends, in turn, upon establishing trust: "Only after he has gained the trust of the common people does the gentleman work them hard, for otherwise they would feel themselves illused. Only after he has gained the trust of the lord does the gentleman advise him against unwise action, for otherwise the lord would feel himself slandered" (19/9).

At first glance, Confucius appears to think of trust in a manner not all that different from Western theorists. Trust is the trustor's expectation of good will on the part of the trustee. Trust is something we can bestow on or refuse to other people. Trust must be gained and, if we are not careful when reposing trust, we will feel ourselves betrayed. On closer examination, though, we find that Confucius diverges from many Western theorists because he regards the virtue of trustworthiness as more important than trust per se.

To be worthy of our trust a person does not have to cater to our needs. While a good leader will try to ensure that those ruled have enough to eat and drink, people will still honor a leader in hard times: "Death has always been with us since the beginning of time, but when there is no trust, the common people will have nothing to stand on" (12/7). This saying suggests that we should trust as long as the good will of the trustee is evident, regardless of whether the trustee promotes our material well-being or conforms to our expectations. Virtuous persons, who look beyond their own narrow self-interest and who seek the spiritual as well as merely material welfare of all of their fellow citizens, merit our trust. Cultivated individuals display good will by never treating the multitude with contempt. Instead he always praises the good while taking pity on the backward (19/3). To excessively hate those who are not refined only provokes them to unruly behavior (8/10), and the trustworthy person seeks to avoid war and conflict (7/13).

Those who are devoted to the way of virtue take instruction from anyone who speaks well. Anyone who truly is trying to be virtuous is eager to learn, and she never dismisses what is said on account of who is speaking (15/23). The person of jen* will even speak with a madman (18/5). In general, the person of jen* is intent upon helping others realize what is good in them (12/16). He neither looks for the evil nor denounces others as evil (17/24). He hates evil, not evil people: "To attack evil as evil and not as evil of a particular man, is that not the way to reform the depraved?" (12/21). If we focus upon evil persons, we will not discern opportunities for realizing the good in others. We will not merit the trust of others because we will not be acting so as to refine people. Instead, our judgments will foster hatred and discord.

Many Western ethics of trust contend that we are justified in accusing those who fall short of our expectations of betrayal. Confucius asks us to consider instead whether we have demanded more of those we have trusted than we should have. We ought to err on the side of making allowances for people (15/15), remembering that individuals have different strengths. Virtue exists as a continuum. The person of jen* has good relations with others precisely because she does not expect complete virtue from everyone:

> A man good enough as a partner in one's studies need not be good enough as a partner in the pursuit of the way; a man good enough as a partner in the pursuit of the way need not be good enough as a partner in a common stand; a man good enough as a partner in a common stand need not be good enough as a partner in the exercise of moral discretion (9/30).

It is up to us to choose our partners and friends carefully. In some cases, our business associates, friends, and family members may fail to keep their promises to us or may not show us due respect. However, we should not waste our energy accusing them of being untrustworthy. It is not the failure of others to appreciate our abilities that should trouble us, but rather our own lack of abilities (14/29). The Confucian ethic sees the value of trust but always directs our attention back to our own performance and attitudes. When there is trouble, we should look inward (4/17) and bring charges against ourselves, instead of blaming or scapegoating others (5/26).

The Confucian ethic takes the energy out of our anger at others for slighting us and redirects that energy back into self-examination. This redirection is appropriate for several reasons. First, there is little point in getting angry with others. If they have harmed us out of ignorance, then the correct response is to try to educate them, not to harm them in return. If they intend us harm, we should still try to dissuade them, rather than retaliate in kind. Second, even if others persist in trying to wrong us, we should not let their actions distract us from the arduous work of becoming an authoritative person. Since refinement or jen* is within our control, we always should look to our own behavior and not worry overly much about what others are or are not doing to us. Warned that Huan T'ui would try to assassinate him, Confucius retorted: "Heaven is the author of the virtue that is in me. What can Huan

T'ui do to me?" (7/23). The person of jen* is free from anxieties (7/37) because he keeps his eye on what is most important: "If, on examining himself, a man finds nothing to reproach himself for, what worries and fears can he have?" (12/4). Confucius was famous for maintaining his composure in the face of insults: "To be transgressed against yet not to mind. It was towards this end that my friend [Confucius] used to direct his efforts" (8/5). It is our trustworthiness, not others' machinations or venom, that should be our primary concern.

Third, it is easy to misjudge another. We may think, for example, that someone is not a good leader because the community or corporation he leads is in disarray. Yet "even with a true king, it is bound to take a generation for benevolence to become a reality" (13/12). Or we may conclude we have been betrayed when a trusted party deviates from a stated plan of action. Sometimes, though, to change one's mind is the right course. A "man who insists on keeping his word and seeing his actions through to the end . . . shows a stubborn petty-mindedness" (13/20). We cannot hope to assess accurately the "betrayals" of other people if we are not striving simultaneously to be as mindful as possible (15/8). Followers have a responsibility, therefore, to be thoughtful as their leaders. If those who are led are not mindful, they will not be able to grasp the wisdom in what the leader is saying and simply may dismiss her out of hand.

Finally, we humans are only too prone to self-deceit. Scrupulous self-examination is necessary if we are not to err. For example, we may be inclined to dismiss younger workers as undisciplined and undeserving of our trust and regard. Yet, we are far from infallible. How "do we know that the generations to come will not be equal of the present?" (9/23). In other cases, our judgment may be motivated by bad faith. One should never oppose a lord or ruler without first making certain of one's own honesty (14/22). If all of us would engage in routine self-scrutiny, we would be more worthy of trust. We then would trust one another more fully. With more trust, we would be able to educate each other even better, thereby increasing the level of trustworthiness and engendering still more trust. If people are failing to live up to their potential and living in

discord, then perhaps it is because we are failing to lead by example (13/4). When Confucius wanted to settle in the midst of the "barbarians." one of his disciples asked, "But could you put up with their uncouth ways?" Confucius bitingly retorted, "Once a gentleman settles amongst them, what uncouthness will there be?" (9/14).

For all of these reasons, Confucius warns that to love trust without loving learning can lead an individual to do harm (17/8). Judging other people's good will without simultaneously turning a critical eye on our own standard and trust-worthiness is a recipe for disaster. It does not follow that we should tolerate any and all abuse. The person of jen* is not angered by abuse, but neither does she stick around to be mistreated. She tries to choose her friends carefully, refusing to accept anyone as a friend who is not as good as herself (9/25; see also 16/4). That does not mean she chooses only completely virtuous individuals as her friends. It does mean she looks for others who are as critically mindful as she is. Her friends should be eager to learn. She advises them as best she can but stops if her advice is not being heeded. She does not ask to be snubbed (12/23) and does not waste her words on those who are incapable of improving themselves (15/8). The superior person does not look for evil but she quickly discerns it because she is thoughtful. So, "without anticipating attempts at deception or presuming acts of bad faith, [she] is, nevertheless, the first to be aware of such behavior" (14/31). Her responses to others' acts are similarly nuanced. An injury should not be taken personally but neither should it be rewarded. Confucius rejects a student's suggestion that one should repay an injury with a good turn. For if you did so, then "what do you repay a good turn with? You repay an injury with straightness, but you repay a good turn with a good turn" (14/34).

By judging and responding with a high degree of discretion, we show ourselves to be worthy of trust. In turn, we should trust those who are consistently thoughtful. There probably is no such thing as a perfect friend or colleague. However, if we use good judgment and do not expect too much of our colleagues and associates; and if our friends use good judgment as well and do not take on too much responsibility, then we can have strong, secure, and trusting relations with our fellow employees and friends.

## SUSPICION OF CONTRACTS

Like the Japanese, the Chinese historically have been loathe to rely upon contracts. They often will not even read long contracts and may insist the document be shortened. A contract is merely a commercial agreement not to be taken as the gospel: "You might say they [the Chinese] sign long complicated contracts only as a formal confirmation that they intend to do business with you, not how they are going to conduct the business." The Confucian emphasis on trustworthiness makes reliance on contracts less attractive for several reasons. First, use of detailed contracts encourages parties to think of the contract as the basis for trust. The parties then feel entitled to accuse each other of betrayal whenever one appears to the other to have deviated from the terms of the contract. The contract thus contributes to an atmosphere of distrust. By contrast, if people enter into relationships and transactions with the understanding that they will need to work hard to accommodate their partner's interests and to keep their own biases and self-righteousness in check, then they will have put their relationship on a sounder footing. They may still decide to use some simple written document to lay out key terms or to serve as a talking document, but they will not make adherence to a contract the entire basis of the relation.

Second, reliance on contracts can prevent people from focussing on the larger picture and from being as mindful as they should be. A number of disputes between the Chinese and their joint venture partners have involved transfer of technology issues. The foreign partner typically accuses the Chinese side of failing to meet contractual requirements to supply land or capital, while the Chinese claim that the foreign partner has not provided the technical training the two had agreed upon. The foreign partner has generally viewed this counter-claim as a fabrication. It did provide training and the Chinese are simply trying to justify their own breach of contract. While that might be true in some cases, the person of jen* would look beyond the contractual dispute to the larger cultural and economic issues.

The Chinese have good reason to be sensitive about technical training. The government has made a conscious decision to modernize the country by importing technology and then adapting it to suit their needs and their level of development. Mao Tse Tung imported "turnkey" facilities—i.e., entire factories. The current policy is to build their own facilities using imported technology. In an effort to acquire technology as cheaply as possible, the Chinese have been willing to acquire slightly older hardware and software in the secondhand market. This modernization strategy obviously will not succeed if they do not also learn to use the technology. Therefore, the Chinese place great emphasis on jishu jiaoliu or technical presentations conveying technical information. They will bring in successive groups. Each group asks most of the same questions their predecessors posed. The Chinese use these sessions not only to brief all members of their team on the status of the project but also to train their people in the technology. They do not see themselves as "using" these presenters for their own purposes. They simply see themselves as obtaining an education that any person of genuine good will would wish to help them obtain.

Given their history of being colonized, the Chinese are understandably afraid of being exploited. Many have noted that, as late as the beginning of World War II, Shanghai's British quarters still had signs proclaiming "Chinamen and dogs are not permitted to enter." They do not want to give up hard currency and to provide land and other resources to their former masters in exchange for technology they are unable to use. Nor do they want to become a dumping ground for obsolete or non-functioning software. If they cannot get the software to run, they naturally suspect that they have been duped. What Westerners view as a rather cut-and-dried contractual dispute— did the Chinese live up to their end of the bargain or not?—is a major cultural issue for the Chinese. The future of China and Chinese pride and self-respect is at stake in each of these deals. Contracting to do business with the Chinese will never build trust unless each side consistently looks beyond the contract to discern the economic, psychological, and cultural factors at work.[7] Parties will be more inclined to take this broad and more generous point of view if they remind themselves that they may not know as much about the situation as they think they do. Contractual disputes will prove more resolvable if each side shifts its attention away from the other's alleged betrayal and to the question of whether it has been behaving trustworthily.

## THE PROMINENCE OF GUANXI

The Chinese reliance on connections or guanxi is another important feature of the Chinese business scene. Does the Confucian ethic endorse such a reliance? Guanxi is typically seen as an outgrowth of the Confucian emphasis on personal relations. And it is true that, for Confucius, good order requires that each person fulfill his particular role-based duties. Children should be filial. The ruler should be a ruler and a father should be a father (12/11). Persons should acknowledge their role in the hierarchy. Historically these roles were relatively fixed by custom. There was little public law to which people could appeal if the authorities abused their power. In such a system, it became vitally important to cultivate relations with powerful people in the event one needed some sort of help from an authority. Family and local ties were especially important. To this day Chinese businesspeople will often treat classmates, friends, and family members preferentially when making hiring or other business decisions.

Public authorities, especially local authorities, continue to exercise a phenomenal degree of power in China. Kristoff and Wudunn argue that China still has an imperial system. The party leader is the new emperor, but local chieftains share in this absolute power:

> Each lower official acts like a prince on his own turf, from the ministry to the department to the section to the team, from the factory manager to the production manager to the workshop director. The petty autocrats are often the worst, as well as the most difficult to escape. In many villages, the local chief rules even more absolutely than [the national leader], for he decides who can marry, who can get good land, who can get water for irrigation, who can be buried where. He is almost as powerful as God, but not so remote.

Businesspeople, therefore, are well advised to cultivate guanxi. However, it would be a mistake to conclude, as Francis Fukuyama does, that China is a low-trust, family-oriented society whose members have little practice or interest in interacting with outsiders or in dealing with others on an equal basis. If this were true, the Chinese would never have been able to achieve their economic miracle: China now ranks first in the world in the production of coal, cement, grain, fish, meat, and cotton; third in steel production; and fifth in crude oil output; its annual growth rate has averaged more than 9 percent since 1978. The Chinese would never have succeeded if they had not imported their technology and had not formed numerous joint ventures with foreign companies. Nearly 10 percent of China's industrial output comes from foreign-owned and private businesses.

It should also be noted that the fastest-growing countries during the last decade—China, Japan, Hong Kong, Singapore, Taiwan, and South Korea—either have a large Chinese population or have been heavily influenced by Chinese culture. The ethnic Chinese may be the most economically successful ethnic group in the world. Although they constitute only 1.5 percent of the Philippine population, they are responsible for 35 percent of the sales of locally owned firms. In Indonesia, they are 2 percent of the population but may own as much as 70 percent of private domestic capital. Again, these minority Chinese populations would never have done as well as they did if they had refused to deal with non-family members.

## CONCLUSION

Although recent Western discussions of trust have tended to focus on conditions for reposing trust, Confucius asks us to see trustworthiness as the more important phenomenon: How should we behave if we are to make ourselves into beings truly worthy of trust? What responsibility do we have for ensuring that our judgment of someone's trustworthiness is sound? The Confucian ethic calls into question whether a business leader can earn the trust of her followers simply by adhering to select rules (e.g., "avoid conflicts of interest") or by adopting certain techniques. Being thoughtful is ultimately the only way to earn and merit the trust of one's fellow citizens.

## NOTE

All references to Confucian sayings are to the chapter and paragraph listing in Confucius, *The Analects*, trans. D. C. Lau (London: Penguin Books, 1979).

## QUESTIONS

1. What elements of Confucian Ethics are similar to Western ethics?
2. Why do the Chinese and Japanese dislike contracts?
3. What are the strengths and weaknesses of business ethics that rely more on trust and relationships than on rules and regulations?

# CASES

## CASE 11.1
# The Oil Rig
Joanne B. Ciulla

You have just taken over as the new chief executive officer of Stratton Oil Company, an exploration and drilling firm under contract to a major multinational oil company. Your enterprise has experienced ups and downs over the past few years because of the fluctuation of international oil prices and complications with overseas operations.

Many of the operational problems stem from difficulties with Stratton's offshore oil-drilling rigs. Maintenance and equipment costs have skyrocketed. You have received several reports of strained labor relations on the platforms. One incident caused such an uproar that the rig manager halted operations for over a week. In addition, there have been a number of complaints from conscientious shareholders who are concerned with the environmental impact of these rigs.

In an attempt to address these issues, you decide to get a firsthand look at the offshore drilling operations. On your first excursion, you visit a rig off the coast of Africa, dubbed the "Voyager 7." You discover that an oil rig is really a small society, separate and distinct from the rest of the world.

Stratton's Voyager 7 is a relatively small "jackup" (a platform with legs) with dimensions of about 200 feet by 100 feet. The platform houses a crew of 150 men, made up of skilled laborers, "roustabouts" or unskilled laborers, maintenance staff, and 30 expatriates. The expatriates work as roughnecks, drillers, technicians, or administrators. The top administrator on the Voyager 7 is the "tool pusher," an expatriate who wields almost absolute authority over matters pertaining to life on the rig.

Stratton engineers modified the crew quarters on the Voyager 7 for operations in Africa. They installed a second galley on the lower level and enlarged the cabins to permit a dormitory-style arrangement of 16 persons per room. This lower level of the rig makes up the "African section" of the rig, where the 120 local workers eat, sleep, and socialize during their 28-day "hitch."

The upper level of the platform houses the 30 expatriates in an area that is equal in square footage to that of the African section. The "expatriate section" contains semiprivate quarters with baths and boasts its own galley, game room, and movie room. Although not explicitly written, a tacit regulation exists prohibiting African workers from entering the expatriate section of the rig except in emergencies. The only Africans who are exempt from this regulation are those who are assigned to the highly valued positions of cleaning or galley staff in the expatriate section. The Africans hold these positions in high esteem because of the potential for receiving gifts or recovering discarded razors and other items from the expatriates.

Several other rig policies separate the African workers from the expatriates. African laborers travel to and from the rig by boat (an 18-hour trip), whereas expatriates receive helicopter transportation. An expatriate registered nurse dispenses medical attention to the expatriates throughout the day, but the Africans have access to treatment only during shift changes or in an emergency. The two groups also receive disparate treatment when serious injuries arise. For instance, if a finger is severed, expatriates are rushed to the mainland for reconstructive surgery. However, because of the high cost of helicopter transportation, African workers must have an amputation operation performed on the rig by the medic.

The company issues gray coveralls to the Africans, while the expatriates receive red coveralls. Meals in the two galleys are vastly different: The expatriate galley serves fine cuisine that approaches gourmet quality, while the Africans dine on a somewhat more proletarian fare. Despite the gross disparity in the numbers served, the catering budgets for the two galleys are nearly equal.

Communication between the expatriates and the Africans is notably absent on the Voyager 7, since none of the expatriates speaks the native language and none of the Africans speaks more that a few words of the expatriate's language. Only the chef of the catering company knows both languages. Consequently, he acts as an interpreter in all emergency situations. In the everyday working environment, management must rely upon sign language or repetition of examples to train and coordinate efforts.

From time to time, an entourage of African government officials visits the Voyager 7. These visits normally last only for an hour or so. Invariably, the officials dine with the expatriates, take a brief tour of the equipment, and then return to shore by helicopter. No entourage has never expressed concern about the disparity in living conditions on the rig, nor have officials ever bothered to speak with the African workers. Observers comment that the officials seem disinterested in the situation of the African workers, most of whom come from outside the capital city.

The presence of an expatriate black worker has little effect on the rig's segregated environment. The expatriate black is assigned to the expatriate section and partakes in all expatriate privileges. However, few expatriate blacks participate in the international drilling business, and the few who do are frequently not completely welcomed into the rig's social activities.

You leave the oil rig feeling uneasy. You know that there has always been a disparity in living conditions on the drilling platforms. However, you want to make Stratton a socially responsible and profitable company. You wonder how you can best accomplish your dual goals.

## QUESTIONS

1. What do you think is really bothering the workers?
2. What kinds of inequalities are tolerable and intolerable on an oil rig, in operations away from home, and inside an organization at home?
3. Does an international corporation have an obligation to give employees benefits that they do not ask for or expect from an employer?

## CASE 11.2

## Foreign Assignment

Thomas Dunfee and Diana Robertson

Sara Strong graduated with an MBA from UCLA four years ago. She immediately took a job in the correspondent bank section of the Security Bank of the American Continent. Sara was assigned to work on issues pertaining to relationships with correspondent banks in Latin America. She rose rapidly in the section and received three good promotions in three years. She consistently got high ratings from her superiors, and she received particularly high marks for her professional demeanor.

In her initial position with the bank, Sara was required to travel to Mexico on several occasions. She was always accompanied by a male colleague even though she generally handled similar business by herself on trips within the United States. During her trips to Mexico she observed that Mexican bankers seemed more aware of her being a woman and were personally solicitous to her, but she didn't discern any major problems. The final decisions on the work that she did were handled by male representatives of the bank stationed in Mexico.

A successful foreign assignment was an important step for those on the "fast track" at the bank. Sara applied for a position in Central or South America and was delighted when she was assigned to the bank's office in Mexico City. The office had about twenty bank employees and was headed by William Vitam. The Mexico City office was seen as a preferred assignment by young executives at the bank.

After a month, Sara began to encounter problems. She found it difficult to be effective in dealing with Mexican bankers—the clients. They appeared reluctant to accept her authority and they would often bypass her in important matters. The problem was exacerbated by Vitam's compliance in her being bypassed. When she asked that the clients be referred back to her, Vitam replied, "Of course that isn't really practical." Vitam made matters worse by patronizing her in front of clients and by referring to her as "my cute assistant" and "our lady banker." Vitam never did this when only Americans were present, and in fact treated her professionally and with respect in internal situations.

Sara finally complained to Vitam that he was undermining her authority and effectiveness; she asked him in as positive a manner as possible to help her. Vitam listened carefully to Sara's complaints, then replied: "I'm glad that you brought this up, because I've been meaning to sit down and talk to you about my little game-playing in front of the clients. Let me be frank with you. Our clients think you're great, but they just don't understand a woman in authority, and you and I aren't going to be able to change their attitudes overnight. As long as the clients see you as my assistant and deferring to me, they can do business with you. I'm willing to give you as much responsibility as they can handle your having. I *know* you can handle it. But we just have to tread carefully. You and I know that my remarks in front of clients don't mean anything. They're just a way of playing the game Latin style. I know it's frustrating for you, but I really need you to support me on this. It's not going to affect your promotions, and for the most part you really will have responsibility for these clients' accounts. You just have to act like it's my responsibility." Sara replied that she would

Case study by Thomas Dunfee and Diana Robertson, "Foreign Assignment," the Wharton School of Business, The University of Pennsylvania. Reprinted by permission of the authors.

try to cooperate, but that basically she found her role demeaning.

As time went on, Sara found that the patronizing actions in front of clients bothered her more and more. She spoke to Vitam again, but he was firm in his position, and urged her to try to be a little more flexible, even a little more "feminine."

Sara also had a problem with Vitam over policy. The Mexico City office had five younger women who worked as receptionists and secretaries. They were all situated at work stations at the entrance to the office. They were required to wear standard uniforms that were colorful and slightly sexy. Sara protested the requirement that uniforms be worn because (1) they were inconsistent to the image of the banking business and (2) they were demeaning to the women who had to wear them. Vitam just curtly replied that he had received a lot of favorable comments about the uniforms from clients of the bank.

Several months later, Sara had what she thought would be a good opportunity to deal with the problem. Tom Fried, an executive vice president who had been a mentor for her since she arrived at the bank, was coming to Mexico City; she arranged a private conference with him. She described her

problems and explained that she was not able to be effective in this environment and that she worried that it would have a negative effect on her chance of promotion within the bank. Fried was very careful in his response. He spoke of certain "realities" that the bank had to respect and he urged her to "see it through" even though he could understand how she would feel that things weren't fair.

Sara found herself becoming more aggressive and defensive in her meetings with Vitam and her clients. Several clients asked that other bank personnel handle their transactions. Sara has just received an Average rating, which noted "the beginnings of a negative attitude about the bank and its policies."

## QUESTIONS

1. Do you think that Vitam and Tom are correct about the "realities" of the culture concerning women? If these cultural assumptions are correct, what are the ethical implications of following the "when in Rome" principle?

2. Was Sarah treated fairly in her evaluation?

3. Where would you draw the line between personal dignity and serving the interests of your company?

# CASE 11.3
## The Quandary at PureDrug
Karen Marquiss and Joanne B. Ciulla

You are the Chief Executive Officer of PureDrug, a large pharmaceutical company with sales and operations throughout the world. Your firm has an outstanding reputation for quality as well as a long-term record of growth and profitability. Over the past 10 years, sales grew at an average annual compound

rate of 12 percent and profits increased by an average of 15 percent per annum. The company had not experienced losses since 1957, and stock prices remained consistently healthy.

In spite of PureDrug's impeccable record, by October 1991 your company is in trouble. Due to a

Karen Marquiss & Joanne B. Ciulla "The Quandary at PureDrug" in Paul Minus, ed., *The Ethics of Business in a Global Economy* (Boston: Kluwer Academic Press, 1993), pp. 130–131.

general economic downturn and a few product development problems, the firm faces a declining market share and weakened corporate profits. Although still profitable, PureDrug fell far short of its goals established for 1990. As of the end of the third quarter of 1991, you project a $4 million loss for the year. The value of your corporate stock has already dropped by one-fifth of its 1990 year-end value, and a loss for the year could result in an even more substantial devaluation. Small investors might switch to pharmaceutical companies with better results. Even worse, a disappointing year could cause large institutional investors such as pension funds to support a takeover by one of your competitors.

In an attempt to remedy the immediate situation, you call an emergency meeting of your top managers to poll their suggestions. Charles Dunn, head of the International Export Division, reminds you that his department has an opportunity to sign an $8 million contract with the Philippine government. The contract involves the sale of Travolene, a new injectable drug, developed by PureDrug for the treatment of serious viral infections, including measles. The drug remains difficult and expensive to manufacture and has been in very short supply since its introduction. The 1991 budget did not include this sale due to the lack of product availability.

Dunn mentions that at this time PureDrug's inventory contains a large lot of Travolene, produced at a cost of about $2 million. The government rejected the batch for the domestic market on the basis of a new, very sensitive test for endotoxin. The authorities recently adopted this test in addition to the standard method that had been used for many years. The more sensitive test revealed a very low level of endotoxin in the batch of Travolene, while the old procedure uncovered no endotoxin whatsoever.

You ask Ann Doe, the company's Chief Medical Safety Officer, whether this rules out shipping the batch to the Philippines. She explains that the Philippines and many other countries still rely exclusively on the old test. Ann said, "It always takes them a while to adopt more sophisticated practices, and sometimes they never do. Endotoxin might cause high fever when injected into patients, but I can't tell you that the level in this batch is high enough to cause trouble. Still, how can we have a double standard, one for our nation and one for Third World countries?"

Charles Dunn interrupts, "It's not our job to overprotect other countries. The health authorities in the Philippines know what they are doing. Our officials always take an extreme position. Measles is a serious illness. Last year in the Philippines half of the children who contracted measles died. It's not only good business but also good ethics to send them the only batch of Travolene we have available."

As the other senior members of PureDrug's management begin to take sides on the issue, you contemplate your options. In the short run, the profit margin on the lot of Travolene would boost PureDrug's bottom line into the black for the year. In addition, the sale to the Philippines could foster a lucrative long-term relationship and lead to expansion into other Asian markets.

You leave the meeting with an uneasy feeling. You have only 72 hours before you must present a plan to PureDrug's Board of Directors.

## QUESTIONS

1. Is it ethical for PureDrug to practice one standard of safety at home and another in a foreign country?

2. If children in the Philippines die as the result of taking Tavolene, is Puredrug morally responsible for it?

3. Do foreign clients have the right to make dangerous decisions about your country's products?

# CASE 11.4

## IBM's Business with Hitler: An Inconvenient Past

Judith Schrempf-Stirling, and Guido Palazzo

Judith Schrempf-Stirling is an Assistant Professor of Management, Robins School of Business, University of Richmond; and Guido Palazzo is Professor of Business Ethics, HEC, University of Lausanne.

**September 9, 1939: IBM Headquarter, New York.**
With full attention Thomas J. Watson, president of International Business Machines (IBM) read the business letter from Herman Rottke, manager of IBM's German subsidiary, Dehomag which arrived by mid-September 1939, only a few days after Adolf Hitler had invaded Poland.

*Dear Mr. Watson:*

*During your last visit in Berlin at the beginning of July, you made the kind offer to me that you might be willing to furnish the German company machines from Endicott in order to shorten our long delivery terms. I . . . asked you to leave with us for study purposes one alphabetic tabulating machine and a collator out of the American machines at present in Germany. You have complied with this request, for which I thank you very much, and have added that in cases of urgent need, I may make use of other American machines. . . .*

*You will understand that under today's conditions, a certain need has arisen for such machines, which we do not build as yet in Germany. Therefore, I should like to make use of your kind offer and ask you to leave with the German company for the time being the alphabetic tabulating machines which are at present still in the former Austria. . . . This offer, made orally by you, dear Mr. Watson . . . will undoubtedly be greatly appreciated in many and especially responsible circles. . . . We should thank you if you would ask your Geneva organization, at the same time, to furnish us the necessary repair parts for the maintenance of the machines. . . .*

*Yours very truly,*

*H. Rottke*

Watson stared at the letter and wondered what to respond while recalling the economic, political, and social climate in Germany.

## PERSECUTION OF JEWS IN GERMANY

When Adolf Hitler became Reich Chancellor in 1933, he announced his ambition to strengthen Germany's economic and territorial position and to create the (Jew-free) Master Race. Many of his initiated regulations and activities were aimed at bringing this vision into reality. He passed critical discriminating regulations, and he initiated and supported boycotts against the Jewish population.[1] The extermination of Jews (genocide), however, was not planned from the beginning but gradually developed. Only in 1942 the "Final solution to the Jewish question" was decided at the Wannsee Conference. In total, Hitler's fight against Jews developed in six phases: identification, exclusion, confiscation, ghettoization, deportation, and extermination.[2] The last two phases took place after the Wannsee Conference (1942).

First, Hitler's Nazi regime identified those people who—according to Nazi philosophy— were of the minor race, i.e. Jews. Hitler ordered that a census be carried out to find out how many Jews lived in Germany and where they lived.[3] According to Nazism, it did not matter whether a Jew was a practicing Jew or not. Using complicated racial mathematics, the Nazis derived at different categories of Jews (full Jew, half Jew).[4] Having Jewish ancestors made a person Jewish. For the Nazis, all kinds of Jews were a threat to the Aryan race and needed to be identified and excluded from society.

This second stage, exclusion, began with the introduction of the *Aryan Paragraph* in 1933. The Aryan paragraph entitled only Aryans to be members of an organization, institution, or corporation.[5] This clause was first applied to the officialdom, which displaced Jewish official servants. The Aryan Paragraph was gradually applied to other professions such as notaries and lawyers.[6] Furthermore, the Nazi regime appealed for a public boycott of Jewish shops and businesses since April 1933. Step by step, Jews were socially and culturally isolated from society.

The third phase—confiscation and expropriation—started with the Nuremberg Decrees in 1935.[7] The Nazi government passed "The law for the protection of German blood" and the "Reich Citizenship Law," which deprived Jews of their German citizenship and all related rights. The Jewish population was increasingly deprived of their assets and possessions. Jewish shop owners were forced to transfer their business to Aryans and hand over other valuable possessions to the Nazi regime. The segregation between Jews and Aryans became more and more visible. From 1935 on, Jews were, for instance, not allowed to marry or to have sexual relationships with Aryans. The first climax of the Anti-Semitism fostered by the Nazis was the Kristallnacht (the Night of Broken Glass) on November 9, 1938. Numerous synagogues, Jewish shops, and Jewish apartments were destroyed and depredated. Around 100 Jews were killed that night and over 20,000 were arrested.

The Nazi policies during their first years of power aimed at banishing the Jewish population out of Germany. Until November 1938, around 170,000 Jews emigrated from Germany as their living conditions had changed dramatically: Nazi regulations did not allow Jews to own land, have health insurance, own a car, get child allowances, work, and participate in social or cultural life.[8] Since 1938, Jews had to add the names Sarah (for women) and Israel (for men) in their passports and any other official documents. Besides, the letter "J" was stamped on their passports to signal immediately their Jewish origins. When Hitler annexed Austria and Czechoslovakia in 1938, those regulations were also introduced in these countries.[9]

With the occupation of Poland in September 1939, the fourth phase, ghettoization, started. Ghettos functioned as a tool to control and segregate Jews

from Aryans. Jews were forced to wear badges and armbands with the Star of David. They had to perform forced labor during their stay in the ghettos. Jewish Councils were established which were responsible for the organization of daily ghetto life. After the resolutions at the Wannsee Conference in 1942, the ghettos became intermediate stations for Jews. From there, they were deported to concentration camps.

The Jewish Councils in the ghettos were responsible for administering the deportation, which was the fifth stage of the Holocaust. Concentration camps were already established in 1933 and 1937 (Dachau and Buchenwald, respectively). Their numbers increased exponentially with the blitzkrieg against Poland in September 1939. In the first years of Hitler's regime, mainly political opponents were sent to concentration camps. Later, people who did not correspond to the Nazi race ideology were herded off to the camps. Those included "antisocials," homosexuals, Jehovah Witnesses, and gypsies. Since the Kristallnacht, more and more Jews were deported to the camps. Concentration camps had various functions. They gathered Jews to specific locations, but also functioned as working camps. Prisoners were assigned work according to their physical strength and skills. Inmates worked in quarries and brickyards or did any other work related to the preparation or the support of Germany's war machine. The working and living conditions in the camps were devastating. Prisoners suffered from hunger and contagions. Some were exposed to inhuman medical experiments like those carried out by Dr. Josef Mengele, who conducted cruel experiments with twins in Auschwitz.[10] During the war years, from 1939 to 1945, some camps evolved to extermination (death) camps where the "final solution" (destruction of the Jewish population in Europe as decided at the Wannsee Conference) was executed.[11]

## INTERNATIONAL BUSINESS MACHINES (IBM)

IBM was founded by Herman Hollerith in 1889 and became known as the "Computing Tabulating

Recording Corporation" in 1911. In 1924, the company name changed to "International Business Machines (IBM). IBM's revenue and number of employees increased steadily since 1915, which is linked to the company's expansion to Europe, Asia, South America, and Australia. In 1915, the company had a gross income of $4M with an employee base of around 1600. Only five years later, its income increased threefold, and the number of employees increased to 2700.[12] The 1920s and 1930s constituted a period of steady growth for IBM, despite the Great Depression. In 1930, IBM employed 6700 people worldwide and had an income of nearly $20M.[13] IBM was a flourishing company and cared for its employees. IBM was one of the first companies to introduce group life insurance, survivor benefits, and paid vacation.[14]

### *IBM's Business: Punched Card System*

IBM's core business consisted of punched card data processing equipment and technology. Punch cards became the key medium for data entry, data storage, and processing in institutional computing. IBM was the main manufacturer and marketer for a variety of unit record machines for creating, sorting, and tabulating punched cards. In its earlier years, IBM worked mainly with the U.S. government on population censuses, but soon the company also provided large-scale, custom-built tabulating and punch card solutions for businesses. IBM enjoyed an almost worldwide monopoly in its punch card technology.

A punch card contains information represented by the absence or presence of holes in predefined positions. In 1928, IBM introduced the Eighty-column punch card with 12 punch locations and one character per column. Each column stood for a predefined characteristic according to a client's wishes and information purposes. Punch cards could offer information such as names, addresses, gender, and any other personal data. Eighty columns with 12 horizontal positions lead to 960 punch hole possibilities yielding thousands of demographic permutations. The original usage of the punch card system was the national census, but

the IBM punch card system was also used for other purposes such as train schedules, warehouse goods, and financial transactions and for the identification of people. Tabulating machines summarize, sort, and count the punch card data.

Over the years, IBM continuously improved its tabulating machines in order to make data processing, sorting, and accounting more convenient and time efficient. In 1920, for example, IBM introduced the printing tabulator, which improved speed and accuracy. In the 1930s, IBM further developed alphabetizer–tabulating machines, which created high–speed alphabetized lists. IBM did not sell those tabulating machines, but leased them to its clients. This ensured the company (and its subsidiaries) monthly payments. IBM headquarters in New York kept a detailed book with information as to the location and usage of the machines worldwide. The machines were tailored to the demands of the customer. IBM usually asked its client to disclose the purpose and use of the technology so that engineers could prepare the punch card systems accordingly. Leasing the machines also included a service and maintenance contract. In case repairs and regular maintenance were necessary, IBM technicians traveled to their clients' offices to check that the IBM machines were functional.

### *IBM President: Thomas J. Watson*

Thomas J. Watson was a born salesman and a self-made industrialist. He started his career as a salesman at the National Cash Register Company in 1895 in Ohio.[15] After a short time, Watson became the best salesman on the East Coast. Applying an "anything-goes strategy" and some tricks such as phony transactions and second-hand businesses, Watson ran one competitor after the other out of business.[16] His business practices did not remain unnoticed. In 1913, he was prosecuted for breaching anti-trust legislation and received a $5000 fine. The trial did not harm Watson's business career. In 1914, he joined IBM as a general manager and worked his way to the top with an adamant focus on sales increase. Within only a few years, Watson became the president of IBM and made the company one of the most effective selling organizations. Watson introduced successful business practices at IBM such as generous sales incentives and an evangelical fervor for instilling company pride and loyalty in every worker. Watson's attitude shaped IBM's corporate culture, and the media called him "the Leader."[17]

Watson's business success can be traced back to his strict management style. He did not leave anything to chance. He was the president of one of America's most influential companies and no decision was made without his approval—be it business deals or the decision as to which office color should be chosen.

Under Watson's leadership, IBM established subsidiaries in different parts of the world—Asia, Australia, South America and Europe.[18] One of the most important European subsidiaries was Dehomag in Germany, which was acquired in 1922 thanks to Watson's persistence and tough negotiation skills. Watson decided to keep the German name Dehomag instead of changing it to IBM Germany due to the already strong national consciousness in the 1920s in Germany. Whether the name was Dehomag or IBM Germany did not change anything: It was a wholly owned IBM subsidiary. Watson saw a glorious financial future in Europe, especially in Germany. He took personal care of the German market and managed its business tightly by setting sales quotas. Watson frequently visited Germany in order to get first-hand information and impressions from how well his German subsidiary was performing and which future profit prospects would still lie ahead. Watson learned from his past clash with the law and made sure to do most business activities by untraceable oral agreements.

## DEHOMAG—IBM'S SUBSIDIARY IN NAZI GERMANY

Willy Heidinger founded Dehomag in 1910. From its early years, the company rented and later also built tabulating machines under IBM license. In 1922, Dehomag became a fully owned IBM subsidiary. It had a history of success in the 1920s, despite the post-war hyperinflation in Germany.

With the rise of Hitler and his Nazi party, IBM's business opportunities increased tremendously. For Hitler's plans to separate the Aryan race from the non-Aryan race as described earlier, he needed a powerful computer system. He needed the best available technology, which would allow him to identify Jews, keep track of their possessions, and finally deport them to ghettoes and concentration camps. IBM's punched card data processing system and technology turned out to be exactly the technology that Hitler required. Governments were a normal type of customer for IBM, and Hitler was therefore not an exception. The German government became a significant and important business partner for Dehomag (IBM). More than 2000 IBM machines would be installed throughout Germany from 1933 onwards and thousands more throughout occupied Europe after 1939. Approximately 1.5 billion punch cards would be produced annually for the German market.[19] The profitable relationship between Hitler and IBM's subsidiary Dehomag started with the first German population census in 1933.[20]

### *First Population Census: April 1933*

IBM's and Hitler's business relationship started only a few months after Hitler became chancellor in 1933. Hitler wanted to conduct a nationwide census, which would give him a demographic overview of the German population. For IBM, a government that aimed at monitoring and counting its population was a promising business client.

Only a few weeks after Hitler's inauguration, IBM headquarters decided to expand its German subsidiary Dehomag by investing over 7 million Reichsmarks.[21] In May 1933, Dehomag's special consultant for government contracts, attorney Karl Koch, secured the contract with the German government for the Prussian census.[22]

As with each customer, Dehomag tailored its punched card system according to the Nazi's wishes. The Nazi regime briefed Dehomag engineers on the aim of the census. For the German government, this census functioned as an identification process, especially in relation to Eastern Jews who became the initial targets in the Nazi anti-Semitic movement. The punch cards provided all the required demographic information such as the person's county, community, gender, age, religion, mother tongue, current occupation, and work. Special attention in this census was given to column 22 "Religion": hole 1 for Protestant, hole 2 for Catholic, and hole 3 for Jew.[23] When Jews were identified during the census, a special "Jewish counting card" was created to indicate the place of birth. This data enabled the Nazi government to identify the Jews in the Prussian population. This first identification of Jews in Germany enabled the Nazi regime to plan and organize its anti-Jewish policies and activities. For example, the census helped to identify the jobs that Jews occupied. Combined with the Aryan paragraph, it became easy for the Nazis to deprive Jews from their work and increasingly deprive them from social life as discussed earlier.

The successful implementation of the Prussian census encouraged Watson to follow his ambitions to increase IBM's presence also in other European countries (e.g., Netherlands, Belgium, and Sweden). Watson ordered all existing IBM subsidiaries in Germany to merge together with Dehomag.[24] He went to Germany and granted Dehomag manager Willy Heidinger special commercial powers outside Germany. This allowed Dehomag to offer and deliver punch card systems directly to customers in other European countries, even if IBM agencies and subsidiaries already existed in those countries. Watson put lots of confidence into the business with the Nazis and Dehomag. He had a personal interest in the success of IBM's business, as he received a five percent bonus on every dollar of after tax, after dividend. Hence, every business relation and transaction with the Reich meant direct profit for Watson. Therefore, Watson was delighted with Dehomag's contract for a second, even bigger population census in 1937.

### Second Population Census: May 1939

In 1937, the Nazi regime planned another census. IBM—as basically the only company offering this technology—secured the 3.5 million Reichsmark contract ($14M today).[25] The census was delayed due to Hitler's absorption of Austria. It was not until May 1939 that the census took place. The large majority of Germany's 22 million households, 3.5 million farmhouses, and 5.5 million shops and factories were registered.[26] This census included almost all of the 80 million citizens in Germany, Austria, the Sudetenland and the Saar. To carry out this census, IBM transferred 70 card sorters, 60 tabulators, 76 multipliers, and 90 million punch cards to Germany.[27]

This census was purely racial and aimed at tracing all Jewish ancestry. Citizens had to indicate their religious faith and material possessions. Additionally, there were special blanks where each citizen had to indicate whether he or she was of pure "Aryan" blood. Finally, the Aryan/Jewish status of each individual's grandparents had to be provided. Only pure Aryans were acceptable according to Nazi ideology. The family statistics helped the Nazis to determine full Jews, half Jews, and even quarter Jews. In total, 330,530 "racial Jews" were identified. The census database was then used to locate Jews, to organize their transportation to ghettos (phase 4) and later to concentration camps (phases 5 & 6). Also the organization of the railways in the German Reich was managed with the IBM punch card technology. The German Reichsbahn (state railway) was one of the largest IBM customers. Most train stations and depots had punch card installations. IBM's technology was used to efficiently manage train scheduling and ensure that detailed lists of rail cargo (humans or commodities) were created. The final destination for most Jews was a concentration camp. At concentration camps, new arrivals were registered by IBM technology.[28]

### Concentration Camps

Concentration camps were assigned IBM code numbers to facilitate the recordkeeping of inmate registration and transfers. Auschwitz, for instance, was 001, Buchenwald was 002, and Dachau was 003.[29] Each concentration camp operated a department where IBM tabulators, sorters, and printers kept track of inmates. Most IBM activity took place in the Labor Assignment Office of the camp, which dealt with daily work assignments and processed inmate data and labor transfer rosters.[30] The office also kept a camp hospital index and kept track of all kinds of inmate statistics. This allowed the full tracking of each single inmate. The Nazis knew where the inmates came from (from another concentration camp or ghetto), what their working skills were, why they were deported, what their health status was, and why they were sent to the camp.

The tabulating machine departments in concentration camps needed experts operating the machines and keeping track of all the processed data. The people working in those departments were directly trained by IBM in Germany or in another country depending on the IBM location and the concentration camps. This was included in the leasing, service, and maintenance contract between IBM and its client. The service contract between Dehomag and the Nazi regime also included regular maintenance services of the machines. Dehomag (IBM) technicians and workers made on-site visits to check, repair, and replace machines. Whether those machines were in concentration camps or regular office buildings did not matter. Hence, IBM workers repaired and checked IBM equipment in concentration camps like Buchenwald and Dachau.

## WATSON'S GERMANY VISITS IN THE 1930S

Watson regularly visited Germany in the 1930s. After the election of Hitler, Watson visited Germany to oversee the merger of IBM's German subsidiaries with its major subsidiary Dehomag.[31] At that time, Nazi anti-Semitic politics were clearly visible in a typical Jew's every day's life. The Nazi party was the only political party remaining. All other political parties had disappeared during 1933. Likewise, critical newspapers and journals had disappeared. People who criticized the Nazi regime in any form or were a threat to the German nation equally disappeared. According to Nazi information, some

committed suicide; others just disappeared. No one knew whether they had left the country or had died. No one seemed to care. Other prevalent events in 1933 were the book burnings, where books, which did not correspond to Nazi ideology, were publicly burned.[32] Between March and October 1933 nearly 100 burnings took place in 70 cities in Germany.

When Watson made his business trips to Germany in the early 1930s, violence against the Jews was apparent. The persecution of Jews started with the boycott of Jewish stores in April 1933. Aryans were no longer allowed to shop in Jewish shops or to be patients of Jewish doctors. The doorways of Jewish shops were blocked by Nazi troops, and signs saying "Jews not wanted" were posted on the streets. Hitler's stormtroopers—a paramilitary organization—made sure that the anti-Semitic regulations were executed. The stormtroopers entered universities and other public institutions, shouted "Jews out" and forced all non-Aryans to leave public buildings immediately. To check whether the boycott was being implemented, stormtroopers went to the medical practices of Jewish doctors to check that there were indeed no patients. On the streets, Jews were confronted with similar antipathy: Insults to the effect of "Judah die" ("Juda verrecke") belonged to their daily lives. Those Germans who managed to sympathize with Jews or who helped them were referred to as national betrayers and were themselves subject to boycotts and sanctions. The atmosphere in Germany became increasingly tense during the 1930s.

For Dehomag's 25th anniversary, Watson traveled to Germany irrespective of the *New York Times* headlines which read "Nazi warns Jews to stay at home." In 1935 anti-Semitic actions became more severe. Jewish shops were systematically destroyed. By the end of 1935, approximately 125,000 Jews had left Nazi Germany.[33] Watson did not have much time to deal with the anti-Semitic attitude in Germany as he focused on the business of his German subsidiary. Dehomag was performing very well. "The company deftly controlled the data operations of the entire Reich."[34] Dehomag's customer base included all important German businesses and public institutions: the Reichsbank (state bank), Reichsbahn (state railway), and companies from central industries such as the aircraft, metal, chemical, car, and ship industries. IBM's and Watson's cooperation with German industry and particularly with the German government was well perceived by the Nazis. As the first international businessman, Watson received the *Merit Cross of the German Eagle with Star* by Hitler for his outstanding activities for Germany in 1937.

Watson saw the political climate and anti-Semitism first-hand during his frequent visits to Germany in the 1930s, but for him his visits were business travels. After one of his visits to Germany, he stated:

> "You can cooperate with a man without believing in everything he says and does. If you do not agree with everything he does, cooperate with him in the things you do believe in. Others will cooperate with him in the things they believe in."[35]

Watson's focus on business corresponded to the manager zeitgeist of the time. Having governments as customers was not unusual. It was actually desirable. Many corporate CEOs and managers shared the viewpoint of "business as usual" in the 1930s and during the war. Alfred P. Sloan, CEO of General Motors (GM) at that time, once said that a global corporation should focus its activities solely on the business level, without any consideration for political opinion of its management or of the states within which it operates.[36]

**September 9, 1939: IBM Headquarters, New York.** Watson looked at Rottke's letter again and then at the newspaper from last week, which was still on his desk: Following Hitler's invasion to Poland, France and Great Britain declared war on Germany.

## NOTES

1. Sebastian Haffner, *Defying Hitler: A Memoir* (London, UK: Phoenix, 2003); Christopher R. Browning, *The Origins of the Final Solution: The Evolution of Nazi Jewish Policy, September 1939–March 1942.* (Jerusalem: Yad Vashem, 2004).

2. Edwin Black, *IBM and the Holocaust: The Strategic Alliance Between Nazi Germany and America's Most Powerful Corporation* (Washington, DC: Dialog Press, 2001). Please note that the case takes place in September

1939. The last three phases of Hitler's fight against Jews (ghettoization, deportation and extermination) took only place after September 1939. Those phases are still described to provide a complete review of the persecution of Jews in Germany. IBM's president Watson, however, could not have known any of the developments at the time he had to make a decision about the machine transfer.

3. Gotz Aly and Karl Heinz Roth, *Nazi Census: Identification and Control in the Third Reich* (Philadelphia: Temple University Press, 2004).

4. Browning, 2004.

5. Marion Kaplan, *Between Dignity and Despair: Jewish Life in Nazi Germany* (New York: Oxford University Press, 1998).

6. Haffner, 2003.

7. Martin Dean, *Robbing the Jews: The Confiscation of Jewish Property in the Holocaust, 1933–1945* (New York: Cambridge University Press, 2008); Ian Kershaw, *Hitler: 1889–1936: Hubris.* (New York: WW Norton & Company, 2008).

8. Black, 2001; Alex Grobman, *Genocide: Critical Issues of the Holocaust: A Companion to the Film Genocide* (Chappaqua, NY: Rossel Books, 1982).

9. Saul Friedlander, *Nazi Germany and the Jews. The Years of Persecution: 1933–1939* (London, UK: Phoenix, 1997); Jean Ziegler, *The Swiss, the Gold and the Dead: How Swiss Bankers Helped Finance the Nazi War Machine* (New York: Penguin Putnam Inc., 1998).

10. Edwin Black, *Nazi Nexus* (Washington, DC: Dialog Press, 2009); Gerald L. Posner and John Ware, *Mengele: The Complete Story.* (Lanham: Cooper Square Publishing Inc., 2000).

11. Yisrael Gutman and Michael Berenbaum, *Anatomy of the Auschwitz Death Camp* (Bloomington: Indiana University Press, 1998); Francois Furet, *Unanswered Questions: Nazi Germany and the Genocide of the Jews* (New York: Schocken, 1989).

12. IBM, *IBM Highlights, 1885–1969 (2001),* http://www.03.ibm.com/ibm/history/documents/pdf/1885–1969.pdf

13. Ibid.

14. Black, 2001.

15. Kevin Maney, *The Maverick and His Machine: Thomas Watson, Sr. and the Making of IBM* (Hoboken: John Wiley & Sons Inc., 2004).

16. William Rodgers, *Think: A Biography of the Watsons and IBM* (New York: Stein and Day, 1969).

17. Black, 2001, p. 71.

18. Rodgers, 1969; Black, 2001.

19. Ibid.

20. Aly and Roth, 2004.

21. Black, 2001.

22. Aly and Roth, 2004.

23. Ibid.

24. Black, 2001.

25. Ibid.

26. Aly and Roth, 2004.

27. Black, 2001.

28. Black, 2009.

29. Black, 2001.

30. Johannes Tuchel, *Die Inspektion der Konzentrationslager* (Berlin: Hentrich, 1994).

31. Ibid.

32. Theodor Verweyen, *Buecherverbrennungen* (Heidelberg: Universitaetsverlag, 2000)

33. Alex Grobman, *Genocide: Critical Issues of the Holocaust: A Companion to the Film Genocide* (Chappaqua, NY: Rossel Books, 1982).

34. Black, 2001, p. 151.

35. Ibid, p. 254.

36. Charles Higham, *Trading with the Enemy. The Nazi-American Money Plot 1933–1949* (Lincoln: iUniverse, Inc, 2007); Henry A. Turner, *General Motors and the Nazis: The Struggle for Control of Opel, Europe's Biggest Carmaker* (New Haven: Yale University Press, 2005).

## QUESTIONS

1. What are the (legal, economic, and ethical) arguments for and against signing the order to transfer the machines to the German IBM subsidiary?

2. In 2002, a group of gypsies filed a lawsuit against IBM. The lawsuit alleged that the American corporation assisted the Nazis in Holocaust killings during World War II by providing the Nazis with punch card machines and computer technology that resulted in the coding. Does today's IBM still have a responsibility for the historic injustices to which it was connected? Please summarize arguments for and against IBM's responsibility for historic injustices.

3. Today, corporations operate in zones of conflict, terror, and war (similar to IBM's situation between 1939 and 1945)—think about diamond and mineral sourcing in African countries. What are the lessons learned from the IBM case, and how can we apply these to current business operations in conflict zones?

# CASE 11.5

## Suicides at Foxconn

Emily Black and Miriam Eapen

Emily Black and Miriam Eapen are 2012 graduates of the Jepson School of Leadership Studies, University of Richmond.

In 1974, Terry Gou founded the Taiwanese company Hon Hai Precision Industry, with only $7500. With Hon Hai Precision Industry as the flagship, Gou created a subsidiary, Foxconn Technology Group, based in China. Foxconn is the largest employer in China, and it accounts for almost 40% of the revenues in the consumer electronics industry. It employs about a million workers—half of them work at the plant in Shenzhen. The company is driven by an aggressive management approach that caters to the needs of its clients, no matter what the costs.[1] Its clients include companies such as Dell, Hewlett-Packard, and Motorola. Foxconn's most successful and technologically demanding client is Apple, Inc. Apple chose to incorporate Foxconn as an integral part of their supply chain because it is the largest electronic manufacturing services provider in the world.

According to Gou, Foxconn aims to recruit people with talent, "those who are willing to continue making progress, building their abilities and taking on bigger responsibilities."[2] Yet, while Foxconn recruits some of the best and brightest to work in its prestigious company, the majority of workers are inexperienced and unskilled. Furthermore, those with experience and inexperience are confined to the production line, with a worker explaining, "I do the same thing every day . . . I have no future."[3]

The factory complexes at Foxconn look like college campuses enclosed by tall fences and security gates. Officials boast that their facilities offer "free meals and accommodation . . . complimentary bus and free laundry . . . free swimming pools, tennis courts . . . exercise programs . . . chess, calligraphy, mountain climbing, or fishing clubs."[4] Yet, many workers complain that they do not have the time to enjoy these benefits. A report conducted by 20 universities across China describes Foxconn "as a concentration camp of workers in the 21st century."[5] Moreover, inside these enclosed facilities "around 50% of employees reported being subjected to some form of abuse, with 16% of cases allegedly perpetuated by supervisors or managers."[6]

Foxconn gained a reputation for being able to turn out quality products for its clients fast. As its client list grew, so did their demands for speedy production. This placed a heavy burden on employees, many of whom worked as much as 80 to100 hours of overtime per month, which is three times the legal limit. Some workers were not allowed to take breaks to eat because they failed to reach production targets. In addition to stressful working conditions, employees were exposed to dangerous chemicals and aluminum dust without proper equipment and protection.[7] While the working conditions are not good, most workers feel fortunate to be employed by a prestigious company that pays better than other available employment options. For personal and cultural reasons, few employees complain.

In 2010 Foxconn came under public scrutiny because in the span of 3 months, 9 of its employees committed suicide at the Shenzhen factory. It then came to light that there had been 17 suicides in the past 5 years. At least 16 of the people jumped to their deaths from the upper floors of the factory and about 20 other people were stopped before they could jump.[8] Although the direct causes of these suicides are unknown, a variety of factors may have contributed to a worker's unhappiness at Foxconn. The company did not think that working conditions were the cause of the suicides. It responded to the suicides by blocking windows, locking the doors to roofs and balconies, and placing over three million square meters of yellow-mesh netting around the buildings to catch jumpers. During a visit to the Foxconn plant in Shenzhen, journalist Joel Johnson described the sight of these nets, "it's hard not to look at the nets. Every building is skirted with them. They drape over precipice, steel poles jutting 20 feet above the sidewalk, loosely tangled like volleyball nets in winter."[9] Although these nets serve as a constant reminder to employees about the suicides, they have deterred other suicides.

Company officials believed that some workers killed themselves to receive compensation for their families from Foxconn, so they decided to make employees to sign an Anti-Suicide Pledge. Employees promise that they will not attempt to kill themselves and that if they do, their families will only receive minimal compensation. It says, "in the event of non-accidental injuries (including suicide, self-mutilation, etc.), I agree that the company has acted properly in accordance with relevant laws and regulations, and will not sue the company, bring excessive demands, take drastic actions that would damage the company's reputation or cause trouble that would hurt normal operations."[10]

Foxconn set up a 24-hour counseling center and gave its employees a 30 percent raise, with a promise for a second raise later in the year. The company also plans to move some plants closer to where worker's families live. Foxconn is building a facility in the city of Zhengzhou, the capital of Henan province, which has a population of more than 100 million. Henan is the home of about a fifth of Foxconn's workforce. "We want to go to the source of abundant workers and where there is a support group of family and friends."[11]

In a September 2010, a journalist from *Business Week* asked Gou how he felt about the suicides. He said, "I should be honest with you. The first one, second one, and third one, I did not see this as a serious problem. We had around 800,000 employees . . . we are about 2.1 square kilometers. At the moment,

170

I'm feeling guilty. But at that moment, I didn't think I should be taking full responsibility."[12] He continued by explaining that it was not until the fifth suicide that he began to think the company had an issue to address. It was at this time that Gou hired the New York Public Relations firm Burson–Marsteller to help devise a formal strategy for addressing the public and the media. Despite Gou's initiatives to address the crisis at Foxconn, he said that dealing with the suicides is not necessarily the responsibility of Foxconn. Instead, he believes "we need to change the way things are. Businesses should be focused on business, and social responsibility should be government responsibility."[13]

The suicides at Foxconn also had an impact on one of its largest clients, Apple. Apple was preparing to roll out its next major product, the iPhone, and it needed Foxconn to produce it on time. Apple's CEO, Steve Jobs, insisted that Foxconn is not a sweatshop. At a June 2010 All Things Digital Conference, Jobs explained, "You go in this place and it's a factory but, my gosh, they've got restaurants and movie theaters and hospitals and swimming pools. For a factory, it's pretty nice."[14] He continued by acknowledging that while the suicides were "very troubling . . . we are on top of this."[15] One month after the suicides, Apple publicized the visit of its Chief Operating Officer Tim Cook and other Apple to the factory in China. Apple's 2011 Progress Report stated that Cook and the executives "met with Foxconn CEO Terry Gou and members of his senior staff to better understand the conditions of the site and to assess the emergency measures Foxconn was putting in place to prevent more suicides."[16] Because Apple believed "we would need additional expertise to help prevent further tragedies," the company commissioned an independent "team of suicide-prevention experts" to survey Foxconn workers about their quality of life and the factory's living conditions.

Apple's independent research revealed "several areas for improvement, such as better training of hotline staff and care center counselors and better monitoring to ensure effectiveness."[17] The Progress Report concluded, "Foxconn incorporated the team's specific recommendations into their long-term plans for addressing employee well-being."[18] With the

Apple executives' trip to the factory and the investigative report publicly underway, Jobs insisted that "Apple does one of the best jobs of any company understanding the working conditions of our supply chain."[19]

## NOTES

1. Frederik Balfour, and Tim Culpan, "The Man Who Makes Your IPhone—BusinessWeek." Businessweek—Business News, Stock Market & Financial Advice. September 9, 2010. Accessed September 30, 2011.

2. Ibid.

3. Stephanie Wong, "Why Apple Is Nervous about Foxconn—Business—US Business—Bloomberg Businessweek—Msnbc.com." Msnbc.com—Breaking News, Science and Tech News, World News, US News, Local News- Msnbc.com. June 7, 2010. Accessed October 01, 2011. http://www.msnbc.msn.com/id/37510167/ns/business-us_business/t/why-apple-nervous-about-foxconn.

4. Malcolm Moore, "A Look inside the Foxconn Suicide Factory—Telegraph." Telegraph.co.uk—Telegraph Online, Daily Telegraph and Sunday Telegraph—Telegraph. May 27, 2010. Accessed September 30, 2011. http://www.telegraph.co.uk/finance/china-business/7773011/A-look-inside-the-Foxconn-suicide-factory.html.

5. Dylan Bushell-Embling, "Foxconn a 'concentration Camp': Report." Telecom Asia. October 11, 2010. Accessed September 30, 2011. http://www.telecomasia.net/content/foxconn-concentration-camp-report.

6. Dylan Bushell-Embling, Ibid.

7. Dylan Bushnell-Embling, Ibid.

8. Malcolm Moore, Ibid.

9. Joel Johnson, Wired Magazine, February 28, 2011 http://www.wired.com/magazine/2011/02/ff_joelinchina/

10. Killian Bell, "Foxconn Workers to Sign 'Anti-Suicide Pledge' & Promise Not to Sue | Cult of Mac." Cult of Mac | Apple News, Reviews and How Tos. May 6, 2011. Accessed September 30, 2011. http://www.cultofmac.com/93674/foxconn-workers-to-sign-anti-suicide-pledge-promise-not-to-sue.

11. Frederik Balfour, and Tim Culpan, Ibid.

12. Frederik Balfour, and Tim Culpan, Ibid.

13. Frederik Balfour, and Tim Culpan, Ibid.

14. Michelle Maisto, "Apple CEO Jobs Says Foxconn Conditions Not So Bad." EWeek.com. June 2, 2010. Accessed September 30, 2011. http://www.eweek.com/c/a/Mobile-and-Wireless/

To: You
From: The Philosopher
Subject: Interns at Foxconn

I can't believe that Foxconn! First, their workers are jumping out the windows and then in September of 2012, they make student interns help them pump out the Apple's new iPhone. You've got to admit, free labor is a great way to keep costs down! According to a *New York Times* (September 10, 2012), nearby vocational schools required students to do an internship at Foxconn. Instead of learning about the company, students had to make cables for iPhones. I guess that will teach them *something* about Foxconn. The students weren't slaves. They could leave at any time; however, they had to complete the internship to graduate.

Apple had hired a group called the Fair Labor Association to audit Foxconn after the suicides. When they found out about the intern labor, the Fair Labor Association took steps to make sure that they interns could resign and still graduate and that Foxconn linked their jobs to their outside studies. Problem solved?

Apple-CEO-Jobs-Says-Foxconn-Conditions-Not-So-Bad-566877/.

15. Ibid.

16. Apple, "Apple Supplier Responsibility." Accessed September 30, 2011. http://images.apple.com/supplier responsibility/pdf/Apple_SR_2011_Progress_Report.pdf.

17. Apple, Ibid.

18. Apple, Ibid., p. 19.

19. Michelle Maisto, Ibid.

## QUESTIONS

1. What do you think of Terry Gou's personal response to the suicides? What do you think of the initiatives that Foxconn took in response to the suicides?

2. What are Apple's responsibilities in this case? Do you think that Apple's investigation was sufficient?

3. Is Foxconn like a sweatshop? What does this case tell us about the social responsibility of a corporation for the behavior of businesses in their supply chain?

# CASE 11.6
# Personal Luxury or Family Loyalty?
Motorola University

*Joe* was a native of *Ganzpoor*, a megacity in the developing nation of *Chompu*. Joe entered this life as the first of five children of an impoverished cloth peddler. Against all odds, by means of sheer guts, hard work and ability, Joe had brought himself to the United States and managed to earn a prestigious

From R. S. Moorthy, Richard T. De George, Thomas Donaldson, William J. Ellos, Robert C. Solomon, and Robert B. Textor, *Uncompromising Integrity: Motorola's Global Challenge* (Schaumburg, IL: Motorola University Press, 1998) pp. 88–89.

degree in engineering from *Cornford University*. Motorola snapped him up a week after graduation, and during the next five years gave him challenging assignments in Florida, Phoenix, Scotland and Mexico. Joe had thoroughly "bought into" the Motorola Culture. Or so it seemed.

Meanwhile, Motorola's business in Chompu began taking off. The Chompu Group was eager for more engineers. But the Human Resources Office was having great difficulty finding candidates willing to accept assignment to Ganzpoor. The news of all this reached Joe, who soon began a vigorous campaign for a transfer. "Look," he argued, "I speak native Ganzpoori and near-native Chompunese, and can hit the ground running." HR saw him as a guy too good to be true: qualified both professionally and culturally. Joe got his transfer.

Upon his assignment to Ganzpoor, Joe was informed in writing that he was expected to reside in a safe and seemly residence of his choice, and would be reimbursed for the actual cost of his rent and servants, up to a maximum of $2,000 per month. "Joe, just give us your landlord's and servants' receipts, and we'll get you promptly reimbursed," explained *Pierre Picard*, a French Motorolan assigned as financial controller for Motorola/Chompu.

Joe found a place to live, but even months later, other Motorolans were not sure exactly where it was because he never seemed to entertain at home. Some of his colleagues thought this was a bit strange, but then realized that Joe hardly had time for entertaining, given his executive responsibility for sourcing contracts for the construction of a new office and factory complex.

Each month Joe would send Pierre a bill for $2,000, accompanied by a rental and service receipt for exactly that amount, duly signed by his landlord. Each month Pierre would reimburse Joe accordingly. This went on for several months, until one day, a traditionally dressed Chompunese man came to see Pierre. He complained bitterly that Joe was his Master, and that Master had cheated him of his servant's wages for the past three months. At this point Pierre, despite his personal regard for Joe, had no

alternative but to check into the facts of Joe's living arrangements.

Pierre and the local HR manager, *Harry Hanks*, had trouble getting the facts of the case, so finally they got a car and driver and went looking for Joe's address. It took almost two hours. The address turned out to be on the edge of a slum area of Ganzpoor, where houses were poorly marked. When they finally got there, they were shocked. Joe was living in what was, by Western standards, not much more than a shack.

Their first concern was for Joe's safety. In this part of the world, there were good reasons why transpatriates chose not to live in slums. Also, they felt, Joe's unseemly residence was hardly good for Motorola's image. Aside from these considerations, though, was the fundamental matter of simple integrity.

Harry felt he had no choice but to report the case to the regional HR director, who had no choice but to order a full-scale investigation.

When Joe learned that he was under investigation, he exploded in fury. He complained to HR that his right to personal privacy was being invaded. Further, he argued that his receipts were legitimate, despite the fact that the investigation revealed that rent plus service in so humble a dwelling could not possibly have cost Joe more than $400 a month, and probably cost much less.

Joe finally explained: Yes, it was true that he actually paid "less than" $2,000 a month (though he refused to say how much less). But, he argued, just because he was willing to "make sacrifices" should not mean that he should receive less than the full $2,000, which "all of my fellow Motorolans receive." To clinch his defense, Joe argued, "Look, I'm a Chompunese as well as a Motorolan, and here in Chompu this kind of thing happens all the time."

The hearings officer pressed further. Finally Joe, near tears, explained that all four of his younger siblings were now of college or high school age, and that he was putting all four of them through school with the reimbursements he received from Motorola, plus a sizeable chunk of his salary. "Look," said Joe, "My family is *poor*—so poor in fact that most Westerners wouldn't believe our poverty even if they saw it. This money can mean the difference between hope and despair for all of us. For me to do anything less for my family would be to defile the honor of my late father.

"Can't you understand?"

A week later Joe was asked to step into the director's office to learn his fate. . . .

## QUESTIONS

1. Do employees have a right to spend their living allowance in a foreign country any way they want?

2. If you were the director, what would you do with Joe?

3. Do employees have the right to spend their living allowances any way that they please in a foreign country?

# CHAPTER QUESTIONS

1. Whose values should prevail when operating in another culture? Who decides what is best for the people in a country?

2. What kind of responsibilities does a firm have for things that happen outside of their business in a foreign country?

3. How can one bridge the gap between people who have different moral priorities?

Printed in the USA/Agawam, MA
October 21, 2021

783148.045